Studies in Music Literature

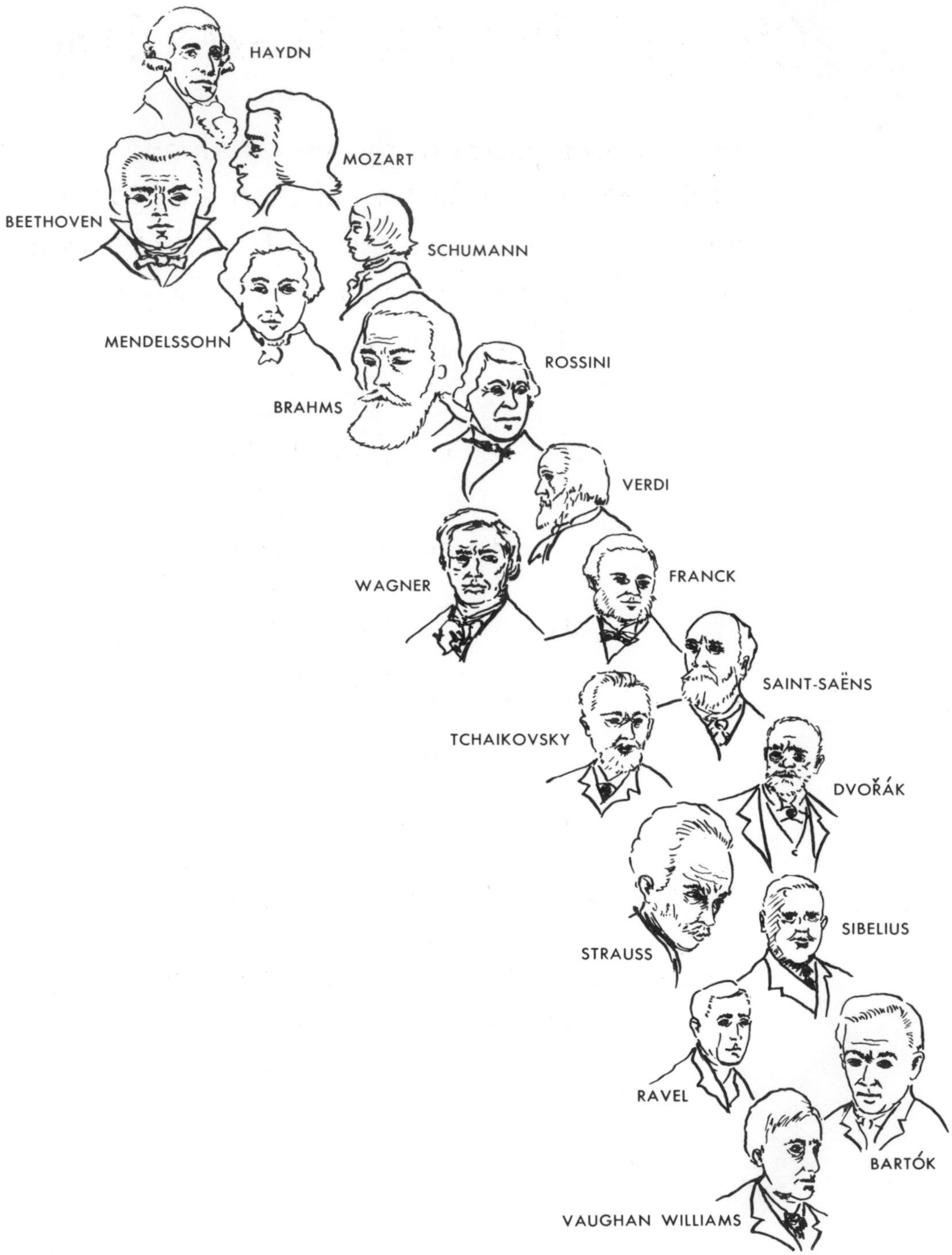
HAYDN
MOZART
BEETHOVEN
SCHUMANN
MENDELSSOHN
BRAHMS
ROSSINI
VERDI
WAGNER
FRANCK
SAINT-SAËNS
TCHAIKOVSKY
DVOŘÁK
STRAUSS
SIBELIUS
RAVEL
BARTÓK
VAUGHAN WILLIAMS

Studies in Music Literature

Classical Period to Present Day

Selected Composers of the 18th, 19th and Early 20th Centuries: A Survey of Orchestral Music, Concertos and Pieces with Orchestra, Chamber Music, Choral Works, Compositions for the Stage, and Solo Compositions

A Synopsis in Topical Form

Prepared by 1368

Verne W. Thompson

Formerly Professor of Music Literature

and

Eugene J. Selhorst

Associate Dean for Graduate Professional Studies
and
Chairman of the Department of Music Literature
Eastman School of Music of the University of Rochester

WM. C. BROWN COMPANY PUBLISHERS

Dubuque, Iowa

MUSIC SERIES

Consulting Editor

Frederick W. Westphal
Sacramento State College

Library of Congress Catalog Card Number: 68–14579

Printed in U. S. A.

Preface

For many years a close associate of the late Verne W. Thompson, the writer is both delighted and honored to assist in the publication of Dr. Thompson's book.

As Dr. Thompson acquired experience in the difficult art of introducing large classes of students to the literature of music, he became more and more convinced of the necessity for some kind of printed orientation or guide which his students could use as a point of departure in their studies. A textbook could not fulfill this function on several grounds. The study was intended to be more than a superficial survey, and the content could not possibly be treated in depth within the limits of a single volume. Moreover, since graduate students were involved, it seemed appropriate to maintain stress on independent research rather than to encourage reliance on a text. On the other hand, a bare syllabus of the course seemed an equally unsatisfactory alternative. After considerable thought and experiment he concluded that a synopsis providing systematic lists of the literature together with a minimal amount of commentary, practical bibliographical suggestions, and a selection of works to be singled out for special attention would best solve the problem.

Particularly interested in such a synopsis for the later historical periods of music—the Classic, Romantic, and Contemporary—Dr. Thompson began work on the present volume in 1960, completing a draft of it by 1962. He made this draft available to his classes on an experimental basis. Greatly pleased with the result, he revised the work further in 1963 and had begun preparing it for publication at the time of his death.

Representing the experience and the mature thought of a highly successful teacher, Dr. Thompson's *Studies in Music Literature* will be of great interest to fellow teachers in the field, many of whom will wish to adopt it for their courses. They will find it an efficient tool for organizing their presentation of the vast musical repertoire of the eighteenth, nineteenth, and twentieth centuries.

At the same time they will see its usefulness as a focus for class discussions. Their students will find it indispensable as a guide to independent study and listening. Properly applied, it will bring the subject matter within workable limits so that the learning experience can be unified and meaningful.

Studies in Music Literature will also find application in music history courses, both graduate and undergraduate. For the independent student, the professional performer, and the interested amateur this book will be attractive as a convenient reference as well as a springboard for advanced study.

Since the book was very near publication at the time of Dr. Thompson's death, the present writer has limited his efforts to details that were necessary to complete it. Proofreading, correction of minor errors, updating the material to incorporate later information, addition of significant new books to the bibliography—these have been the main contributions. It must be emphasized that the underlying idea, the plan of organization, the format, the compilation of the material—including the agonizing decisions as to what to omit and what to retain—these are the work of Dr. Thompson. *Studies in Music Literature* is *his* book. May it disseminate widely the thought and achievement of one who was a fine teacher and a fine man.

Eugene J. Selhorst
Rochester, N.Y.

Introduction

The *Synopsis* surveys the literature and materials of music from the middle of the eighteenth century to the present day. Within this historical span it seeks to point out the chief developments and to outline the important artistic personalities by reference to representative composers and typical compositions. Intended to be merely suggestive, it is in no sense a complete coverage.

Composers are grouped, as shown in the Contents, according to style periods, and are largely arranged in chronological order under the period headings.

Six categories have been set up, and—where appropriate—the composer's works are considered under these categories.

A General Bibliography gives a selected list of music histories and study helps that are easily available and found in the personal libraries of most music students. The growing library of paperbound books is represented here. Symbols are indicated for the books, and these symbols are used throughout the *Synopsis*.

Each composer is introduced by a brief summary of style characteristics which attempts to define his position in music history and to suggest his unique contributions to the materials of music.

Under subheadings indicating the six categories, there is given first a list of principal works (the "compositional output"). Secondly, specific works are suggested for study as a means of establishing a composer profile.

Under Suggested Reading and by means of the symbols, pages are given in books chosen from the General Bibliography. The intent is that the student will use those works at hand and not feel responsible for all the sources listed in every case.

Under References are selected bibliographical materials such as thematic indexes, important musical sources, and books dealing with specific composers.

As organized, the *Synopsis* is to be used as a check list of materials, the plan suggested being that of filling in where past experience and knowledge of the music seem to indicate a lack of familiarity. Class discussions and performances are, of course, an important part of the project. Phonograph disks, tapes, and well-chosen radio programs (FM is more productive than AM, usually) are also helpful parts of the total experience. It goes without saying that opportunities to hear essential works authoritatively performed in recitals and concerts should never be overlooked.

American music is not included. For valuable help in the music of our own country, the student is referred to *America's Music* by Gilbert Chase; *Music in a New Found Land* by Wilfred Mellers; and the *Anthology of American Music* compiled by Harold Gleason and Thomas Marrocco.

Without the interest and approval of Dr. Howard Hanson, Director of the Eastman School of Music, and Dr. Eugene Selhorst, Associate Dean for Graduate Professional Studies, the *Synopsis* could not have been assembled. The treasures of Sibley Music Library, as administered by Dr. Ruth Watanabe, are a vital part of any Eastman project (such as this one) having to do with musical essentials. Appreciation is also due the following for work on materials: Vivian Clemons, John Paton, Charles Brown, Jr., Martha Powell, Cameron Johnson, Gayel Panke, Robert Finster, Karen Edmiston, and Margaret Whitfield.

Verne W. Thompson

Contents

Chapter 1. Antecedents and Forerunners of Classical Style

Chapter 2. The Viennese Classicists

Chapter 3. The Early Romanticists

Spellings of composers' names are in accordance with those given in Baker's *Biographical Dictionary of Musicians.*

Chapter 4. Representative Nineteenth-Century Opera Composers: Grand, Lyric, and Comique Types; The Music Drama

Chapter 5. The Late Romanticists

Chapter 6. The Nationalistic Composers

Chapter 7. The Post-Romanticists

Chapter 8. The Impressionists

Chapter 9. Composers of Modern and New Music; Conflicting Trends and Styles

CHAPTER

1

Antecedents and Forerunners of Classical Style

I. Background

IDEAS AND IDEALS OF EIGHTEENTH-CENTURY THOUGHT

Basic ideas included faith in experimental knowledge and faith in the value of natural feeling, with importance of the individual emphasized and his well-being made the basis of judgments in the several fields. The common humanity of men; universal human brotherhood; the rising "middle class" bringing a new market for art expressions and giving emphasis to the importance of the musical amateur; rationalism and reasonableness in place of Baroque mysticism, passion, and grandeur—these were some of the concepts and conditions mirrored in eighteenth-century art and music.

The Enlightenment

A movement in eighteenth-century philosophy in which distinguishing traits were the questioning of authority, the emphasizing of empirical methods in science, and an intense interest in political and cultural matters. It was given impetus and strength by the writings, teachings, and theories of such earlier thinkers as John Locke (1632-1704, English philosopher), Pierre Bayle (1647-1706, French philosopher and critic), and Sir Isaac Newton (1642-1727, English mathematician and natural philosopher). It was centered in France, where Voltaire (1694-1778) the skeptic, Rousseau (1712-78) the adherent of naturalism, Condillac (1715-80) the sensationalist, together with Diderot (1713-84) and d'Alembert (1717-83) the encyclopedists, were leaders.

In Germany (equivalent term is *Aufklärung*), representatives were Lessing, Moses Mendelssohn, and Herder. As far away as America, Benjamin Franklin (1706-90), Thomas Paine (1737-1809) and the leaders of the Revolution were exponents.

Sturm und Drang (Storm and Stress)

Stands for the intellectual turbulence in late eighteenth-century Germany where moves toward freedom from French literary domination, together with a new emphasis on subjectivity, intensity of feeling, and expression, were characteristic. Term derived from a drama by Klinger (1752-1831) called *Sturm und Drang*. The *Robbers* of Schiller also added to the feeling and mood of the movement.

A NEW MUSICAL STYLE

In place of the Baroque style came the Rococo (small structure rather than large; overdecoration and ornament) or *Style galant et touchant* (gallant and pathetic; simple melody plus simple harmony in place of counterpoint, short phrases as musical motifs). Later came the Style of Sensitivity (Fr., *sensibilité*; Ger., *Empfindsamkeit*; response to sentimental expression, use of such musical elements as the "sigh," diminished intervals, chromatics, "color" chords, feminine cadences).

II. The Pre-Classic Homophonic Orchestra Style; Sonata and Symphony

NEW STANDARDS

New concepts of melody . . . New texture as harmonic-melodic style replaced the old, contrapuntal style . . . New forms . . . New extremes in dynamics and expression . . . New instruments, new instrumental combinations, and new methods in their use . . . Development of the art of orchestration.

THE ITALIAN GROUP

1. Alessandro Scarlatti (1659-1725) in Naples.
2. Guiseppe Tartini (1692-1770).
3. Giovanni Battista Sammartini (1701-1775).
4. Giovanni Battista Pergolesi (1710-1736).
5. Johann Christian Bach (1735-82, the "Milan" or "English" Bach) and the "Singing Allegro."
6. Luigi Boccherini (1743-1805), cellist and chamber-composer.

THE AUSTRIAN SYMPHONY SCHOOL

1. Georg Christoph Wagenseil (1715-77), court composer and organist.
2. Georg Matthias Monn (1717-50), organist of the Karlskirche in Vienna.
3. Karl Ditters von Dittersdorf (1739-99), violinist and composer.

THE MANNHEIM SCHOOL (STYLE OF CRESCENDO AND CONTRAST)

1. Johann Stamitz (1717-57), violinist and conductor.
2. Franz Xaver Richter (1709-89).
3. Johann Schobert (*c.* 1720-67), composer and harpsichordist, translated the Mannheim style features to the keyboard in Paris.
4. Anton Filtz (*c.* 1730-60), Bohemian 'cellist.
5. François-Joseph Gossec (1734-1829), director of *Concerts spirituels* in Paris; employed, in his own way, Mannheim characteristics.
6. Christian Cannabich (1731-98), prominent member of younger generation of Mannheim composers.

THE NORTH GERMAN SCHOOL

1. Johann Gottlieb Graun (1702-71), violinist and composer; leading exponent of the "heroic" style.
2. Franz Benda (1709-86), Bohemian violinist, teacher, orchestra leader for the Crown Prince (afterwards Frederick II).
3. K. P. E. Bach (1714-88), "Berlin" or "Hamburg" Bach, representative of both *Sturm und Drang* and German *Empfindsamkeit.*

III. The Neapolitan *Opera Seria*

Plots often lacked unity and consistency, with little attention to realism or dramatic details. Music (stressing melody with light, homophonic accompaniment) featured the singer (*castrati* employed for both male and female roles), who added embellishments and improvised cadenzas. Arias (*da capo* aria, a favorite, became standard type) were separated by recitatives (both *secco* and *accompagnato*) which highlighted the action. The *pasticcio* was popular.

1. Alessandro Scarlatti (1659-1725) played a vital part in the transition from earlier Venetian to Neapolitan style. The Italian overture (Fast-Slow-Fast), emphasis on vocal ensembles, use of larger orchestras and the accompanied recitative were among his contributions.
2. Apostolo Zeno (1668-1750) and Pietro Metastasio (1698-1782) were important librettists.
3. In the works of Nicola Jommelli (1714-74), Tommaso Traetta (1727-79), and J. C. Bach (1735-82) are seen a deepening of texture, a less rigid pattern of arias and recitatives, a closer connection between music and drama, and increased emphasis on harmonic variety, the vocal ensemble, and the orchestra.
4. Nicola Piccini (Piccinni) (1728-1808), champion of the pure Italian school, opposed Gluck in the Paris "Quarrel of the Gluckists and Piccinists."

IV. Comic Opera of the Eighteenth Century

Comic episodes were deleted from tragic operas, thus separating comic opera from *seria.* Satirical and humorous subjects with popular tunes; the *genre* divided into national forms; spoken dialogue employed in all but Italian *opera buffa.* At the end of the century comic opera was elevated to a position of real respectability.

Italian *opera buffa* developed in Naples through *intermezzi.* The ensemble finale featured. Giovanni Pergolesi (*La Serva padrona*), Giovanni Paisiello (1740-1816; *Il Barbiere di Siviglia,* 1782), Piccini (*La buona figliuola,* 1760), Baldassare Galuppi

(1706-85; *Il filosofo da campagna*), and Domenico Cimarosa (1749-1801; *Il Matrimonio segreto,* 1792) were important in this style.

French *opéra comique,* initiated in the Baroque era by Lully and Molière in their *comédie-ballets,* attained new importance. The *Théâtre de l'Opéra-comique* opened in Paris in 1715. Broad subject matter included archetypal peasantry and idealized Orientals. Simple, appealing music at first consisted largely of borrowed *vaudevilles* (popular tunes); later, of original *ariettes.* Spoken dialogue. Some vocal ensembles, but no ensemble finales.

Composers of importance: Egidio Romualdo Duni (1709-75; *L'Isle des fous,* 1760), Jean-Jacques Rousseau (1712-78; *Devin du village,* 1752), François André Danican-Philidor (1726-95; *Tom Jones,* 1764), Pierre-Alexandre Monsigny (1729-1817; *Le Déserteur,* 1769), and André-Ernest-Modeste Grétry (1741-1813; *Richard Coeur-de-Lion*).

English ballad opera aimed against foreign musical domination was established by Gay and Pepusch in *The Beggar's Opera* (1728; satiric, borrowed music, presented inferior characters using commonplace language). Charles Coffey (*The Devil to Pay,* 1731), Dr. Thomas Arne (1710-78; *Thomas and Sally,* 1744), and William Shield (1748-1829; *A Flitch of Bacon,* 1778) were prominent.

German *Singspiel* traces back to the popular dramas of itinerant players who introduced simple music patterned on the *lied.* Around the middle of the eighteenth century, English ballad operas, with texts translated into German, were presented in Berlin and other German cities. These performances gave impetus to German poets and composers who at first followed the English model but soon transformed it into something essentially German. Johann Adam Hiller (1728-1804) in North Germany, in collaboration with Christian Felix Weisse, produced *Der Teufel ist los* (1766) and *Die Jagd* (1770), characterized by picturesqueness and sentimental idyllicism. Karl Ditters von Dittersdorf (1739-99; *Doktor und Apotheker,* 1786) in South Germany offered works with more liveliness and display, strongly influenced by Italian *opera buffa.*

Spanish *Zarzuela* and *Tonadilla* presented pastoral and mythological subjects by use of solo songs, dialogues, dancing. Composers included Don Pablo Estevo y Grimau (dates unknown) and Don Blas de Laserna (1751-1816).

V. Melodrama and Reform Opera

Melodrama (spoken text accompanied instrumentally) featured by Rousseau (*Pygmalion,* 1770; music by Coignet) and Benda (1722-95; *Ariadne auf Naxos,* 1775).

The opera form, much criticized over a long period, was re-evaluated by Christoph Willibald von Gluck (1714-87), assisted by librettist Ranieri di Calzabigi (1714-95), who revised the balance between drama and music with more attention to drama, divested both music and libretto of unnecessary ornament, and attempted the correction of current vocal abuses. *Orfeo ed Euridice* (1762) and *Alceste* (1767), both composed in Vienna, are "reform" works. *Iphigénie en Tauride* (considered his masterpiece) belongs to his Paris period, as also *Iphigénie en Aulide.*

SUGGESTED READING

1.	*Ca-Jo-WaAM*	287-97
2.	*GroutHWM*	411-36
3.	*GroutSHO*	181-225 (Neapolitan Opera), 226-45 (The Operas of Gluck), 246-73 (Eighteenth-Century Comic Opera)
4.	*PaulyMCP*	11-28 (Rococo), 28-32 (Pre-Classic Symphony), 167-175 (Gluck)
5.	*SachsCA*	163-76
6.	*UlCM*	145-77 (The Emergence of Classical Style)
7.	*Ul-PiHM*	312-30 (Emergence of Classical Style), 331-51 (The Classical Period: Opera), 360-65 (The Classical Period: Other Vocal Music)
8.	*UlSM*	50-66 (The Rococo and the Style Galant)

REFERENCES

1. Berlin, I., *The Age of Enlightenment,* New York: Mentor Books.
2. Demuth, N., *French Opera: Its Development to the Revolution,* Sussex: The Artemis Press, 1963.
3. Newman, W. S., *The Sonata in the Baroque Era,* Chapel Hill: University of North Carolina Press, 1959.
4. ———, *The Sonata in the Classic Era,* Chapel Hill: University of North Carolina Press, 1963.
5. Windelband, W., *A History of Philosophy,* vol. II, *Renaissance, Enlightenment, and Modern,* New York: Torchbooks, 1958.

CHAPTER

2

The Viennese Classicists

VI. (Franz) Joseph Haydn (1732-1809)

By nationality an Austrian (of pure German lineage), Haydn early became familiar with the culture and music of other groups, absorbing impressions to be used later in his own compositions. Born into the Rococo and *Empfindsamer* periods, he moved consistently and surely toward the new instrumental style and musical forms of the classicists, contributing both to the growth of the sonata pattern toward its full maturity and also to the solution of problems arising from redistribution of *continuo* elements. The Esterházy seclusion, inconvenient at times, offered ideal conditions for experiment and development ("I was forced to become original"), his completed style commanding the full complement of moods and emotions, from the joyous and gay to the tender and passionate.

ORCHESTRAL MUSIC

One hundred four symphonies; many divertimentos, serenades, overtures.

Symphonies

D Major, No. 6, "Le Matin" }
C Major, No. 7, "Le Midi" } (1761-62)
G Major, No. 8, "Le Soir" }
E-flat Major, No. 22, "The Philosopher" (1764-65)
E Minor, No. 44, "Trauersinfonie" (1772-73)
F-sharp Minor, No. 45, "Farewell" (*c.* 1773)
B-flat Major, No. 85, "La Reine" (1784)
G Major, No. 92, "Oxford" (*c.* 1790)
G Major, No. 94, "Surprise" (1792)
G Major, No. 100, "Military" (perf. 1794)
D Major, No. 101, "Clock" (1794?)
B-flat Major, No. 102 (1794?)
E-flat Major, No. 103, "Drum Roll" (1795)
D Major, No. 104, "London" (1795)

CONCERTOS AND PIECES WITH ORCHESTRA

Three violin; 2 cello; 1 flute; a *symphonie concertante* for oboe, violin, bassoon, cello, and orchestra; 1 trumpet; 2 horn; 15 piano.

Cello

D Major (1783)

Piano

D Major (1784)

Violin, Oboe, Cello, Bassoon

Symphonie Concertante, Op. 84 (1792)

CHAMBER MUSIC

Eight sonatas for piano and violin (including transcriptions and arrangements); 6 duets for violin and viola; numerous string trios (18 for 2 violins and cello); 31 trios for piano, violin, and cello; 84 string quartets (including "Interludes to the Seven Last Words," the "Lost Heir," and the incomplete Op. 103); a great number of works for baryton in various combinations.

String Quartets

F Major, Op. 3, No. 5 (*c.* 1755-65)
F Minor, Op. 20, No. 5 (*c.* 1772)
E-flat Major, Op. 33, No. 2, "The Joke" (1781)
C Major, Op. 33, No. 3, "The Bird" (1781)
E-flat Major, Op. 64, No. 6 (1790)
C Major, Op. 76, No. 3, "Emperor" (1797-98)

CHORAL WORKS

Several cantatas, 4 oratorios, 14 masses, 2 *Te Deums,* a *Stabat Mater,* Offertories.

Cantata

Miseri Noi, Misera Patria (*c.* 1790; large-scale work of late period, for soprano and orchestra)

Oratorios

Il Ritorno di Tobia ("The Return of Tobias," 1774-75)
Die Sieben Worte des Erlösers am Kreuze ("The Seven Last Words of Our Saviour on the Cross," 1785)
Die Schöpfung ("The Creation," 1798)
Die Jahreszeiten ("The Seasons," 1801)

COMPOSITIONS FOR THE STAGE

Nineteen operas and *Singspiele,* plus incidental music to various plays.

SOLO COMPOSITIONS

Sixty piano sonatas (52 extant); 32 arrangements for mechanical clock; numerous vocal arias; *c.* 45 songs with piano accompaniment; over 150 arrangements of Scotch, Irish and Welsh melodies.

SUGGESTED READING

1.	*Ca-Jo-WaAM*	297-316
2.	*CobCM*	I, 515-45; II, 603
3.	*GleCM*	Outline II
4.	*GroutHWM*	438-454
5.	*HiCon*	38-48
6.	*HiSym*	22-54
7.	*RobCM*	13-55
8.	*PaulyMCP*	76-87, 98-105, 116-119, 148-159
9.	*SachsCA*	176-79
10.	*ToveyEMA*	I
11.	*UlCM*	179-209
12.	*Ul-PiHM*	365-68, 372-75, 378-86, 396-403
13.	*UlSM*	66-78, 97-104, 107-112, 179-209
14.	*VeiCon*	71

REFERENCES

THEMATIC INDICES

1. POHL, C. F. *Joseph Haydn* 3 vols., vol. 3 by Hugo Botstiber, Berlin: A. Sacco Nachfolger, 1875, 1882; Leipzig, 1927.
2. LARSEN, J. P., *Drei Haydn Katalogc in Faksimile,* Copenhagen, 1941. Contains the so-called *Entwurf Katalog* (draft catalogue) written by Haydn and/or his copyist, Joseph Elssler, with 17 sheets giving thematic beginnings. Written mostly between 1765 and 1777; now in State Library in Berlin.
3. HAYDN, J., *Verzeichnis aller derjenigen Compositionen, welche ich mich beyläufig erinnere von meinem 18ten bis in das 73ste Jahr verfertiget zu haben.* (Catalogue of all those compositions that, as nearly as I can remember, I composed between my 18th and 73rd year.) In the hand of Johann Elssler. Facsimile.
4. ———, *Werkverzeichnis,* Leipzig: Breitkopf & Härtel, 1930(?).
5. HOBOKEN, A. VAN, *Joseph Haydn. Thematisch-bibliographisches Werkverzeichnis,* Mainz: Schott's Söhne, 1957-

MUSIC

1. HAYDN, J., *Kritische Gesamtausgabe* 80 vols., projected under editorship of G. Adler, H. Kretzchmar, E. Mandyczewski, M. Seiffert, etc., 10 vols. issued, Leipzig: Breitkopf & Härtel, 1907-33.
2. ———, *Werke* 24 vols. to date. Haydn Institute in Cologne. Munich-Duisburg: G. Henle Verlag.
3. LARSEN, J. P., ed., *The Works of Joseph Haydn* 4 vols.; Boston: The Haydn Society, 1950-

BOOKS

1. BARBAUD, P., *Haydn,* New York: Grove Press, 1959.
2. GEIRINGER, K., *Haydn, a Creative Life in Music,* New York: W. W. Norton Company, Inc., 1946.
3. ROBBINS LANDON, H. D., *The Symphonies of Joseph Haydn,* London: Universal, 1956.
4. ———, *Supplement to the Symphonies of Joseph Haydn,* London: Barrie and Rockliff, 1961.

VII. Wolfgang Amadeus Mozart (1756-1791)

Mozart's art was entirely spontaneous, being unhindered by theory and unhampered by prevailing and accepted tenets. His creative ability was the most comprehensive known to music. His sense of form was perfect and intuitive, his qualities of workmanship complete and faultless. He utilized generally accepted forms (sonata, variations, rondo), making of them suitable vehicles for the expression of his musical thought. Of all the great composers, he was the least distinguished by national characteristics. He took no special notice of Nature and showed little sympathy for the music of the common folk. Much of his music is Italian in spirit and manner, exemplifying Italian polish, refinement, and musical thoroughness. To the casual listener, his music is bright, cheerful, and serene. Beneath, however, are qualities deep and profound, with evidences of underlying tenderness and melancholy.

ORCHESTRAL MUSIC

Forty-nine symphonies; 2 symphonic movements; 31 divertimentos, serenades, and cassations.

Symphonies

D Major, K. 385, "New Haffner" (1782)
C Major, K. 425, "Linz" (1783)
D Major, K. 504, "Prague" (1786)
E-flat Major, K. 543 (June 26, 1788)
G Minor, K. 550 (July 25, 1788)
C Major, K. 551, "Jupiter" (August 10, 1788)

CONCERTOS AND PIECES WITH ORCHESTRA

Six violin; a *Concertone* for 2 violins; a *Sinfonia concertante* for violin and viola; 2 concertos for flute; 1 for flute and harp; 1 clarinet; 1 bassoon; 4 horn; 23 piano (including 1 for 2 pianos and 1 for 3 pianos); 35 cadenzas to piano concertos.

Violin
D Major, K. 218 (June, 1775)
A Major, K. 219 (1775)

Flute
D Major, K. 314 (Ke 285d) (1777?)

Clarinet
A Major, K. 622 (1791)

Bassoon
B-flat Major, K. 191 (Ke 186e) (1774)

Piano
E-flat, K. 482 (1785)
D Major, K. 537, "Coronation" (1788)
B-flat Major, K. 595 (1791)

Violin, Viola
Sinfonia concertante in E-flat Major, K. 364 (1779)

CHAMBER MUSIC

Forty-two sonatas for violin and piano; an allegro and 2 sets of variations for piano and violin; sonata for bassoon and cello; 2 duos for violin and viola; 1 duo for 2 violins; 7 trios for piano, violin, and cello; 1 trio for piano, clarinet, and viola; 26 string quartets; 2 piano quartets; 4 quartets for flute, violin, viola, and cello; quartet for oboe, violin, viola, and cello; 7 string quintets with 2 violas; 1 quintet for violin, 2 violas, cello, and horn; 1 quintet for clarinet and string quartet; one quintet for piano, oboe, clarinet, horn, and bassoon; 11 pieces for string and wind combinations (including several with basset-horn); *Eine kleine Nachtmusik* for strings, including double bass.

A. String Instruments

Quartets
G Major, K. 387 (1783)
C Major, K. 465, "Dissonant" (1784-85)
D Major, K. 575, "Prussian" (1789-90)

B. Piano and String Instruments

Trios
E-flat Major, K. 498, for piano, clarinet, viola (1786)

Quartets
G Minor, K. 478 (1785)

C. Miscellaneous

Quintets
A Major, K. 581, for clarinet and string quartet (1789)
E-flat Major, K. 452, for piano, oboe, clarinet, horn, and bassoon (1784)

CHORAL WORKS

Four cantatas; 15 masses (all for 4 voices); 4 litanies; 1 *Magnificat*; 1 *Te Deum*; many small pieces of church music including the motet, *Ave, verum corpus* (K. 618), and 3 small cantatas for Masonic use.

Masses
C Major, K. 257, "Credo Mass"
C Major, K. 317, "Coronation"
D Minor, K. 626, "Requiem" (1791; completed by Süssmayr)

COMPOSITIONS FOR THE STAGE

A sacred play, a Latin comedy, 18 operas and *Singspiele.*

Operas and Singspiele
Bastien und Bastienne, operetta in one act, K. 50 (1768)
Idomeneo, re di Creta ("Idomeneus, King of Crete"), *Opera seria,* K. 366 (1780-81)
Die Entführung aus dem Serail ("The Elopement from the Seraglio"), Singspiel, K. 384 (1781-82)
Le nozze di Figaro ("The Marriage of Figaro"), *Opera buffa,* K. 492 (1785-86)
Don Giovanni ("Don Juan"), *Opera buffa,* K. 527 (1787)
Così fan tutte: ossia la Scuola degli amanti ("Thus Do They All: or the School for Lovers"), *Opera buffa,* K. 588 (1790)
Die Zauberflöte ("The Magic Flute"), German opera, combination of Singspiel and Oratorio, K. 620 (1791)

SOLO COMPOSITIONS

For piano: 10 pieces for 4 hands 1 keyboard; 2 pieces for 4 hands 2 keyboards; 17 sonatas; a *fantasia* and fugue; 3 *fantasias*; 16 sets of variations; 35 cadenzas to piano concertos. For organ: 17 sonatas, mostly with 2 violins and cello. For voice: 27 arias; 34 songs; and various ensemble pieces. Also pieces for harmonica, clockwork organ, etc.

SUGGESTED READING

1. *Ca-Jo-WaAM* 316-28
2. *CobCM* II, 150-83
3. *GleCM* Outline III

4.	*GroutHWM*	454-69
5.	*GroutSHO*	274-96
6.	*HiCon*	49-118
7.	*HiSym*	55-91
8.	*PaulyMCP*	87-97, 105-114, 119-132, 134-147, 159-166, 175-185
9.	*RobCM*	60-93, 293-299
10.	*UlCM*	210-38
11.	*Ul-PiHM*	351-59, 368-72, 386-96
12.	*UlSM*	79-97, 104-7
13.	*VeiCon*	72-124

REFERENCES

THEMATIC INDEX

1. Köchel, L., *Chronologisch-thematisches Verzeichnis sämtlicher Tonwerke* Wolfgang Amadeus Mozart, 6th edition by F. Giegling, A. Weinmann, G. Sievers, Leipzig: Breitkopf & Härtel, 1964.

MUSIC

1. Mozart, W. A., *Werke* 55 vols, Leipzig: Breitkopf & Härtel, 1876-1886, reprinted by J. W. Edwards, Ann Arbor: University of Michigan Press, 1951-56.
2. ———, *Werke,* 45 vols., edited by Ernst Fritz Schmid of the *Mozart-Archiv der deutschen Mozart-gesellschaft* in Augsburg, Germany, Kassel: Bärenreiter Verlag, 1955.

BOOKS

1. Biancolli, L., ed., *The Mozart Handbook,* Cleveland: World Publishing Co., 1954.
2. Blom, Eric, *Mozart,* New York: E. P. Dutton & Co., Inc., 1949.
3. Burk, J. N., *Mozart and His Music,* New York: Random House, Inc., 1959.
4. Deutsch, O. E., *Mozart,* Stanford: Stanford University Press, 1965.
5. Einstein, A., *Mozart: His Character, His Work,* translated by A. Mendel and N. Broder. New York: Oxford University Press, 1945.
6. Turner, W. J., *Mozart, the Man and His Works,* London: V. Gollancz, 1938, reprint, Garden City, N.J.: Doubleday & Company, Inc.

VIII. Ludwig Van Beethoven (1770-1827)

Born in a propitious period in the history of human thought, Beethoven accepted the spirit of Kant's philosophy and the tenet of Schiller that art was an elevating force. He took advantage of the change in position of the individual toward his society and of the movement toward emancipation of the individual. Symbolic of the nineteenth century, he served only his art and composed according to the direction of his musical spirit. Often characterized as the "Liberator of Music," Beethoven established the composer's work upon a professional basis, placed music democratically in the concert hall, freed it from formalism and literary connotations, introduced new harmonic and modulatory techniques, and made personality and emotion vital elements in musical construction.

ORCHESTRAL MUSIC

Nine symphonies; *The Battle of Vittoria;* music to ballet *Prometheus* and Goethe's *Egmont,* both with overtures; 9 additional overtures.

Symphonies

1. C Major, Op. 21 (1800)
2. D Major, Op. 36 (before 1803)
3. E-flat Major, Op. 55, "Eroica" (1803-04)
4. B-flat Major, Op. 60, (1806)
5. C Minor, Op. 67, (1807)
6. F Major, Op. 68, "Pastoral" (1807-08)
7. A Major, Op. 92, (1812)
8. F Major, Op. 93, (1812)
9. D Minor, Op. 125, "Choral" (1817-23)

Overtures

The Creations of Prometheus, Op. 43 (1802)
Leonore No. 2, Op. 72a (1805)
Leonore No. 3, Op. 72a (1806)
Coriolanus, Op. 62 (1807)
Fidelio, Op. 72b (1814)
Egmont, Op. 84 (1810)
The Consecration of the House, Op. 124 in C Major (1822)

CONCERTOS AND PIECES WITH ORCHESTRA

One violin; 2 Romances for violin and orchestra; 2 cadenzas to the violin concerto; 6 piano concertos plus Rondo in B-flat (completed by Czerny), also an arrangement for piano of the violin concerto; 8 cadenzas to the first 4 piano concertos and 2 cadenzas to Mozart's D Minor (K. 466); Triple concerto for piano, violin, cello.

Violin

D Major, Op. 61 (1806)

Piano

B-flat Major, Op. 19 (1794-95)
C Major, Op. 15 (1797-98)
C Minor, Op. 37 (1800)
G Major, Op. 58 (1805-06)
E-flat Major, Op. 73 (1809)

CHAMBER MUSIC

For violin and piano: 10 sonatas, rondo in G, 12 variations in F, 6 *Deutsche Tänze.* For cello and piano: 5 sonatas, 3 sets of variations. For horn and piano: 1 sonata. Five string trios. One trio for 2 oboes and English horn; also a serenade for flute, violin and viola. Nine trios, 2 sets of variations for piano, violin, and cello. Two trios for piano, clarinet (or violin) and cello. One trio for piano, flute, and bassoon. Sixteen string quartets, and a Grand Fugue for string quartet. Four quartets for piano and strings. Three *Equali* for 4 trombones. Quintet for piano and winds. Three quintets for strings and a fugue for string quintet. Sextet for winds. Septet for strings and winds. Two octets for winds.

A. String Instruments

Quartets

F Major, Op. 18, No. 1 (1798-1800)
E Minor, Op. 59, No. 2, "Rasoumovsky" (*c.* 1806)
F Minor, Op. 95, "Serioso" (1810)
A Minor, Op. 132 (1824-25)
B-flat Major, Op. 130 (1825-26)
Grand Fugue, Op. 133, in B-flat Major (1825)
C-sharp Minor, Op. 131 (1826)
F Major, Op. 135 (1826)

B. Piano with Other Instruments

Trios

B-flat Major, Op. 97, "Archduke" (1811)

CHORAL WORKS

Cantatas and ensemble works with orchestra and with piano; 1 oratorio; 2 masses; *Choral Fantasy.*

Oratorio

Christus am Oelberg ("Christ on the Mount of Olives"), Op. 85 (1803)

Mass

Missa Solemnis in D, Op. 123 (1819-23)

Other Works

Choral Fantasy for piano, chorus, and orchestra, Op. 80 (1808)

COMPOSITIONS FOR THE STAGE

Opera

Fidelio (1805; revised 1806, 1814)

SOLO COMPOSITIONS

For piano 38 sonatas and 2 sonatinas, 21 sets of variations; for voice 75 songs with piano accompaniment, 23 canons, 7 books of English, Scotch, Irish, Welsh, and Italian songs with piano, violin and cello; for organ a 2-part fugue.

SUGGESTED READING

1.	*Ca-Jo-WaAM*	328-40
2.	*CobCM*	I, 81-111
3.	*GleCM*	Outline IV
4.	*GroutHWM*	470-91
5.	*GroutSHO*	311-14
6.	*HiCon*	119-42
7.	*HiSym*	92-125
8.	*PaulyMCP*	197-206
9.	*RobCM*	94-140
10.	*SachsCA*	180-84
11.	*UlCM*	239-80
12.	*UlSM*	113-49
13.	*Ul-PiHM*	375-77, 404-24
14.	*VeiCon*	125-50

REFERENCES

THEMATIC INDICES

1. Nottebohm, G., *Thematisches Verzeichnis der im Druck erschienenen Werke von Ludwig van Beethoven,* Leipzig: Breitkopf & Härtel, 1925. Incomplete and not fully reliable.
2. Kinsky, Georg and Halm, Hans, *Das Werk Beethovens; Thematisch-Bibliographisches Verzeichnis,* München-Duisburg, G. Henle Verlag, 1955.

MUSIC

1. Beethoven L. van, *Werke* 46 vols, Leipzig: Breitkopf & Härtel, 1864-90, reprinted by J. W. Edwards, Ann Arbor: University of Michigan Press, 1949.

BOOKS

1. Burk, J. N., *The Life and Works of Beethoven,* New York: Random House, 1943.
2. Grove, Sir Geo., *Beethoven and His Nine Symphonies,* New York: Dover Publications, 1898.
3. Kerman, J., *The Beethoven Quartets,* New York: Alfred A. Knopf & Co., 1967.
4. Marliave, Joseph de, *Beethoven's Quartets,* translated by Hilda Andrews, New York: Dover Publications, 1961.
5. Mason, D. G., *The Quartets of Beethoven,* New York: Oxford University Press, 1947.
6. Thayer, A. W., *The Life of Ludwig van Beethoven,* rev. and ed. by Elliot Forbes, Princeton: Princeton University Press, 1964.
7. Tovey, D. F., *Beethoven,* London, 1956 (an unfinished final work).

CHAPTER

3

The Early Romanticists

IX. Franz Schubert (1797-1828)

The least "schooled" of the German masters, but reared in a music-saturated environment; made up for his lack of formal training with a keen musical intuition and a never-ending reserve of melody. Marked by lack of public recognition, by humiliation and disappointment, his short life was a constant struggle against sickness and poverty. In circumstances a musical Bohemian, but with the encouraging love of a few friends, he composed ceaselessly and with care. Equally at home with voice or instrument, and in secular or sacred fields, it was only in opera that Schubert was not successful. Sensitive to external influences (Haydn, Mozart, Beethoven, the "Italianism" of Rossini), he was still a unique personality, with traits that marked him as a Romanticist. His music characterized by a self-generated type of melody, a feeling for harmonic color, new sonorities, imaginative use of wind instruments (flute, trombone, horn), and widely-ranging modulations. Considered the creator of the modern German *lied,* his songs captured the emotional essence of the poem and made true partners of singer and pianist. Finally, with equal inspiration, he transferred the "Liedform" to the solo piano in *Moments musicaux* and *Impromptus.*

ORCHESTRAL MUSIC

Nine symphonies (including the unfinished and unpublished E minor of 1821; but not including the "Gastein," of 1825, the score of which has not been found), 8 overtures (1, at least, "in the Italian style").

Symphonies
No. 4 in C Minor, "Tragic" (1816)
No. 5 in B-flat Major (1816)
No. 6 in C Major (1817)
No. 8 in B Minor, "Unfinished" (1822)
No. 9 in C Major (1828)

PIECES WITH ORCHESTRA

Concertstück for violin

CHAMBER MUSIC

Rondo brillant (B minor, Op. 70), *Phantasie* (C, Op. 159) Sonata (A, Op. 162), 3 Sonatinas (Op. 137) for vln. and pf.; Introduction and Variations for fl. and pf. (Op. 160); String Trio (vln., vla., vcl.; B-flat), 2 Piano Trios; 15 str. quartets; str. quintet (C, Op. 163, with 2 cellos); pf. quintet (A, Op. 144, the "Trout" with double bass); Octet (5 strings, horn, bassoon, and clarinet, Op. 166).

A. String Instruments

Quartets
No. 14 in D Minor, "Death and the Maiden" (1824)

Quintets
C Major, Op. 163, for 2 violins, viola, 2 cellos (1828)

B. Piano with Other Instruments

Duos
Rondo brillant, Op. 70, for violin and piano (1826)

Trios
B-flat Major, Op. 99, for piano, violin, cello (1827)
E-flat Major, Op. 100, for piano, violin, cello (1827)

Quintets
A Major, Op. 114, for piano, violin, viola, cello, double bass, "The Trout" (1819)

C. Miscellaneous

Octet

F Major, Op. 166, for clarinet, horn, bassoon, string quartet, and double bass

CHORAL WORKS

Six Latin Masses, 1 German Mass (4-pt. mixed cho. with organ); *Lazarus* (oratorio fragment); Psalm 92 (baritone solo, mixed cho.); 2 *Tantum ergo* (4-pt. mixed cho., orch.); 2 *Stabat Mater* (4 voices, orch.); several *Salve regina; Miriams Siegesgesang* (sop. solo, cho., orch.); Prayer, *Vor der Schlacht* (soli, mixed cho., pf.); *Herr unser Gott* (hymn, 8-pt. men's cho., wind instr.); *Hymne an den Heiligen Geist* (8-pt. male cho., orch.); *Morgengesang im Walde* (4-pt. male cho., orch.); *Nachtgesang im Walde; Nachthelle* (4-pt. male cho., horns); *Schlachtlied* (8-pt. male cho., pf.); *Glaube, Hoffnung und Liebe* (mixed cho., wind).

Masses

In G Major, D. 167 (1815) for SATB, str. orch., and organ

In A-flat Major, D. 678, for SATB, orch., and organ (1822; later emendations)

In E-flat Major, D. 950, for SATB and orch. (1828)

COMPOSITIONS FOR THE STAGE

Die Zauberharfe (3-act melodrama, Vienna, 1820); *Alfonso und Estrella* (3-act opera, 1821-22, perf. Weimar, 1854, by Liszt); *Die Verschworenen* (renamed *Der häusliche Krieg*, 1-act operetta, 1823; perf. Karlsruhe, 1897); *Rosamunda von Cypern* (incidental music, 1823; Overture from *Die Zauberharfe*); *Die Bürgschaft* (1816).

SOLO COMPOSITIONS

For the piano: twenty-two sonatas (7 left incomplete; the C major was completed by Ernst Křenek); 31 dances, 16 other works for 1 performer; 32 4-hand pieces (including the Fantasy in F minor, Op. 103; Sonata in C major, Op. 140; *Grand Rondeau* in A major, Op. 107). For solo voice and piano: 634 songs, 44 of them in the great cycles *Die schöne Müllerin*, Op. 25, and *Die Winterreise*, Op. 89.

SUGGESTED READING

1.	*Ca-Jo-WaAM*	341-56
2.	*CobCM*	II, 352-66
3.	*GleCM*	Outline V
4.	*GroutHWM*	500-03, 506-14, 523-25, 530-31, 560
5.	*HiSym*	126-48
6.	*RobCM*	141-74
7.	*SachsCA*	184-90
8.	*UlCM*	281-99
9.	*Ul-PiHM*	425-28, 430-44
10.	*UlSM*	150-59

REFERENCES

THEMATIC INDICES

1. Deutsch, O. E., *Schubert, Thematic Catalogue of all his Works in Chronological Order,* London: J. M. Dent & Sons, Ltd., 1951.
2. Nottebohm, G., *Thematisches Verzeichnis,* Vienna: Schreiber, 1874.

MUSIC

1. *Werke,* 21 vols. in 39, Leipzig: Breitkopf & Härtel, 1884-1897.

BOOKS

1. Abraham, G. E., ed., *The Music of Schubert,* New York: W. W. Norton & Company, Inc., 1947.
2. Deutsch, O. E., *Schubert, a Documentary Biography,* translated by Eric Blom, London: J. M. Dent & Sons, Ltd., 1947.
3. Einstein, A., *Music in the Romantic Era,* New York: W. W. Norton & Company, Inc., 1947.

X. Hector Berlioz (1803-1869)

The most important figure in the French Romantic movement, Berlioz added new luster to French Romantic opera, pioneered the symphonic poem, and pointed the way toward modern orchestration. At the Paris Conservatoire he challenged the restrictions of the classical school as set down by his instructors (Lesueur and Reicha) and gave full rein to his own imagination. Influenced by the writings of Virgil, Shakespeare, and Goethe, as well as by the symphonies of Beethoven, he attempted from the first to exceed the accepted limits of both composition and performance. As the foremost music critic of his time and a brilliant journalist (articles in *Journal des Débats* and *Gazette Musicale*), he roused interest in new musical ideas both by his writings and by his compositions. Dreaming of huge orchestras sufficient to express the power and scope of his ideas, and abandoning the classical method of thematic development, he fathomed the full resources of the symphony orchestra for the portrayal of personal feeling, and established the use of the *idée fixe*, or recurring theme. With artistic designs tending to run in parallel literary and musical channels, he employed novel melodic and rhythmic effects, and he enriched the orchestral ensemble by dividing, combining, and otherwise exploiting its acoustic resources. According to his compositional creed, not only beauty but ugliness merited musical representation as segments of truth, and this conviction led to still further explorations in vivid color. With all of this, it must be recorded that at times Berlioz seemingly lacked in self-criticism and selectivity, so that crudities and banalities may at times be found in his scores. His *Traité d'instrumentation et d'orchestration modernes* (1844) has been translated into all European languages, with revised and enlarged German editions issued by Felix Weingartner (1904) and Richard Strauss (1905). An English edition was published by Kalmus in 1948.

ORCHESTRAL MUSIC

Symphonie fantastique (1829-30, revised 1846 and pub. as Op. 14); *Lelio, ou le Retour a la vie* (sequel to *Symphonie fantastique,* for actor, soloists, chorus, pianists, and orch.; 1832); *Harold en Italie* (solo viola and orch., completed 1834); 7 Overtures inc. *Waverly* (1827, Op. 1); *Le Roi Lear* (1831, Op. 4); *Rob Roy* (1832); *Le Carnaval romain* (1844, Op. 9, written for 2nd act of *Benvenuto Cellini*); and *Le Corsaire* (1855, Op. 21).

Symphonies

Symphonie fantastique, "Episode in the Life of an Artist," Op. 14 (revised 1846)
Lelio or The Return to Life
Harold en Italie, Op. 16 (1834)

Overtures

Benvenuto Cellini (1838)
Le Carnaval romain (1844)

CHORAL WORKS

Grand Messe des Morts (Requiem Mass, 1837), *Roméo et Juliette* (a "dramatic symphony" for soloists, chorus, and orch.; 1839), *Symphonie funèbre et triomphale* (for military band, strings, and cho.; 1840; Op. 15), *La Damnation de Faust* ("opéra de concert," final form 1846), *Te Deum* (for tenor, 3 choirs, orch., brass band and organ; 1849), and *L'Enfance du Christ* (a sacred trilogy, 1854).

Secular Texts

Roméo et Juliette, Op. 17 (1839)
La Damnation de Faust (1846)

Sacred Texts

Grand Messe des Morts (1837)
Te Deum (1849)
L'Enfance du Christ (1854)

COMPOSITIONS FOR THE STAGE

Operas *Benvenuto Cellini* (1838), *Les Troyens* (1856-59), and *Béatrice et Bénédict* (*opéra comique* in 2 acts, 1862).

Operas

Benvenuto Cellini (1838)
Les Troyens (1856-59)
Béatrice et Bénédict (1862)

SOLO COMPOSITIONS

Voice

Song cycles *Irlande* (1830) and *Nuits d'été* (1834-41, also with orchestra)

SUGGESTED READING

1.	*Ca-Jo-WaAM*	368-72
2.	*GroutHWM*	494-98, 535-38, 549-550
3.	*GroutSHO*	323-28
4.	*HiSym*	149-61
5.	*Ul-PiHM*	461-2, 489-93
6.	*UlSM*	184-93
7.	*VeiCon*	174-79

REFERENCES

MUSIC

1. *Werke* 20 vols., edited by Charles Malherbe and Felix Weingartner (operas *Benvenuto Cellini* and *Les Troyens* not included; also see Supplement 5 in Barzun, *Berlioz* for errors, musical and otherwise. Leipzig: Breitkopf & Härtel, 1900-).

BOOKS

1. Barzun, Jacques, *Berlioz and the Romantic Century,* New York: Little, Brown & Company, 1950. Reprint under title, *Berlioz and His Century,* New York: Meridian Books, 1959.
2. Elliott, J. H., *Berlioz,* New York: E. P. Dutton & Co., Inc., 1938.
3. Turner, W. J., *Berlioz, the Man and His Work,* London: Dent & Sons, Ltd., 1934.
4. Wotton, T. W., *Hector Berlioz: four works.* London: Oxford, 1929.

XI. Felix Mendelssohn (1809-1847)

One of the world's most gifted musicians. Born into a home of culture, position, and wealth, Mendelssohn had every advantage in environment and education. His music, like his life, was well ordered and harmonious, the pleasant aspects being always emphasized. By training, inclination, and conviction Mendelssohn was a classicist, and his works displayed formal perfection, faultless craftsmanship, and an unerring sense of proportion. At the same time he was fully responsive to Romantic trends, his compositions being imbued with sentiment, passion, and delicate color. The youthful Mendelssohn proved his musical maturity at age seventeen with the composition of the *Midsummer Night's Dream* Overture, in which were evidenced the same mastery and finish of form as were to appear sixteen years later in the remaining numbers. Accomplished in the graphic arts (landscape painting especially), he was frequently pictorial in his writing, his music showing, however, more expression of mood than actual depiction—merely describing in tones the feelings aroused in the composer by scenes or objects. His ideas were always thought out before being committed to paper (he used no sketch books as Beethoven did). From 1820, at his father's suggestion, he copied all works in a series of forty-four manuscript volumes, the place and date of composition usually being given. While not an innovator or pioneer, and while his music often lacks virility and resourcefulness, his influence on German, English, and American music for some time after his death was substantial. His symphonies, chamber music, and oratorios are still very much a part of the world repertory.

ORCHESTRAL MUSIC

Five symphonies (Op. 1 in C minor; Op. 52, *Lobgesang,* with voices; Op. 56 in A minor, *Scotch;* Op. 90 in A major, *Italian;* Op. 107 in D minor, *Reformation*); 10 overtures (inc. Op. 21, *A Midsummer Night's Dream;* Op. 26, *Hebrides* or *Fingal's Cave;* Op. 27, *Calm Sea and Prosperous Voyage;* Op. 32, *The Lovely Melusine;* Op. 95, *Ruy Blas;* Op. 101, Trumpet Overture).

Symphonies

D Minor, Op. 107, "Reformation" (1832, known as No. 5)
A Major, Op. 90, "Italian" (Completed 1833, known as No. 4)
A Minor, Op. 56, "Scotch" (Completed 1842, known as No. 3)

Overtures

Midsummer Night's Dream, Op. 21 (1826)
Calm Sea and Prosperous Voyage, Op. 27 (1828)
Fingal's Cave (Hebrides), Op. 26 (1830-32)
Ruy Blas, Op. 95 (1839)

CONCERTOS AND PIECES WITH ORCHESTRA

Two for 1 piano (Op. 25 in G minor; Op. 40 in D minor), 2 for 2 pianos (A-flat major and E major, both having been extracted from parts in Berlin *Staatsbibliothek* and recorded), plus *Capriccio brillante* (Op. 22), *Rondo brillante* (Op. 29), *Serenade and Allegro giojoso* (Op. 43) for pf. and orch.; 2 vln. (one written at age 12 was rediscovered and pub. in 1952, with 1st perf. by Yehudi Menuhin same year; Op. 64 in E minor, one of finest for the instrument).

Violin

E Minor, Op. 64 (1844)

Piano

G Minor, Op. 25 (1831)
D Minor, Op. 40 (1837)

CHAMBER MUSIC

For piano and violin, 1 sonata (Op. 4); for pf. and vcl., 2 sonatas (Op. 45, 58), *Variations concertantes* (Op. 17) and *Lied ohne Worte* (Op. 109); for clarinet and pf., 1 sonata; 2 trios for clar., basset-horn, and pf. (Op. 113, 114); 2 piano trios (Op. 49, 66); 3 pf. quartets (Op. 1, 2, 3); 7 string quartets (Op. 12, 13, 44, 44a, 44b, 80, 81); a pf. sextet (Op. 110); 2 string quintets (Op. 18, 87); octet for strings (Op. 20).

A. String Instruments

Quartets

E-flat Major, Op. 44, No. 3 (1837-38)

Octets

E-flat Major, Op. 20 (1825)

B. Piano with Other Instruments

Trios (piano, violin, cello)

D Minor, Op. 49 (1839)
C Minor, Op. 66 (1845)

CHORAL WORKS

Oratorios *St. Paul* and *Elijah*; *Lobgesang* (symphony-cantata, Op. 52; also designated as symph. No. 2); ballade, *Die erste Walpurgisnacht,* (Op. 60, for soli, cho., orch.); various vocal works without orch.; 21 quartets for men's voices; 28 quartets for mixed voices.

Oratorios

St. Paul, Op. 36 (1836)
Elijah, Op. 70 (1846)

Symphony-Cantata

Lobgesang, Op. 52 (Hymn of Praise, on texts from the Holy Scriptures) (1840)

COMPOSITIONS FOR THE STAGE

An early opera, *Die Hochzeit des Camacho*; various fragments of projected works.

SOLO COMPOSITIONS

For piano, 3 sonatas (Op. 6 in E major, Op. 105 in G minor, Op. 106 in B-flat major); 3 sets of var.

(Op. 54 in D minor, *Variations sérieuses*; Op. 82 in E-flat major; Op. 83 in B-flat major); 49 Songs Without Words (8 books with 6 each, 49th discovered 1951 in England); 7 Characteristic Pieces (much Scarlatti influence, Nos. 4 and 7 most individual); Andante and Rondo Capriccioso in E-e, Op. 14); 6 Preludes and Fugues (Op. 35 in e-E, D, b, A-flat, f, B-flat). For solo voice and piano, 83 songs. Music for four hands. Organ music (inc. 3 preludes and fugues, Op. 37, plus 6 organ sonatas).

SUGGESTED READING

1.	*CobCM*	II, 128-36
2.	*GleCM*	Outline VI
3.	*GroutHWM*	514-15, 525-26, 531-34
4.	*HiCon*	154-61
5.	*HiSym*	162-72
6.	*RobCM*	175-82
7.	*UlCM*	299-301, 303-8
8.	*Ul-PiHM*	469-74
9.	*UlSM*	165-70, 173-77
10.	*VeiCon*	179-87

REFERENCES

THEMATIC INDEX

1. Mendelssohn-Bartholdy, F., *Thematisches Verzeichnis der im Druck erschienenen Compositionen von Felix Mendelssohn-Bartholdy,* Leipzig: Breitkopf & Härtel, 187-

MUSIC

1. Mendelssohn-Bartholdy, F., *Werke* 19 vols. in 37, Leipzig: Breitkopf & Härtel, 1874-77.
2. *Mendelssohn's Chamber Music,* Miniature scores, Leipzig: Eulenburg, 188- Vol. I: Quartets, Op. 12, 13, 44 (Nos. 1-3), 80, 81; Vol. II: Quintets, Op. 18, 87; Octet, Op. 20; Trios Op. 49-66.

BOOKS

1. Jacob, H. E., *Felix Mendelssohn and His Times,* translated by Richard and Clara Winston, New York: Prentice-Hall, Inc., 1963.
2. Kaufman, S., *Mendelssohn, a Second Elijah,* New York: Thomas Y. Crowell Company, 1934.
3. Stratton, S. S., *Mendelssohn,* New York: E. P. Dutton & Company, Inc., 1934.
4. Werner, Eric, *Mendelssohn: A New Image of the Composer and His Age,* translated by Dika Newlin, New York: Free Press of Glencoe, 1963.

XII. Robert Schumann (1810-1856)

Youngest son of a bookseller and interested from the first in poetry, he contributed at fourteen to a work published by his father, and at seventeen composed musical settings of his own poems. With burning admiration for the extravagantly romantic outpourings of Byron and Jean Paul Richter, and because of an unfortunate injury to his hand, he devoted himself to musical composition and literary work. In 1834 he founded (with others) the *Neue Zeitschrift für Musik,* serving as editor from 1835 to 1844. Writing under pen names "Florestan," "Eusebius," "Meister Raro," and signing his essays with numerals "2" or "12," he represented musical journalism at its best. On the side of liberal and progressive musical art he exerted a strong influence on musical thought and tastes, encouraging the highest ideals and discouraging mediocrity and sham. The acknowledged leader of the German Romantic school, he evidenced in his music concentrated passion, intense emotion, poetic restraint, freshness, and exuberance. He took up one department of musical composition at a time and devoted himself intently to that one. Op. 1 to 23, with 26, 28, and 32 (to end of 1839) were for piano solo; under inspiration of his love for Clara, he then turned (1840) to song writing, after which symphonic works (1841), chamber music (1842), and choral works (1843) occupied his attention. In 1845 he resumed the writing of piano works (Op. 56, 68, 76, and others). His keyboard compositions express many of the most characteristic piano idioms of the nineteenth century. His songs show an intuitive understanding of Romantic poetry in their varied forms and intimate expression. Although it is somewhat the fashion to criticize his orchestration, his "thick" scoring, and the ineffective organization and expansion of his musical inspirations, the fact remains that his music lives because of the sheer beauty of ideas, enthusiasm, humor, charm, and eloquence. Because of tragic ill health, there is a gradual waning of his musical and compositional powers at the end of his career. However, Robert Schumann remains one of the most romantic of the German Romantics, a musical genius of many sides, and the embodiment of imagination, sentiment, individualism in thought and profundity of expression.

ORCHESTRAL MUSIC

Four symphonies (Op. 38 in B-flat, Op. 61 in C, Op. 97 in E-flat, Op. 120 in D minor); *Ouvertüre, Scherzo und Finale* (Op. 52); 4 concert overtures (*Die Braut von Messina,* Op. 100; *Festouvertüre,* Op. 123; *Julius Caesar,* Op. 128; *Hermann und Dorothea,* Op. 136).

Symphonies

B-flat Major, Op. 38 (1841)
D Minor (1841, 1st called No. 2; revised 1853 as No. 4, Op. 120)
C Major, Op. 61 (1846; now known as No. 2)
E-flat Major, Op. 97 *Rhenish* (1850; now known as No. 3)

Overtures
Genoveva, Op. 81 (1847-48)
Manfred, Op. 115 (1848)

CONCERTOS AND PIECES WITH ORCHESTRA

One for piano (A minor-major, Op. 54); *Konzertstück* (Introduction and Allegro appassionato in G minor, Op. 92); *Konzert-Allegro* (D minor, Op. 134) for piano; *Konzertstück* (Op. 86) for 4 horns; Concerto (A minor, Op. 129) for cello; *Fantasia* (Op. 131) and Concerto (written 1853, pub. 1937) for vln.

Violin
D Minor, (1853; resurrected 1937)

Cello
A Minor, Op. 129 (1850)

Piano
A Minor-Major, Op. 54 (1841, 1845)

CHAMBER MUSIC

Adagio and Allegro (Op. 70) for piano and horn; 3 *Fantasiestücke* (Op. 73) for pf. and clarinet; 3 *Romanzen* (Op. 94) for pf. and oboe; 5 *Stücke im Volkston* (Op. 102) for pf. and vcl.; 2 sonatas (A minor, Op. 105; D minor, Op. 121) for pf. and vln.; 4 *Märchenbilder* (Op. 113) for pf. and vla.; 4 *Märchenerzählungen* (Op. 132) for pf., clarinet, and viola; 3 pf. trios (D minor, Op. 63; F major, Op. 80; G minor, Op. 110); 4 *Fantasiestücke* (Op. 88) for pf., vln., and vcl.; 3 string quartets (A minor, F major, and A major, Op. 41); quartet (E-flat, Op. 47) for pf. and strings; quintet (E-flat, Op. 44) for pf. and strings.

A. String Instruments

Quartets
A Minor, Op. 41, No. 1 (1842)
F Major, Op. 41, No. 2 (1842)
A Major, Op. 41, No. 3 (1842)

B. Piano with Other Instruments

Trios
D Minor, Op. 63, for piano, violin, cello

Quartet
E-flat Major, Op. 47, for piano, violin, viola, cello (1843)

Quintet
E-flat Major, Op. 44, for piano and string quartet (1843)

CHORAL WORKS

Cantata *Das Paradies und die Peri* (solo, cho., orch., after T. Moore's *Lalla Rookh* Op. 50); *Adventlied* (Soprano, cho., orch.; Op. 71); *Beim Abschied zu singen* (cho. with woodwind or pf.; Op. 84); *Requiem für Mignon* (Op. 98b); *Nachtlied* (cho., orch., Op. 108); cantata *Der Rose Pilgerfahrt* (Op. 112); ballade *Der Königssohn* (Op. 116); ballade *Des Sängers Fluch* (Op. 139); 4 ballades (*Vom Pagen und der Königstochter,* Op. 140,); ballade *Das Glück von Edenhall* (men's cho., orch., Op. 143); *Neujahrslied* (Op. 144); *Missa sacra* (Op. 147); Requiem Mass (Op. 148); many choruses a cappella for men, mixed voices, women; choruses with piano.

Cantata
Das Paradies und die Peri, Op. 50 (1843)

COMPOSITIONS FOR THE STAGE

An opera, *Genoveva* (Op. 81, 1850); music to Lord Byron's *Manfred* (Op. 115); Scenes from Goethe's *Faust.*

SOLO COMPOSITIONS

For the piano: three sonatas (Op. 11 in F-sharp minor, Op. 14 in F minor, Op. 22 in G minor); 3 "sonatas for the young" (Op. 118 in G, D, C); a Fantasie in 3 mvts. (Op. 17 in C); 12 studies on Caprices by Paganini; Variations on *Abegg;* Impromptus on a Theme by Clara Wieck; 12 Studies in the form of Variations (*Etudes symphoniques,* Op. 13); sets with titles *Papillons* (Op. 2), *Davidsbündlertänze* (Op. 6), *Scenes of Childhood* (Op. 15), *Carnaval* (Op. 9), *Fantasiestücke, Kreisleriana* (Op. 16), *Album für die Jugend* (Op. 68), *Toccata* (Op. 7 in C), *Humoreske* (Op. 20 in B-flat); four-hand pieces and pieces for pedal-piano. Solo Voice: a wealth of lyrical gems, inc. cycles *Frauenliebe und Leben* (poems by Chamisso, Op. 42) and *Dichterliebe* (16 numbers, poems by Heine, Op. 48).

SUGGESTED READING

1.	*Ca-Jo-WaAM*	356-58
2.	*CobCM*	II, 368-94
3.	*GleCM*	Outline VII
4.	*GroutHWM*	494-99, 503-4, 513-16, 534-35
5.	*HiCon*	170-178
6.	*HiSym*	173-190
7.	*RobCM*	183-190
8.	*UlCM*	301-303, 308-316
9.	*Ul-PiHM*	474-80
10.	*UlSM*	177-183
11.	*VeiCon*	187-194

REFERENCES

MUSIC

1. SCHUMANN, R., *Werke* 14 vols., Leipzig: Breitkopf & Härtel, 1883-93.
2. WIER, A. E., *Miscellaneous Chamber Works,* New York: Longmans, Green & Company, 1940.

BOOKS

1. BOUCOURECHLIEV, ANDRÉ, *Schumann,* translated by Arthur Boyars, New York: Grove Press, 1959.
2. EVANS, E., *Schumann,* London: Novello, 1944.
3. FULLER-MAITLAND, J. A., *Schumann's Concerted Chamber Music,* London: Oxford University Press, 1929.
4. SCHAUFFLER, R. H., *Florestan: the Life and Work of Robert Schumann,* New York: Henry Holt & Company, Inc., 1945.

XIII. Frédéric Chopin (1810-1849)

Called by Schumann (*Neue Zeitschrift für Musik,* 1839) "the boldest and proudest poetic spirit of the time," Chopin was an experimenter in small forms, an innovator in harmonic practice, and the liberator of the piano from the orchestral and choral influences which were traditional at his time. Representing the chromatic branch of the nineteenth century, he was in the forefront of his contemporaries in the unconventionality and daring of his tonal thinking. By hinting at keys that often were not fully realized or secured by tonics, by constant chromatic alteration of sonorities, by chordal respellings and transient modulations, Chopin helped prepare the way for the "suspensive writing" of Wagner and others to follow. Living in Paris from 1831 on, and destined never to revisit his native Poland, he nevertheless carried the adversities and misfortunes of his homeland close to his heart. National rhythms, forms, harmonies, and melodic characteristics are features of his writing. His fully-developed style was a compound of many elements, among them being the coloratura embellishments in Rossini and Bellini operas, the ornaments and figurations formerly employed to prolong the harpsichord tone, and the counterpoint featured in Bach's part-writing. After a few early works which combined the piano with other instruments—composed when he was seeking to establish himself by means of public programs—he confined his creative talents to the piano as a solo instrument. In this field he showed to the full his indefinable spontaneity, his penchant for introspective and improvisatory writing, his mastery of the art of suggestion, and his ingenuity and subtlety in the use of such expressive elements as *tempo rubato.*

CONCERTOS AND PIECES WITH ORCHESTRA

Two concertos; *Andante spianato* and *Polonaise;* Fantasia on Polish Airs; *Rondo à la Krakowiak;* Variations on "Là ci darem la mano" of Mozart (Op. 2).

Piano

F Minor, Op. 21 (1829)
E Minor, Op. 11 (1830)

CHAMBER MUSIC

Piano trio; cello sonata; Introduction and Polonaise for cello and piano.

SOLO COMPOSITIONS

For piano: Three sonatas, 4 Ballades, 3 *Écossaises,* 27 Études, 3 Impromptus, *Fantaisie-Impromptu,* 51 Mazurkas, 19 Nocturnes, 12 Polonaises, 25 Preludes, 4 Scherzos, 17 Waltzes, *Barcarolle, Berceuse,* Fantasie in F Minor. For voice: 17 Polish Songs (Op. 74; edited with English text and published in New York).

SUGGESTED READING

1. *Ca-Jo-WaAM* 358-360
2. *CobCM* I, 275f
3. *GroutHWM* 515-519
4. *Ul-PiHM* 465-469
5. *UlSM* 172
6. *VeiCon* 214-220

REFERENCES

THEMATIC INDEX

1. BROWN, M. J. E., *Chopin, An Index of his Works,* London: Macmillan and Company, Ltd., 1960.

MUSIC

1. CHOPIN, F., *Werke* 14 vols., Leipzig: Breitkopf & Härtel, 188-

BOOKS

1. ABRAHAM, G., *Chopin's Musical Style,* London: Oxford University Press, 1939.
2. BOURRIQUEL, C., *Chopin,* translated by Sinclair Road, New York: Grove Press, 1960.
3. KELLY, E. S., *Chopin the Composer,* New York: G. Schirmer, 1913.

XIV. Franz Liszt (1811-1886)

Acknowledged as the greatest pianist of his day, with sheer virtuosity probably still unsurpassed, he lived one of the most brilliant and stimulating lives of the nineteenth century. Among the first piano "recitalists," his stated ideal in the use of his fabulous technique was the full revelation of the composer's intention. His accomplishments as a composer were likewise revolutionary. Convinced that new forms were necessary for the expression of new ideas, he worked toward liberation from established patterns, the one-movement symphonic poem being the result. In this genre, the form is the function of a programme, for the execution of which thematic transformation is a foundation principle. In the process, chosen musical elements are kept in a continuous state of change, modifications being conditioned by various time and rhythmic patterns, by the use of different keys and scales, and by the use of picturesque and colorful effects. Added to harmonic alterations and the movement to unusual tonalities by means of chromatic or enharmonic modulations were the varieties of orchestral color which Liszt called to his aid—often by means of large orchestral ensembles. The final objective, however, was not the portraying of a detailed story but the presenting of a mood. Rather than specific scenes, objects and so on, the composer portrayed his feelings "and the adventures of his soul in order to communicate them." In his final period Liszt experimented with new melodic materials (whole-tone scale, etc.) and new harmonic combinations (unusual intervals, bold modulations, extreme chromaticism), pointing the way toward polytonality and atonality. As a practical musician sensitive to the expectations of his public, Liszt at times indulged in exhibitionism on the stage, as well as bombast and insincerity in his compositions (the ornate and showy arrangements of popular operas are cases in point). He remains, however, the most famous composer-performer of his period, with piano works demanding technical fluency and poetic imagination, with songs equal to the best of nineteenth-century *lieder,* and with orchestral works foreshowing elements of twentieth-century "modern" music.

ORCHESTRAL MUSIC

Faust Symphony, *Dante* Symphony, 12 Symphonic Poems (not inc. *From the Cradle to the Grave,* a short work written 1883).

Symphonies

A Faust Symphony (1853-61)
Symphony on Dante's Divine Comedy (1856)

Symphonic Poems

Tasso, Lamento e Trionfo (after Goethe's *Tasso*: 1849, revised, 1854)
Les Préludes (after Lamartine's *Méditations poétiques,* 1854)
Orpheus (1854)
Hamlet (1858)

CONCERTOS AND PIECES WITH ORCHESTRA

For piano: Two concertos (No. 1 in E-flat, "Triangle"; No. 2 in A major); *Danse Macabre* ("Totentanz").

Piano

E-flat Major (*c.* 1848)
A Major (*c.* 1848)
Danse Macabre, "Totentanz" (*c.* 1850)

CHORAL WORKS

Two oratorios; *Gran Festival Mass* (consecration of the Cathedral at Gran, Hungary in 1855); *Hungarian Coronation Mass* (composed for the King, 1876).

Oratorios

The Legend of St. Elizabeth (1862)
Christus (1886)

SOLO COMPOSITIONS

For the piano: 12 books *Technische Studien; Années de Pèlerinage* (3 books: *Suisse,* 1852; *Italie,* 1848; *Troisième année,* posthumously collected, 1890); 12 *Études d'Exécution Transcendante* (1830, 1831, final form, 1854); 3 *Études de Concert* (A-flat, F minor, D-flat; 1849); *Deux Études de Concert* (*Waldesrauschen, Gnomenreigen,* 1849-63), *Deux Légendes* (1866); 20 Hungarian Rhapsodies (19 pub.); *Harmonies poétiques et religieuses* (4 pieces enlarged to 10, 1851; "Funerailles," No. 7); 6 Paganini Études (G minor, E-flat, G-sharp minor, E, E, A minor); Sonata (B minor), many transcriptions (lieder of Schubert, Mendelssohn, and Schumann, Polish songs by Chopin) and operatic paraphrases (Auber, Donizetti, Gounod, Meyerbeer, Rossini, Verdi, Wagner). Solo Voice: about 60 songs with piano. Organ: Fantasia and Fugue on a chorale theme ("Ad nos, ad salutarem undam," from Meyerbeer's *Le Prophète,* 1850); Prelude and Fugue on B-A-C-H.

SUGGESTED READING

1. *Ca-Jo-WaAM*	360-64, 372-75
2. *CobCM*	II, 98
3. *GroutHWM*	495-98, 506-10, 519-21, 538-39
4. *HiCon*	179-186
5. *HiSym*	191-202
6. *Ul-PiHM*	494-99
7. *UlSM*	193-200
8. *VeiCon*	194-202, 204-208

REFERENCES

MUSIC

1. LISZT, F., *Werke* 33 vols., Leipzig: Breitkopf & Härtel, 190-

BOOKS

1. NEWMAN, E., *The Man Liszt, A Study,* New York: Charles Scribner's Sons, 1934.
2. SEARLE, H., *The Music of Liszt,* New York: John de Graff, 1954.

XV. Johannes Brahms (1833-1897)

One of music's greatest masters, his artistic personality was established by the opposition of two contradictory principles. Considered by early admirers to be the standard-bearer of Romanticism, he absorbed and utilized the poetic and sentimental expressiveness of Vienna together with the sensuous charm of gypsy music and German folk song. Resultant musical characteristics were fervor, imagination, and feeling. At the same time he proclaimed himself the champion of the glorious art of the past. He employed the medieval Church modes, emulated the canonic achievements of the old Flemish composers, gave allegiance to the methods and purposes of such forerunners as Palestrina and Beethoven, and chose for his most important works the classic sonata pattern. Remaining a conservative, he revitalized established forms with a mixture of emotional intensity and restraint, working always in the direction of clear and logical structure. With well-defined musical architecture the basis of his creative efforts, he gave emphasis to clear outline rather than to color, and avoided empty virtuosity and meaningless rhetoric. In his art, then, he brought together apparently conflicting ideals of lyricism and conventional form, combining in one organic whole both feeling and intellect, freedom and restraint. While one of the masters of contrapuntal practice and always exemplifying rigid self-discipline in his handling of musical materials, he still departed from convention when his artistic purpose was served by so doing. In addition to this, with unusual melodic patterns, bold harmonies, complicated rhythms, and formal experiments he often pointed the way to the future. Always severe and sternly critical of his own work, he permitted nothing to remain that did not measure up to his personal standards. Many compositions were destroyed as unworthy. His first symphony was not offered to the public until he was forty-three years of age. In the field of the piano his compositions made new demands upon both technique and understanding. In his songs are beauty, sincerity, and earnestness, a new importance being given to the vocal part. In his chamber music he was a worthy follower of Beethoven, writing with warmth, charm, and strength. As editor he was responsible for a long list of works, many of which appeared for the first time.

ORCHESTRAL MUSIC

Two Serenades (D Major, Op. 11, 1857-58; A Major, Op. 16); 4 symphonies; Variations on a Theme of Haydn (Op. 56a, 1873); 2 overtures.

Symphonies

No. 1 in C Minor, Op. 68 (1856-1876)
No. 2 in D Major, Op. 73 (1877)
No. 3 in F Major, Op. 90 (1883)
No. 4 in E Minor, Op. 98 (1884-1885)

Overtures

"Academic Festival," Op. 80 (1880)
"Tragic," Op. 81 (1880)

CONCERTOS AND PIECES WITH ORCHESTRA

One for violin, 1 for violin and cello, 2 for piano.

Violin

D Major, Op. 77 (1878)

Violin and Cello

A Minor, Op. 102 (1887)

Piano

D Minor, Op. 15 (1854-1858)
B-flat Major, Op. 83 (1878-1881)

CHAMBER MUSIC

Two string sextets (Op. 18 in B-flat, Op. 36 in G); 2 string quintets (Op. 88 in F, Op. 111 in G); 3 string quartets (Op. 51 in C minor and A minor; Op. 67 in B-flat); clarinet quintet (Op. 115); piano quintet (F minor); 3 piano quartets (Op. 25 in G minor, Op. 26 in A, Op. 60 in C minor); 3 piano trios (Op. 8 in B, Op. 87 in C, Op. 101 in C minor); trio for clarinet, cello and piano (Op. 114 in A minor); trio for violin, horn and piano (Op. 40 in E-flat); 3 violin sonatas (Op. 78 in G, Op. 100 in A, Op. 108 in D minor); 2 cello sonatas (Op. 38 in E minor, Op. 99 in F); 2 clarinet sonatas (Op. 120 in F minor and E-flat).

A. String Instruments

Quartets

C Minor, Op. 51, No. 1 (1873)
A Minor, Op. 51, No. 2 (1873)
B-flat Major, Op. 67 (1875)

Quintets

F Major, Op. 88, for 2 violins, 2 violas, cello (1882)
G Major, Op. 111, for 2 violins, 2 violas, cello (1890)

Sextets

B-flat Major, Op. 18, for 2 violins, 2 violas, 2 cellos (1860)
G Major, Op. 36, for 2 violins, 2 violas, 2 cellos (1864)

B. Piano with Other Instruments

Duos

Sonatas:

G Major, Op. 78 for piano, violin (1878-79)
A Major, Op. 100 for piano, violin (1886)

D Minor, Op. 108 for piano, violin (1886-88)
E Minor, Op. 38 for piano, cello (1862-65)
F Major, Op. 99 for piano, cello (1886)

Trios

B Major, Op. 8 for piano, violin, cello (1853-54, revised 1889)

E-flat Major, Op. 40 for piano, violin, horn (or cello or viola) (1865)

Quartets

C Minor, Op. 60, for piano, violin, viola, cello (1855-1875)

Quintet

F Minor, Op. 34 for piano and string quartet (first written as string quintet with 2 cellos; rewritten, 1862, as a sonata for 2 pianos; final form completed in 1864)

C. Miscellaneous

Quintet

B Minor, Op. 115 for clarinet in A, 2 violins, viola, cello (1891)

CHORAL WORKS

Vocal ensemble works in many forms and styles include *Ave Maria,* for women's voices, organ and orchestra (Op. 12; 1858); 5 *Soldatenlieder,* for 4-part male chorus a cappella (Op. 41; 1861-62); *Ein deutsches Requiem; Rinaldo*, cantata for tenor, male chorus and orchestra (after Goethe; Op. 50; 1863-68); the "Alto" *Rhapsodie; Schicksalslied; Triumphlied,* for 8-part chorus and orchestra (Op. 55; 1870-71); *Gesang der Parzen*; 13 canons for women's voices and piano (Op. 113; 1863-90).

Secular texts

Rhapsodie, Op. 53 for alto, male chorus and orchestra (after Goethe's *Harzreise*) (1869)

Schicksalslied, Op. 54 for chorus and orchestra (Song of Destiny) (1871)

Gesang der Parzen, Op. 89 for 6-part chorus and orchestra (Song of the Fates, after Goethe) (1882)

Requiem

Ein deutsches Requiem, Op. 45 for soli, chorus and orchestra (1857-68)

SOLO COMPOSITIONS

For Piano: 3 sonatas (Op. 1 in C, Op. 2 in F-sharp minor, Op. 5 in F minor); Scherzo in E-flat minor (Op. 4); Variations on a Theme by Paganini (Op. 35, 2 vols.). Two Pianos: Sonata in F minor (Op. 34b; original version of piano quintet, Op. 34); Variations on a Theme by Haydn (Op. 56b). Piano Duet: Variations on a Theme by Schumann (Op. 23); 16 Waltzes (Op. 39), *Liebeslieder* Waltzes (Op. 52 and Op. 52a, both with optional voice parts). Solo Voice: nearly 200 songs.

SUGGESTED READING

1.	*Ca-Jo-WaAM*	403-8
2.	*CobCM*	I, 158-85
3.	*GleCM*	Outline VIII
4.	*GroutHWM*	504-6, 526-29, 539-42
5.	*HiCon*	187-205
6.	*HiSym*	224-246
7.	*RobCM*	191-201
8.	*UlCM*	317-335
9.	*Ul-PiHM*	480-88
10.	*UlSM*	201-219
11.	*VeiCon*	220-228

REFERENCES

THEMATIC INDEX

1. Braunstein, J., *Thematic Catalogue of the Collected Works of Brahms,* Ars Musica Press, 1956.

MUSIC

1. Brahms, J., *Sämtliche Werke* 26 vols., Leipzig: Breitkopf & Härtel, 1926-28.
2. Wier, A. E., *The Chamber Music of Brahms,* New York: Longmans, Green & Company, 1940.

BOOKS

1. Anderson, W. R., *Introduction to the Music of Brahms,* London: D. Dobson, 1949.
2. Evans, E., *Handbook to the Chamber and Orchestral Music of Johannes Brahms,* London: W. Reeves, 1933-1935.
3. Geiringer, K., *Brahms, His Life and Work,* New York: Houghton Mifflin Company, 1936, reprinted by Doubleday & Company, Inc., 1961.
4. May, F., *Life of Johannes Brahms,* London: W. Reeves, 1948.
5. Niemann, W., *Brahms, A Comprehensive View of the Man and an Exhaustive Critique of his Works,* translated by C. A. Phillips, New York: Alfred A. Knopf, 1929.
6. Schauffler, R. H., *The Unknown Brahms, His Life, Character and Works,* New York: Dodd, Mead & Company, 1933.

CHAPTER

4

Representative Nineteenth-Century Opera Composers

Grand, Lyric, and Comique Types; The Music Drama

XVI. Giacomo Meyerbeer (Jakob Liebmann Beer, 1791-1864); Grand Opera

The foremost composer of grand opera in Paris during the period following 1830, he exerted a potent and widely-felt influence (Wagner's *Rienzi* in 1842 was designed to "out-Meyerbeer Meyerbeer"). Beginning with a fluent but heavy German style (*Alimelek,* perf. in Vienna, Prague, and Dresden), he mastered the flowing melodic style of Rossini by means of study in Italy (*Il Crociato in Egitto,* Venice, 1824), and achieved such typically French qualities as emotionally effective declamation and pungent rhythm with his work in Paris (studying carefully the French operas from Lully onward). All of these characteristics, plus his natural ease and rapidity of production, his originality in orchestral effects, and his skill in theatrical method, combined to make Meyerbeer the operatic power he was—a true dramatic craftsman. His music is marked by tunefulness, technical proficiency, rhythmic strength, clever harmonic patterns, colorful orchestration, and brilliant treatment of the voice. His capabilities were always employed toward the realization of the full dramatic and emotional content of the libretto. Unfortunately, however, his eagerness to meet public demands and his own bent for the spectacular led at times to an inflated and somewhat bombastic style. Here may be found musical and dance numbers not justified dramatically, repetitive and monotonous writing, and showy but pointless cadenzas. The grand operas of Meyerbeer, then, exemplify both the best and worst musical traits of the genre.

Principal works, beside operas, include incidental music to *Struensee* (tragedy by his brother Michael, one of his best works), *Gutenberg* cantata, cantata *Der Genius der Musik am Grabe Beethovens,* seven sacred odes by Klopstock for four voices a cappella, various instrumental numbers (wind band and orchestra), and works in MS.

COMPOSITIONS FOR THE STAGE

Operas

Robert le Diable (1831)
Les Huguenots (1836)
Le Prophète (1849)
L'Africaine (produced 1865)

SUGGESTED READING

1. *GroutHWM*	546-47
2. *GroutSHO*	319-23

XVII. Gioacchino Rossini (1792-1868); *Opera Buffa* and *Opera Seria*

Enjoyed a brilliant and impressive career as opera composer, terminating his activities early, however, and for reasons never made clear. Youthful successes in Italy included *Tancredi* (*opera seria,* Venice, 1813) and *Almaviva ossia l'inutile precauzione* (*opera buffa,*

Rome, February 20, 1816; performed first time as *Il Barbiere di Siviglia* at Bologna, August 10, same year). After spending a very profitable season in London, he established himself in Paris (1824). At first producing French versions of early works, he composed and produced *Guillaume Tell* (*opera seria,* Paris Opera, 1829), tremendously successful and a glorious climax to his career. Then (age thirty-seven) he retired, never again to write an opera. After travels between France, Italy, and Spain, he settled permanently in Paris (1855), where he became famous as a gourmet and wit. The final years of his life were punctuated by the production of *Stabat Mater* (1842), *Petite Messe Solennelle* (1864), *Hymne à Napoléon III,* and several piano pieces, songs, and instrumental works (called by him *Péchés de vieillesse,* "Sins of Old Age"). Pre-eminent as a composer of vigorous and attractive melodies, Rossini gave utmost importance to the voice, used both alone and in ensembles. His music exemplified light and clear texture, harmonic simplicity, and effective, easily recognized thematic materials. His use of instruments was skillful, the famed Rossini crescendo often contributing to steady growth in tension and excitement. One of the last composers to write for castrati, he was at the same time one of the earliest to be sensitive to the musical worth of the contralto and mezzo-soprano voices. He took the precaution to write out coloratura passages and cadences, but this did not prevent singers from supplying their own versions. With resources of melody, theatrics, humor, and pathos apparently unlimited, Rossini paid tribute to the human voice as one of music's most effective instruments.

Partial catalogue of works beside operas (over 40, if revisions are counted). *Orchestral Music*: Overture (1808); Variations for Clarinet and Orchestra (1809); marches and fanfares. *Chamber music*: 6 sonatas for 2 violins, cello, and double bass (very early); *Rondeau fantastique* for horn and piano (1856); *Tema con variazioni* for flute, clarinet, bassoon, horn (1812); 5 string quartets (1808); 6 wood-wind quartets. *Choral Works*: 23 cantatas (1808 to 1861). *Solo Works*: songs and piano pieces.

Rossini's melodies have furnished material for many other composers, among them Paganini (transcription of Prayer from *Mosè*), Respighi (Rossini's *Quelques Riens* used in the ballet *La Boutique fantasque,* other themes in the orchestral suite *Rossiniana*), and Benjamin Britten (in orchestra suites *Soirées musicales* and *Matinées musicales*). An opera, *Rossini in Neapel,* was composed by Bernhard Paumgartner (1936).

COMPOSITIONS FOR THE STAGE

Operas

Barbiere di Siviglia (1816)
Guillaume Tell (1829)

SUGGESTED READING

1. *CobCM* II, 305f
2. *GroutHWM* 551-52
3. *GroutSHO* 344-56
4. *Ul-PiHM* 452-55

BOOKS

1. Bonavia, F., *Rossini,* London: Novello, 1941.
2. Stendhal (pseud. for Marie-Henri Beyle), *Life of Rossini* (1824), translated by R. Coe, New York: Criterion Books, 1957.
3. Toye, J. Francis, *Rossini, A Study in Tragi-comedy,* London: W. Heinemann, 1934.

XVIII. Giuseppe Verdi (1813-1901); Romantic Melodrama, Climax of Italian Tragic and *Buffa* Types

Acknowledged as the dominating figure in nineteenth-century Italian opera, he was supreme for fifty years, bringing the genre to a musical stature and eminence never realized up to his time. Taking the form as left by Bellini and Donizetti and remaining always loyal to native traditions, he evolved a rich and splendid style compounded of drama, lyricism, textual and musical unity, ingenious workmanship, complexity, and sophistication. With complete understanding of the special purpose of music in the theatre, and entirely unconcerned with theories or subtle philosophies, Verdi projected human passions, producing musical structures basically simple and direct in appeal, but which at the same time were examples of great beauty and tremendous power. His compositional career is usually divided into three periods. The first (ending with *Il Trovatore* and *La Traviata*) is characterized by romantic and sensational melodrama, startling contrasts, climactic passion, rapidly-changing situations, and intense realism. In the second period (ending with *Aïda*), and especially in the third period (embracing *Otello* and *Falstaff*), the undisguised savageness, the excessive sentiment, and the violent situations were modified in the direction of more subtlety and refinement, together with more imaginative handling of materials. While the singer—following established Italian tradition—was always supreme, Verdi's scoring for the instruments in his mature period showed more expertness, originality, and evocative clarity. This growing emphasis on the orchestra reached a culmination in the continuous sound fabric woven for *Falstaff*. His fondness for Shakespeare found glorious expression in the two final operas. Thematic materials were re-used effectively, but his treatment did not approach the *leitmotif* system of Wagner. He accepted the vocal ensemble as a natural and expressive medium, and in the achieving of ingenious sound combinations he showed strength in declamation, perfect timing, and a never-failing instinct for climax. Adored by his own people and honored by all the musical world, Verdi gave to the lyric drama a new lustre and to Italian "grand" opera its full measure of human passion and profound emotion.

CHAMBER MUSIC

String Quartet
E Minor (1873)

CHORAL WORKS

Inno delle Nazioni (for the London Exhibition of 1862); *Requiem Mass* (Manzoni Requiem; 1874); *Pater noster* for 5-part chorus a cappella (1880); *4 Pezzi sacri* (his last work, a group of sacred choruses, in one of which Verdi used a "scala enigmatica"): *Ave Maria* for mixed chorus a cappella; *Stabat Mater* for mixed chorus and orchestra; *Laudi alla Vergine Maria* for female chorus a cappella; *Te Deum* for double chorus with orchestra.

COMPOSITIONS FOR THE STAGE

Operas (complete list): *Oberto, Conte di San Bonifacio* (Milan, 1839); *Un Giorno di regno* (Milan, 1840; a failure; also given as *Il finto Stanislao*); *Nabucodonosor* (*Nabucco,* Milan, 1842); *I Lombardi alla prima Crociata* (Milan, 1843; revised as *Jerusalem,* Paris, 1847); *Ernani* (Venice, 1844); *I due Foscari* (Rome, 1844); *Giovanna d'Arco* (Milan, 1845); *Alzira* (Naples, 1845); *Attila* (Venice, 1846); *Macbeth* (Florence, 1847; revised as *Sivardo, il Sassone,* Paris, 1865); *I Masnadieri* (London, 1847); *Il Corsaro* (Trieste, 1848); *La Battaglia di Legnano* (Rome, 1849; also as *L'Assedio d'Arlem*); *Luisa Miller* (Naples, 1849); *Stiffelio* (Trieste, 1850; revised as *Aroldo,* Rimini, 1857); *Rigoletto* (Venice, 1851; immediately popular); *Il Trovatore* (Rome, 1853; immediately popular); *La Traviata* (Venice, 1853; a failure; also given as *Violetta*); *Les Vêpres siciliennes* (Paris, 1855; also as *Giovanna di Guzman*); *Simone Boccanegra* (Venice, 1857; revised, Milan, 1881); *Un ballo in maschera* (Rome, 1859); *La forza del destino* (St. Petersburg, 1862); *Don Carlos* (Paris, 1867); *Aïda* (Cairo, 1871); *Otello* (Milan, 1887); *Falstaff* (Milan, 1893).

For special attention
Rigoletto (1851)
Il Trovatore (1853)
La Forza del Destino (1862)
Aïda (1871)
Otello (1881)
Falstaff (1893)

SUGGESTED READING

1. *Ca-Jo-WaAM* 408f
2. *CobCM* 528f
3. *GroutSHO* 361-73
4. *Ul-PiHM* 524-30

REFERENCES

BOOKS

1. BARKHAM, J., *Verdi, His Music, Life and Times,* New York: Dodd, Mead & Company, 1963.
2. HUSSEY, D., *Verdi,* New York: Farrar, Strauss, and Cudahy, Inc., 1940, paperback, New York: Collier Books, 1962.
3. TOYE, F. J., *Giuseppe Verdi: His Life and Works,* New York: Alfred A. Knopf, 1931, contains full synopses of all the operas.
4. VERDI, G., *Verdi, the Man in His Letters,* edited by F. Werfel and Paul Stefan, translated by E. Downes, New York: L. B. Fischer, 1942.
5. WALKER, F., *The Man Verdi,* New York: Alfred A. Knopf, Inc., 1962.

XIX. Charles-François Gounod (1818-1893); Lyric Opera

Eminent French dramatic composer of the middle nineteenth century, a champion of distinctive French characteristics in serious music. With a many-sided musical background and diverse talents, he showed much versatility, being perhaps most effective in music where his ability to write attractive melodies and his discriminating ear for harmonic color come into full play. He evidenced at times an undeniable depth and pathos—qualities perhaps arising from an inner conflict between his sensuous nature and his strongly religious inclinations. Unusually responsive to the implications of text, he developed a consistent and logical operatic style. *Faust,* probably the most popular French opera ever composed, continues to be widely performed. Representing an operatic type best termed "lyric," it occupies a stylistic position midway between "grand" opera and operetta. Not so magnificent a spectacle as the first nor so trivial as the second, the Lyric Opera is more intimate and subjective than grand opera, more pretentious and meaningful than operetta. Despite its success, *Faust* is often criticized for its melodramatic approach to the Goethe story and for the sentimentality of its music.

ORCHESTRAL MUSIC

Two symphonies; *Marche funèbre d'une Marionette* for orchestra (1873); *Petite Symphonie* for wind instruments (1888).

CHAMBER MUSIC

Three string quartets.

CHORAL WORKS

Oratorios: *La Rédemption* (1882); *Mors et Vita* (1885). Cantatas: *Marie Stuart* (1837); *Gallia* (1871). Church Music: 9 masses (including *Messe solennelle,* 1849); 3 Requiems; *Stabat Mater*; *Te Deum*; motets; etc.

COMPOSITIONS FOR THE STAGE

Operas: *Sapho* (1851); *La Nonne sanglante* (1854); *Le Médecin malgré lui* (1858); *Faust* (1859); *Philémon et Baucis* (1860); *La Reine de Saba* (1862); *Mireille* (1864); *La Colombe* (1866); *Roméo et Juliette* (1867); *Cinq-Mars* (1877); *Polyeucte* (1878); *Le Tribut de Zamora* (1881).

For special attention
Faust (1859)

SUGGESTED READING

1. *GroutHWM*	548-49
2. *GroutSHO*	340-41
3. *Ul-PiHM*	541-44

XX. Carl Maria Von Weber (1786-1826); German Romantic Opera

Born in a musical and theatrical environment, and into a family where music was an hereditary gift, he grew up in the atmosphere of the stage. To dramatically-stimulated interest and imagination were added practical experiences as manager and conductor. Thus equipped, and naturally versatile, he achieved distinction not only as composer and conductor but as pianist, critic, writer, and poet. Of great importance and influence in the development of German music, Weber was called the "First National German Musician," and is honored as the founder of the German Romantic School. His operas especially established the essential characteristics of the new period, both in style and technique. His romanticism, however, was not of the esoteric, withdrawn, and contemplative order, but was on the contrary spectacular, picturesque, and evocative. A master of melody and of the other materials essential to the composer's craft, he broke with the past and pointed in a new direction as he portrayed folk and fairy tales in an atmosphere of the miraculous, the mysterious and the fanciful. One of the musical heroes of the nineteenth-century thought and practice, he foreshadowed Wagner and the music drama in his orchestral coloring and his tentative use of leading themes.

ORCHESTRAL MUSIC

Two symphonies (both C major); *Beherrscher der Geister* (Op. 27, overture to the unfinished opera, *Rübezahl*); *Jubel-ouvertüre* (Op. 59).

CONCERTOS AND PIECES WITH ORCHESTRA

Two for piano (Op. 11 in C Major; Op. 32 in E-flat Major) and *Konzertstück* (Op. 79, F minor); 2 clarinet (Op. 73, F minor; Op. 74, E-flat Major) and *Concertino* for clarinet (Op. 26, E-flat Major); 1 bassoon (Op. 75, F Major); *Concertino* for horn (Op. 45, E minor).

CHAMBER MUSIC

Piano quartet (Op. 8, B-flat Major); 6 sonatas for violin and piano (Op. 13, F Major, G Major, D minor, E-flat Major, A Major, C Major); variations for clarinet and piano (Op. 33, B-flat Major); piano trio (Op. 63, G minor).

CHORAL WORKS

Der erste Ton, for declamation, chorus and orchestra (1808); *Kampf und Sieg* (Op. 44, cantata on the battle of Waterloo, 1815); *L'Accoglienza* for 6 solo voices, chorus and orchestra (1817); *Jubelkantate* (Op. 58, for soli, chorus and orchestra, 1818); 2 Masses (E-flat, G).

COMPOSITIONS FOR THE STAGE

Operas: *Das Waldmädchen* (Freiberg, 1800); *Peter Schmoll und seine Nachbarn* (Augsburg, 1803); *Silvana* (Frankfurt, 1810); *Abu Hassan* (Munich, 1811); *Der Freischütz* (Berlin, 1821); *Euryanthe* (Vienna, 1823); *Oberon or The Elf King's Oath* (London, 1826).

For special attention
Der Freischütz (1820)
Euryanthe (1823)
Oberon (1826)

SOLO COMPOSITIONS

For Piano: 4 sonatas (Op. 24, C Major; Op. 39, A-flat Major; Op. 49, D minor; Op. 70, E minor); *Aufförderung zum Tanz* (Invitation to the Dance, orchestral transcriptions by Berlioz and Weingartner); 8 sets of variations; dances, etc.; for Voice: numerous songs and part songs.

SUGGESTED READING

1. *Ca-Jo-WaAM*	364-68
2. *CobCM*	II, 569f

3. *GroutHWM* 506-7, 558-60
4. *GroutSHO* 383-89
5. *Ul-PiHM* 428-30, 445-50

REFERENCES

INDEX

1. Jähns, F. W., *Carl Maria von Weber in seinen Werken,* Berlin, 1871.

BOOKS

1. Moser, H. J., ed., *Sämtliche Werke,* Munich: *Deutsche Akademie.* Begun 1926; discontinued after 2 vol.: *Early Operas* and *Salzburg Mass.*
2. Saunders, W., *Weber,* New York: E. P. Dutton & Co., Inc., 1940.
3. Stebbins, L. and Stebbins, R. P., *Enchanted Wanderer: the Life of Carl Maria von Weber,* New York: G. P. Putnam's Sons, 1940.

XXI. Richard Wagner (1813-1883); The Music Drama

A colossal figure in history's list of musico-dramatic reformers, he turned every circumstance, every bit of formal or informal training, every experience, and every personal contact to account in the achieving of his consuming ambition—to be successful as an opera composer. With complete disregard for all conventional obligations (financial, social, or whatever), he accepted and demanded support from all about him as he gradually developed his ideas. Beginning in his formative period with works plainly derivative, he demonstrated in *Der Ring des Nibelungen* unique ideas carried to their logical conclusion. Wagner rejected operatic methods and forms of his period (both Italian and French) as artificial and unable to serve dramatic expression and dramatic truth. He found them faulty in subject-materials, in their use of verse-forms, and in the precedence given music over drama. Choosing his subjects from legendary sources (he wrote his own librettos) because of their freedom from requirements of convention or history, he employed a form of alliterative verse to stimulate the emotions, used instrumental music for immediate expression of feeling, gave to the voice a type of musical declamation (*Sprechsingen*), and utilized the cogent power of association by creating a musical texture from characteristic motifs which were developed and varied either alone or in combination. With his concept broadened to include other arts (painting, architecture, the dance), the music drama became the *Gesamtkunstwerk* (complete or composite art work). As a help in understanding the "Music of the future," Wagner's own detailed and voluminous writings are essential sources. His literary works, as well as published volumes of correspondence, are available in English and furnish invaluable aids toward a comprehension of his theories.

Among the various musical elements and procedures which are considered characteristically Wagnerian are chromatic alteration of chords, application of third relationships in chord and key movement, exchange of major and minor modes, use of enharmonic equivalents, acceptance of seventh and ninth chords as consonant sonorities, and the maintaining of a "suspensive" atmosphere by means of deceptive resolutions and emphasis on nonharmonic tones. Wagner's principle that every component of an art work must contribute to the fulfillment of the dramatic objective of that work was of far-reaching influence. He was one of the German Nationalists' greatest heroes, a musical craftsman of tremendous imagination and full command of resources, an idealist insistent and uncompromising in his devotion to convictions.

ORCHESTRAL MUSIC

Several overtures, including Overture in C (1831), Overture to Raupach's *König Enzio* (1832; published 1908), *Eine Faust-ouvertüre* (1839-40; Dresden, July 22, 1844; rewritten and publ. 1855); *Trauermusik* for wind instruments, after motifs from *Euryanthe* (1844; December 14, 1844, on the arrival of Weber's body from London; publ. 1906); *Siegfried-Idyll* (1870; Triebschen, December 25, 1870; publ. 1877); *Grosser Festmarsch,* for the Philadelphia Centennial Exposition (1876; Philadelphia, May 10, 1876; publ. 1876). Symphony in C Major (1832; publ. 1911); and Symphony in E Major (1834; fragment, not publ.).

CHORAL WORKS

Das Liebesmahl der Apostel, for men's chorus and orchestra, on the biblical scene (1843; Dresden, July 6, 1843; publ. 1844); *An Webers Grabe* for men's chorus a cappella, for the burial of Weber's remains (1844; Dresden, December 15, 1844; publ. 1871).

COMPOSITIONS FOR THE STAGE

Operas and Music Dramas: *Die Hochzeit* (fragment, 1832); *Die Feen* (1833; 1st perf. posthumously Munich, 1888); *Das Liebesverbot* (after Shakespeare's *Measure for Measure*; first given as *Die Novize von Palermo,* Magdeburg, 1836; revived Munich, 1923); *Rienzi der letzte der Tribunen* (1840; 1st performance, Dresden, 1842); *Der fliegende Holländer* (1841; 1st perf., Dresden, 1843); *Tannhäuser* (Dresden, 1845; "Paris" version, 1861); *Lohengrin* (1848; 1st performance, Weimar, 1850); *Der Ring des Nibelun-*

gen ("dramatic trilogy" in 3 pts. and introduction) consisting of *Das Rheingold* (1854; 1st perf., Munich, 1869), *Die Walküre* (1856; 1st perf., Munich, 1870), *Siegfried* (1871; 1st performance, Bayreuth, 1876), *Götterdämmerung* (1874; 1st perf., Bayreuth, 1876); *Tristan und Isolde* (1859; 1st perf., Munich, 1865); *Die Meistersinger von Nürnberg* (1867; 1st perf., Munich, 1868); *Parsifal* (Bayreuth, 1882).

SOLO COMPOSITIONS

Piano works include Sonata in D minor (1829; lost); Sonata in B-flat Major (1831; publ. 1832); Polonaise in D Major for 4 hands (1831; publ. 1832); *Albumsonata* in E-flat Major (for Mathilde Wesendonck; 1853; publ. 1877); *Albumblatt* in C (for Countess Metternich; 1861; publ. 1871); *Albumblatt* in E-flat (for Frau Betty Schott; 1875; publ. 1876). Among works for piano and voice are *Sieben Kompositionen zu Goethes Faust, Les deux Grenadiers* (Fr. transl. by Heine himself, 1839), *Trois Romances,* and *Fünf Gedichte* (the "Wesendonck Songs," 1857-58; publ. 1862).

SUGGESTED READING

1.	*Ca-Jo-WaAM*	376-93
2.	*CobCM*	II, 561-63
3.	*GroutHWM*	494-98, 561-67
4.	*GroutSHO*	392-424
5.	*Ul-PiHM*	451, 531-40

REFERENCES

BOOKS

1. BAGAR, R. C., *Wagner and his Music-Dramas,* New York: The Philharmonic Society, 1943.
2. KERMAN, JOSEPH, *Opera as Drama,* New York: Alfred A. Knopf, Inc., 1956.
3. LAVIGNAC, A., *The Music Dramas of Richard Wagner,* translated by E. Singleton, New York: Dodd, Mead, 1908.
4. NEWMAN, E., *The Wagner Operas,* New York: Alfred A. Knopf, Inc., 1949.
5. STEIN, J. M., *Richard Wagner and the Synthesis of the Arts,* Detroit: Wayne University Press, 1960.

XXII. Georges Bizet (1838-1875); *Opéra Comique*

Born of parents both active in music professionally, he studied at the Paris Conservatoire (beginning at age nine), won various prizes (including the Offenbach for *Le Docteur Miracle,* a one-act opera, and the *Grand Prix de Rome*—both at age nineteen) and returned to Paris where he composed and produced (with extremely indifferent success) operas and other works. Even *Carmen,* his masterpiece, was staged only after many difficulties, and then to an apathetic public. Retained in the repertory, however, with thirty-seven performances during its first season (Bizet died on the evening of the thirty-first performance), it finally achieved world-wide success, and is acclaimed today as the most popular and epochal French opera of the late nineteenth century. Called by some a "tragic operetta," *Carmen,* like *Faust,* was first written with spoken dialogue, thus belonging to the genre of *opéra comique.* Today's performances, however, are usually with Ernest Guiraud's recitatives. With its picturesque Spanish background and musical atmosphere (not fully accepted as authentic by Spaniards), the work turns from the sentimental or mythological and exemplifies such new traits as exoticism and stark realism. In his treatment of the violent and sensual plot (written by Halévy and Meilhac after a narrative by Mérimée), the composer wrote music of melodic vitality, rhythmic strength, and dramatic power—the latter accomplished by strikingly economical means. In this monument of French operatic music, Bizet's rare natural abilities are further shown in ingenious harmonization, effective counterpoint, and lean but artistically compelling orchestration. The "fate" motif from the Overture is the only theme that recurs prominently throughout the score, which is divisible into the conventional arias, ensembles, and other set numbers.

ORCHESTRAL MUSIC

Symphony (written at age seventeen, publ. 1935); *Souvenirs de Rome* (symph. suite in 3 mvts., 1869; publ. as 4-movement suite *Roma* in 1880); Incidental music to *L'Arlésienne* (Daudet's Provençal story, 1872); *Patrie* (orchestral overture, 1874).

Symphony
C Major, No. 1 (1855)

CHORAL WORKS

Cantatas: *David* (1856) and *Clovis et Clothilde* (1857); *Vasco da Gama* (Symphonic ode with chorus, 1859).

COMPOSITIONS FOR THE STAGE

In addition to his principal operas given below, the following: *Le Docteur Miracle* (prize-winning 1-act work perf. at *Bouffes-Parisiens* April 9, 1857); *Don Procopio* (2-act Italian *opera buffa,* sent from Rome instead of the prescribed mass; produced March 10, 1906, in Monte Carlo); *La Guzla de l'Emir* (1-act; withdrawn); *Numa* (1871); *Ivan le Terrible* (4 acts;

Bordeaux, October 12, 1951; score found after composer's death). Completed Halévy's biblical opera *Noë* (1869).

Significant works
Les Pêcheurs de perles (Paris, 1863)
La jolie fille de Perth (Paris, 1867)
Djamileh (Paris, 1872; 1-act)
Carmen (Paris, 1875)

SOLO COMPOSITIONS

For the piano (Bizet was an excellent pianist): *Jeux d'enfants* (suite for 4 hands, also for orchestra); about 150 solo pieces of all kinds.

SUGGESTED READING

1. *GroutHWM* 549
2. *GroutSHO* 426-27
3. *Ul-PiHM* 542
4. *UlSM* 230

REFERENCES

BOOKS

1. Curtiss, M. S., *Bizet and his World,* New York: Alfred A. Knopf, Inc., 1958.
2. Parker, D. C., *Georges Bizet—his Life and Works,* London: K. Paul, Trench, Trubner, 1926.

CHAPTER

5

The Late Romanticists

XXIII. Anton Bruckner (1824-1896)

Bruckner was one of the later nineteenth century's most important composers of church and symphonic music. Born in upper Austria, he matured slowly and late. He was teacher of theory and organ at the Vienna Conservatory (1868-91), and an excellent organist. Somewhat overshadowed by Brahms and constantly criticized because of his allegiance to the Wagner school, he seemed unsure of himself and was always open to suggestions. He permitted almost any interested person to make cuts, adjust materials, or revise orchestration in his symphonies—thus presenting a real problem in performance. In 1929 a monumental edition (22 vols.) of his works in original form was begun under the auspices of the National Library in Vienna and the *International Bruckner-Gesellschaft*. His was a lonely, ingenuous, and intensely religious spirit. Fully equipped in music's mechanics (counterpoint, orchestration, etc.), he resolved—in his own, personal way—fundamental musical problems of his period with a coalescence of opposing Classical and Romantic forces. He wrote under the marked influence of his faith (mystic mood, reverence in use of sacred texts, use of liturgical themes), of Wagner (harmonic language, use of sequence, lengthy construction, imposing orchestral forces), of Beethoven (grandeur of concept, strong contrast, cyclical writing), of Schubert and Liszt (formal and constructive procedures), and of the pipe organ (instrumental grouping suggestive of registers or manuals, thematic expansion simulative of improvisation). His symphonies are all in four movements. The first is in sonata-form with exposition expanded by use of third theme, development characterized by contrapuntal devices of diminution, augmentation, inversion, stretto, etc., the recapitulation literal but varied by transpositions. The second movement is an Adagio, either A-B-A, variation-form, or a combination. The third movement is an energetic, Beethoven-like Scherzo flavored with Austrian rustic dances and popular songs. The final movement is like a separate composition—long, filled with new material, and marked by somberness and sublimity. Other characteristics of his style include long pedal-points (tonic or dominant), pizzicati background, tremolo, and the "Bruckner" rhythm (two quarters plus a triplet of quarters in 4/4 time). While his symphonies have not been popular outside Austria, there seems to be a growing awareness of their worth, and his influence on later Viennese composers—such as Mahler and Schoenberg—is considerable.

ORCHESTRAL MUSIC

Nine symphonies (not counting F minor, 1863, discovered and performed in 1923; or D minor, 1864, revised 1869, performed 1924, listed as No. "O" by Bruckner): No. 1 in C minor (1866, performed 1868, revised 1877-91); No. 2 in C minor (1872, performed 1873, revisions 1875 and 1877); No. 3 in D minor (1873, performed 1877, revised 1877 and 1888); No. 4 in E-flat major ("Romantic" 1874, Scherzo and Finale revised 1878-80, performed 1881); No. 5 in B-flat major (1875-77, revised 1878, performed 1894); No. 6 in A major (1879-81, Adagio and Scherzo performed 1883, complete performance 1899 under Mahler); No. 7 in E major (1881-83, performed 1884); No. 8 in C minor ("Apocalyptic," 1884-87, revised 1890, performed 1892 under Richter); No. 9 in D minor (1895-96, Finale unfinished; performed 1903 with the *Te Deum* substituted for the Finale).

Symphonies

No. 3 in D Minor (1873)
No. 7 in E Major (1881-1883)
No. 8 in C Minor (1885-1890)

CHAMBER MUSIC

String Quintet
In F Major

CHORAL WORKS

Requiem
In D Minor (1849)

Missa Solemnis
In B-Flat Major (1854)

Masses
Three (1864, 1866, 1867)

Others
Germanenzug (1863)
Abendzauber (1878)
Helgoland (1893)
Te Deum (1881, revised 1884, performed with orchestra, 1886)
150th Psalm (1892), for soprano, choir, and orchestra

SUGGESTED READING

1. *GroutHWM*	509-10, 542-44
2. *HiSym*	210-223
3. *UlSM*	222-228
4. *CobCM*	I, 215f
5. *Ul-PiHM*	549-52

REFERENCES

1. Engel, G., *Symphonies of Anton Bruckner,* New York: Bruckner Society, 1955.
2. Newlin, D., *Bruckner, Mahler, Schönberg,* New York: King's Crown Press, 1947.
3. Doernberg, E., *The Life and Symphonies of Anton Bruckner,* London: Barrie & Rockliff.

XXIV. César Franck (1822-1890)

Composer and organist. After studies at the Liège and Paris Conservatoires, and after settling permanently in Paris (1844), he taught at the Paris Conservatoire (from 1872). Not only organ music, but composition and French musical education in general received new impetus and direction by means of his devotion to the contrapuntal art of Bach, his emphasis on absolute music (as opposed to opera, which had dominated national musical tastes), and his willingness to consider and use unorthodox procedures. Formation of the "Schola Cantorum" by Bordes, d'Indy, and others in 1894 brought into concrete existence his ideals and teachings. Some years later (1938, after death of d'Indy) important members of the "Schola" resigned and founded the "École César Franck." Franck's compositions are strong in Romantic traits, with melodies that keep diatonic and chromatic elements in splendid balance, a harmonic scheme satisfyingly ample and colorful, and a contrapuntal fabric clear and easily comprehended. Working in the accepted instrumental forms (symphony, symphonic poem, sonata, variations, and the several types of chamber music) and the usual vocal forms (opera, oratorio, mass, motet), he exemplified a logical working-out of ideas, an effective use of the cyclical principle, a moderate but lustrous chromaticism (derived from Bach rather than from Wagner or Liszt), and a basically conventional method in shaping and developing themes. While not prolific as a composer, Franck demonstrated a constant growth in his creative powers as he added years to his life. The Symphony was finished at age sixty-six, the widely acclaimed and universally loved violin sonata was the product of his sixty-third year, and the string quartet marked the final year of his life. As a foundation for his thinking and his achievements he retained at all times a deep-seated religious fervor and an idealistic confidence in the rightness of things and the value to society of the dedicated artist.

ORCHESTRAL MUSIC

Symphonic poems: *Les Éolides* (1877), *Le Chasseur maudit* (1883), *Les Djinns* (1885, piano used), *Psyché* (1888, chorus with orchestra); 1 Symphony.

Symphonies
D minor (1886-1888)

Symphonic Poems
Les Éolides (1876)
Le Chasseur maudit (1882)
Psyché (1888)

CONCERTOS AND SOLO PIECES WITH ORCHESTRA

Piano
Variations Symphoniques (1885)

CHAMBER MUSIC

Piano Trios
Four (1841-42)

Piano and Violin Duo
Duo pour piano et violon concertante (1844, on themes from Dalayrac's *Gulistan*)

Quintet
Piano (F minor, 1879)

Sonata
for Violin and Piano in A Major (1886)

Quartet
for Strings (D major, 1889)

CHORAL WORKS

Oratorios: *Ruth* (1846), *La Tour de Babel* (1865), *Rédemption* (1871, 2nd version 1874), *Les Béatitudes* (1869-79; perf. 1880), *Rebecca* (1881; produced as a 1-act sacred opera at the Paris Opera, May 25, 1918). *Messe solennelle* (1858); *Messe à trois voix* (1860); *Panis angelicus* for tenor, organ, harp, cello, and double bass; *Psalm 150*; motets and offertories.

COMPOSITIONS FOR THE STAGE

Operas: *Hulda* (1882-85, produced Monte Carlo, 1894); *Ghisèle* (unfinished, orchestration completed by d'Indy, Chausson, Bréville, Rousseau, and Coquard; 1st performed Monte Carlo, 1896).

SOLO COMPOSITIONS

Piano

Prélude, choral et fugue
Prélude, aria et final

Organ

Petites pièces (album of 44 numbers)
L'Organiste (album of 55 numbers)
Trois Chorales (E Major, B Minor, A Minor)

SUGGESTED READING

1.	*GleCM*	Outline XI
2.	*GroutHWM*	522-3, 597-8
3.	*HiCon*	433-7
4.	*HiSym*	203-9
5.	*CobCM*	I, 418-29
6.	*RobCM*	363-9
7.	*UlCM*	335-9
8.	*UlSM*	228-32
9.	*VeiCon*	202
10.	*Ul-PiHM*	500-03

REFERENCES

1. Andriessen, H., *César Franck*, translated by W. A. G. Doyle-Davidson, Stockholm: The Continental Book Co., 1947.
2. Demuth, N., *César Franck*, New York: Philosophical Library Publications, 1949.
3. Vallas, L., *César Franck*, translated by H. Foss, New York: Oxford University Press, 1951.

XXV. Camille Saint-Saëns (1835-1921)

Achieved a notable reputation as pianist (first performances of all five of his piano concertos), organist (especially for abilities in sight reading and improvisation), editor (many arrangements of Classical and Romantic composers, special editions of Gluck, Rameau, etc.), writer (essays on philosophy and music, plays and poems), and composer (very prolific, with opus numbers reaching 169 and new compositions extending into the final year of his life). He gave his first public recital at age ten, began the study of composition with Halévy at the Paris Conservatoire at age thirteen, and was active and productive until he passed away in Algiers at age eighty-six while on a tour conducting his own works. While young he made the acquaintance of Liszt, and as a result of that influence he accepted the symphonic poem as an adequate solution of formal problems and the "cyclic" principle as an aid to the development of thematic materials (Symphony No. 3 is compounded from a single theme). His music, more Classical than Romantic as regards salient characteristics, is marked by graceful refinement, delicate taste, economy of means, and conformity to established concepts of order and method. With a firm contrapuntal technic, full understanding of instrumental color, and a certain opulence of harmony, he produced works clear in design, exquisite in detail, and easy of understanding. He was given honors, citations, and degrees in many countries, including his own. And yet Saint-Saëns' inclinations were apparently old- rather than new-fashioned. He was cool toward Debussy and his style, looked with some disdain upon modernity, and was not prone to musical daring or adventurousness. Therefore—not with complete justification, perhaps—time has judged much of his work to be of surface excellence only, and popular approval has declined over the years.

ORCHESTRAL MUSIC

Symphonies No. 1 (Paris, 1853), No. 2 (Leipzig, 1859), No. 3 (with organ, piano 4-hands; London, 1886); Symphonic Poems *Le Rouet d'Omphale* (Paris, 1872), *Phaëton* (Paris, 1873), *Danse macabre* (Paris, 1875); incidental music *Antigone* (Paris, 1893); Ballet, *Javotte* (Lyons, 1896); *Suite algérienne* (Paris, 1880); *Le Carnaval des Animaux* (Paris, 1922).

Symphony

No. 3 in C Minor, Op. 78

Symphonic Poems

The Spinning Wheel of Omphale, Op. 31
Phaëton, Op. 39
Danse macabre, Op. 40

Suites

Le Carnaval des Animaux (Grande Fantaisie Zoologique)

CONCERTOS AND PIECES WITH ORCHESTRA

For piano, 5 concertos (in D, g, E-flat, c, F), *Africa* fantasy; for violin, 3 concertos (in A, C, b), *Introduction et Rondo Capriccioso* (1863, 1st performed in 1913); for cello, 2 concertos (in a, d).

Violin

Introduction and Rondo Capriccioso
Concerto No. 3 in B minor, Op. 61 (1880)

Cello

No. 1 in A minor, Op. 33, (1873)
No. 2 in D minor, Op. 119 (1902)

Piano

No. 2 in G minor, Op. 22 (1868)
No. 4 in C minor, Op. 44 (1875)
No. 5 in F Major, Op. 103, "The Egyptian"

CHAMBER MUSIC

Two violin sonatas; 2 cello sonatas; oboe sonata (1921); clarinet sonata (1921); bassoon sonata (1921); 2 piano trios (1869, 1892); 1 piano quartet (1875); 2 string quartets; 1 piano quintet (1858); septet for trumpet, strings, and piano (1881).

CHORAL WORKS

Oratorio *Le Déluge* (Paris, 1876).

COMPOSITIONS FOR THE STAGE

Operas *La Princesse jaune* (Paris, 1872); *Le Timbre d'argent* (composed 1864-5, produced 1877); *Samson et Dalila* (given by Liszt in German at Weimar in 1877, refused by the Paris Opera until 1892).

SUGGESTED READING

1. *GroutHWM*	598-99
2. *GroutSHO*	434
3. *HiCon*	206-18
4. *UlSM*	232-34
5. *VeiCon*	250-53
6. *CobCM*	II, 321-25
7. *Ul-PiHM*	503-05

REFERENCES

1. Saint-Saëns, C., *Musical Memories,* translated by E. G. Rich. Boston: Small, Maynard, 1919.

XXVI. Vincent D'Indy (1851-1931)

Following early music studies, piano with Diémer and harmony with Lavignac (1862-1865), and service in the Franco-Prussian War, he became a composition student of César Franck. The leading pupil of that master, he remained always loyal to the methods and ideals of his teacher, carrying on the traditions in his own teaching and in his composing. Meeting Liszt and Wagner on the occasion of his first visit to Germany (1873), he also mirrored elements of their styles in his own works. In 1876 he was present for the 1st performance of the *Ring* in Bayreuth, and after that made regular trips to Munich where he heard all of Wagner's works. He also attended the *première* of *Parsifal* (1882). Joining the *Société Nationale de Musique* (1871), he became secretary, then president (after the death of Franck). With Bordes and Guilmant he founded the *Schola Cantorum* (1894), which was first designed for the study of plainchant and the Palestrina style, but which was later broadened to embrace all musical fields. In this organization d'Indy was one of the directors, then a teacher, then (after death of Guilmant) sole director. He wrote in almost every musical form, but gave evidence of greatest ability in the field of large instrumental works. In addition to influential factors already mentioned, the musical characteristics of Gregorian Chant, Bach (contrapuntal writing), and Beethoven were important elements in his style. Somewhat complex at times, and with its emotional content concealed beneath a cloak of self-restraint and severity, his music is occasionally considered difficult to comprehend. Beneath it and through it, however, is poetic power of great depth and religious devotion both consistent and profound. As editor he brought out early works of Monteverdi and Rameau. As arranger, he issued piano versions of orchestral compositions by Chausson, Duparc, etc. His *Cours de Composition musicale* (two books in three parts, 1903, 1909, 1933) and his *Beethoven: Biographie critique* (1911) are notable.

ORCHESTRAL MUSIC

Wallenstein, symphonic trilogy, Op. 12: a) *Le Camp de Wallenstein,* 1880; b) *Max et Thécla,* originally *Les Piccolomini,* 1874; c) *La Mort de Wallenstein,* 1884. *Symphonie Cénevole* (*sur un chant montagnard français,* with piano; Op. 25); *Istar* (symphonic variations, Op. 42; 1897); 2nd Symphony (in B-flat, Op. 57; 1904); *Jour d'été à la montagne* (symphonic poem, "Summer Day on the Mountain," 1905); 3rd Symphony (Op. 70).

Symphonies

Symphony on a French Mountain Air, Opus 25, for Piano and Orchestra
No. 2 in B-flat Major, Op. 57

Symphonic Poems

Jour d'été à la montagne (Summer Day on the Mountain), Op. 61

Symphonic Variations

Istar, Op. 42

CONCERTOS AND PIECES WITH ORCHESTRA

For oboe, *Fantasie* (Op. 31, 1888); for saxophone, *Choral varie* (1904); Concerto for piano, flute, cello, and string orchestra (Op. 89, 1927).

CHAMBER MUSIC

Sonata for violin (Op. 59, 1905); for cello (Op. 84, 1926); Trio for piano, clarinet, and cello (Op. 29, 1888); Trio No. 2 for piano, violin, cello (Op. 98, 1929); piano quartet in A minor (Op. 7, 1878); 3 string quartets (Op. 35, 1891; Op. 45, 1898; Op. 96, 1929); piano quintet (in G minor, Op. 81, 1925); Suite for trumpet, 2 flutes, and string quartet (in D major, Op. 24, 1887); *Chansons et Danses* (*divertissement* for 7 wind instruments, Op. 50, 1899).

CHORAL WORKS

Le Chant de la cloche (dramatic legend, "The Song of the Bell," Op. 18; 1879-1883); *La Légende de Saint-Christophe,* lyric drama, Op. 67 (composed 1908-1915, performed 1920); cantata, *Ste. Marie-Magdeleine* (1885).

Oratorio

La Légende de Saint-Christophe, Op. 67 (1920)

COMPOSITIONS FOR THE STAGE

Lyric dramas *Fervaal* (Op. 40, 1897); *L'Étranger* (Op. 53, 1903).

SOLO COMPOSITIONS

Piano: *Poème des Montagnes* (*Le Chant des Bruyères, Danses rhythmiques, Plein-air;* Op. 15, 1881); Sonata (Op. 63, 1907); *Menuet sur le nom de Haydn* (Op. 65, 1909); *Thème varié, fugue et chanson* (Op. 85).

Organ: various pieces.

SUGGESTED READING

1. *GroutHWM*	597-8
2. *CobCM*	II, 1-8
3. *UlSM*	232
4. *Ul-PiHM*	503

REFERENCES

1. Books by d'Indy on Beethoven, Franck, Wagner and other subjects.
2. D'Indy, V., *Cours de composition musicale,* Paris: Durand, 1909-1930.

XXVII. Ernest Chausson (1855-1899)

After studies with Massenet (Paris Conservatoire) and private lessons with César Franck, he began his career as a composer. Having sufficient private means for comfortable livelihood, he composed relatively little and did not engage in music professionally. His works are typically French in their refined gracefulness and structural clearness. Melodically and harmonically he showed the influence of Wagner as well as Franck. Notwithstanding these musical obligations he developed a unique style of his own, marked by a moderate chromaticism, a certain amount of thematic extravagance, and a sensitive type of Romanticism. He was active in Parisian musical society and served as secretary of the *Société Nationale de Musique.*

ORCHESTRAL MUSIC

Symphony

B-flat Major, Op. 20 (1898)

CONCERTOS AND PIECES WITH ORCHESTRA

Poème for violin (*Concerts Colonne,* Paris, 1897); Concerto for piano, violin, and string quartet (without orchestra); *Poème de l'amour et de la mer* (1882-92) and *Chanson perpetuelle* (1898) for voice.

Violin

Poème, Op. 25

Violin, Piano, String Quartet

Concerto in D Major, Op. 21 (1890-1891)

CHAMBER MUSIC

Piano Trio, Piano Quartet, and String Quartet (unfinished).

A. Piano with Other Instruments

Trio

G minor, Op. 3 for piano, violin, cello

Quartet

A Major, Op. 30 for piano, violin, viola, cello

COMPOSITIONS FOR THE STAGE

Incidental music to *La Légende de Saint Cécile* (Paris, 1892); and the opera *Le Roi Arthus* (perf. posthumously, Brussels, Nov. 30, 1903).

SOLO COMPOSITIONS

Many songs of genuine charm.

SUGGESTED READING

1. *UlSM*	232
2. *VeiCon*	253-4
3. *CobCM*	I, 266-70

REFERENCES

1. Barricelli, J. P. and L. Weinstein, *Ernest Chausson,* Norman: University of Oklahoma, 1955.

XXVIII. Gabriel-Urbain Fauré (1845-1924)

Taken to Paris by his father (after showing early and striking musical abilities), he studied with Louis Niedermeyer and (following Niedermeyer's death in 1861) Camille Saint-Saëns. In his career he filled various organ positions, taught composition at the Paris Conservatoire (from 1896), and became its director (succeeding Théodore Dubois in 1905), serving with distinction until forced to resign (1920) because of acute deafness. Fauré helped to found the National Society for French Music, and was the first president of the Independent Musical Society (organized 1909). He was elected to membership in the *Académie des Beaux Arts* (1909), and was made a Commander of the *Légion d'honneur* (1910). His music reviews appeared in *Le Figaro* (1903-1921) and were published posthumously in 1930 as *Opinions Musicales*. He was a celebrated and influential teacher, and among his pupils were Florent Schmitt, Louis Aubert, Georges Enesco, Roger-Ducasse, Gabriel Grovlez, Charles Koechlin, Maurice Ravel, and Nadia Boulanger. As a composer he developed a unique and expressive musical language, components of which were modality, mild dissonance, vivid coloring, a flowing yet vigorous melody, and a well-calculated but sometimes surprising harmonic structure. His piano works reflect the limpid transparency of the earlier clavecin masters. His songs are impressively lyrical, demonstrate a charming economy of means, and exemplify a refined and subtle type of Romanticism. One medium—that of the orchestra—was not congenial to Fauré, and he published no symphonies or concertos. His chamber works continue to be significant contributions to the repertory, however, and show instrumental skill, strength in design, and a poetic imagination. In general, his music is not marked by display, but rather by balance, clarity, and repose. While examples of freely-moving seventh chords, chromatic progressions, and enharmonic modulations can be found, it is the musical logic, the faultless workmanship, and the aristocratic qualities that stand out most prominently.

ORCHESTRAL MUSIC

Pavane (1887); *Masques et bergamasques* (suite, 1919).

CONCERTOS AND PIECES WITH ORCHESTRA

Piano and Orchestra: *Ballade* (1881); *Fantasie* (1919). Violin and Orchestra: *Romance* (1882).

CHAMBER MUSIC

For cello and piano, *Elégie* (1883), *Sérénade* (1908); for flute and piano, *Fantasie* (1898); 2 violin sonatas (1879, 1886); 2 cello sonatas (1918, 1922); 1 piano trio; 2 piano quartets; 1 string quartet; 2 piano quintets.

A. String Instruments

Quartet

E Minor, Op. 121 (1924)

B. Piano with Other Instruments

Duos

Sonatas: A Major, Op. 13 for Violin and Piano
E Minor, Op. 108 for Violin and Piano
D Minor, Op. 109 for Cello and Piano (1918)
G Minor, Op. 117 for Cello and Piano (1922)

Trio

D Minor, Op. 120 for Piano, Violin, Cello (1923)

Quartets

C Minor, Op. 15 for Piano, Violin, Viola, Cello (1886)
G Minor, Op. 45 for Piano, Violin, Viola, Cello (1886)

Quintets

D Minor, Op. 89 for piano and string quartet (1906)
C Minor, Op. 115 for piano and string quartet (1921)

CHORAL WORKS

Les Djinns (chorus and orchestra, 1875); *Requiem Mass* (soli, chorus, organ, orchestra, 1887).

Requiem

Messe de Requiem, Op. 48 (1887)

COMPOSITIONS FOR THE STAGE

Incidental music: *Shylock* (1889, after Shakespeare); *Pelléas et Mélisande* (1898; after Maeterlinck, often given as an orchestral suite). Operas, *Prométhée* (lyric tragedy, 1900); *Pénélope* (1913).

SOLO COMPOSITIONS

For piano: 5 Impromptus, 13 Nocturnes, 13 Barcarolles, 9 Preludes, 4 waltzes. For voice: 96 songs; includes song-cycles *La Bonne Chanson* (Paul Verlaine, 1892); *La Chanson d'Ève* (Charles van Lerberghe, 1907-10); *Le Jardin clos* (1915-18); *L'Horizon chimérique* (4 songs, Jean de la Ville de Mirmont; 1922); *Mirages* (4 songs; 1919). Among well-known single songs are the following: *Lydia* (1865); *Après une rêve* (1865); *Clair de lune* (1887); *Au cimitière* (1889); *Cinq mélodies* (1890, to poems of Verlaine); *Ici-Bas; Les roses d'Ispahan.*

SUGGESTED READING

1. *AusMTC*	150-55
2. *GleCM*	Outline XII
3. *GroutHWM*	599-601
4. *CobCM*	I, 386-92
5. *UlCM*	359
6. *Ul-PiHM*	505-6

REFERENCES

1. Koechlin, C. L. E., *Gabriel Fauré* (1845-1924), London: D. Dobson, 1945.
2. Suckling, N., *Fauré*, New York: E. P. Dutton & Co., Inc., 1945.

XXIX. Piotr Ilyitch Tchaikovsky (1840-1893)

In his tenth year the family moved to St. Petersburg, where he attended law school, graduating at nineteen to become a clerk in the Ministry of Justice. While in school he began music studies but showed no exceptional promise. When twenty-one he was accepted as a regular student in a music school begun by Anton Rubinstein (later to be the St. Petersburg Conservatory), taking lessons from Zaremba (harmony and counterpoint) and Rubinstein (composition). He graduated in 1865 and the next year joined the faculty of the Moscow Conservatory, which was directed by Nicholas Rubinstein. At this point he began to compose with great diligence, and the unique characteristics of his mature period began gradually to appear. In addition to teaching and composing, he wrote music reviews for Moscow papers (1868-74) and traveled a great deal. From 1878, when he resigned from the Conservatory staff, he devoted himself entirely to composition, being helped (for over thirteen years) by the annuity furnished by Nadezhda von Meck, whose extraordinary connection with the composer is well known. In 1891 he made his only voyage to America, leading concerts of his works and receiving many honors. While the Russian idiom in Tchaikovsky's music is an important factor, and while some Russian folk materials are employed, his nationalism was determined by natural impulse and was not the result of plan or intention. His music is characterized by frank and open sentiment, superlative melodies, and inventiveness of a high order. His compositions are conditioned, however, by personal and introspective emotional states (gloominess, melancholia, acceptance of the irresistible power of Fate, etc.), and often show lack of skill in the handling of formal problems. He was successful in every musical genre, producing works which are especially admired and enjoyed in Anglo-Saxon countries, and which, at the same time, are often pointed to in the Soviet Union as the ultimate examples of what music should be. His *Manual of Harmony* (Moscow, 1870; many eds.) is published in English as *Guide to the Practical Study of Harmony* (1900).

ORCHESTRAL MUSIC

Symphonies No. 1 ("Winter Dreams;" 1868; revised 1874, performed Moscow, 1868); No. 2 ("Little Russian" or "Ukrainian;" 1873); No. 3 (1875); No. 4 (1877, performed 1878); No. 5 (1888, performed 1st in St. Petersburg, very successful from the beginning); No. 6 (St. Petersburg, later called "Pathetique;" 1893); *Manfred* Symphony (1885; after Byron; performed 1886). Overtures *Romeo and Juliet* (1869; revised 1870 with Balakirev's help; finally revised 1879); *The Year 1812* (1880, performed 1882). Symphonic Fantasias *The Tempest* (1873, after Shakespeare); *Francesca da Rimini* (after Dante; 1876; performed 1877); *Hamlet* (overture-fantasy; 1888). Symphonic Poem *Fatum* (1868, performed 1869; showing beginnings of his true style); Three Suites (1879, 1883, 1884); *Capriccio Italien* (1880); Serenade in C for string orchestra (1880, performed 1882).

Symphonies

"Manfred," Op. 58 (1885)
No. 4 in F Minor, Op. 36 (1877)
No. 5 in E minor, Op. 64 (1888)
No. 6 in B minor, "Pathetique," Op. 74 (1893)

Overtures

Romeo and Juliet

CONCERTOS AND PIECES WITH ORCHESTRA

For piano: 3 concertos (B-flat minor, 1875; G major, 1880, revised 1893; E-flat, in 1 movement, 1893); *Concert-fantasia* (1884). For violin, 1 Concerto (1878); for cello, *Variations on a Rococo Theme* (1876).

Violin

D Major, Op. 35 (1878)

Cello

Variations on a Rococo Theme, Op. 33 (1876)

Piano

No. 1 in B-flat Minor, Op. 23 (1875)

CHAMBER MUSIC

For violin and piano, *Souvenir d'un lieu cher*; 1 Piano Trio (A minor, 1882; in memory of Nicholas Rubinstein); 3 string quartets (D major, 1871; F major, 1874, E-flat minor, 1876); 1 String Sextet, *Souvenir de Florence* (begun 1887, revised 1892).

A. Piano with Other Instruments

Trio

Piano Trio in A minor, Op. 50, "To the memory of a great artist" (1882)

COMPOSITIONS FOR THE STAGE

Eleven operas, including *Vakula the Smith* (1876; revived as *The Little Shoes,* 1887; published as *Les*

Caprices d'Oxane); *Eugene Onegin* (1879); *The Maid of Orleans* (1881); *Mazeppa* (1884); *The Enchantress* (1887); *The Queen of Spades* (1890); *Iolanthe* (1892); 3 Ballets, *Swan Lake* (1876); *Sleeping Beauty* (1889); *Casse-Noisette* (1891-92); Incidental music for *Snow-maiden* (1873) and *Hamlet* (1891).

Operas

Eugene Onegin (1879)

SOLO COMPOSITIONS

For piano: Sonata in C-sharp minor (1865); *The Seasons* (1876, 12 characteristic pieces for each month of the year); Grand Sonata in G major (1878); *Children's Album* (1878); *Dumka* (1886). For voice: about 100 songs in various sets.

SUGGESTED READING

1.	*GroutHWM*	544-45
2.	*GroutSHO*	460-61
3.	*HiCon*	219-33, 437-40
4.	*HiSym*	261-75
5.	*UlCM*	341-43
6.	*UlSM*	234-39
7.	*VeiCon*	238-45
8.	*CobCM*	II, 490-500
9.	*Ul-PiHM*	514-18, 548

REFERENCES

1. Abraham, G., ed., *Tchaikovsky: a Symposium,* 2nd ptg., London: Lindsay Drummond, 1946.
2. Blom, E., *Tchaikovsky: Orchestral Works,* London: H. Milford, Oxford University Press, 1927.
3. Evans, Edwin, *Tchaikovsky: a critical and personal analysis of the man and his music,* New York: Avon Book Division of the Hearst Corporation, 1960.
4. Newmarch, R., *Tchaikovsky, his Life and Works,* ed. by Edwin Evans, London: G. Richards, 1908.
5. *Russian Symphony; Thoughts about Tchaikovsky,* articles by Shostakovich and others, New York: Philosophical Library, 1947.
6. Weinstock, H., *Tchaikovsky,* New York: Alfred A. Knopf & Co., 1943.

CHAPTER

6

The Nationalistic Composers

RUSSIAN

XXX. Mikhail Glinka (1804-1857)

Descendant of wealthy landowners and educated in an exclusive St. Petersburg school, Glinka had little formal training in music (among early teachers was visiting pianist John Field, from whom he took three lessons) until middle age (almost thirty when technical equipment completed). He read a great deal, however, and numbered among his friends such noted writers as Pushkin and Zhukovsky. After visits to Italy (where he knew Bellini and Donizetti, and became fully Italian in his musical style) and Berlin (where he studied with Dehn, famous theorist), he was recalled to Russia by his father's death. Acting upon Zhukovsky's suggestion, he composed his first opera (*A Life for the Tsar*) upon a national subject–rescue of the first Romanov Tsar by a peasant, Ivan Susanin. (The same subject had been treated by the Italian-Russian composer, Cavos, twenty years earlier.) Glinka's work was produced December 9, 1836, in St. Petersburg with tremendous success, being recognized as of great import in Russian culture and a decisive factor in Russian national music. Its success was unabated until the Revolution made its libretto unacceptable when it was revised (music unchanged) as *Ivan Susanin*–with the country saved rather than the Tsar. *Russlan and Ludmilla,* the second opera (St. Petersburg, 1842; after fairy tale by Pushkin) also achieved great success. Here, Oriental color and exotic effects are strong characteristics (e.g., first operatic use of whole-tone scale). Both operas, however, are in Italian style with set numbers. In his orchestral *fantasia, Kamarinskaya,* he demonstrated the effective use of folk song as the structural basis of a complicated work. In Paris (1844) he met Berlioz, and in Spain he collected folk songs and composed works in characteristic Spanish style.

ORCHESTRAL MUSIC

Symphony

Symphony on Two Russian Themes

Orchestral Fantasia

Kamarinskaya (1848)

CHAMBER MUSIC

A. String Instruments

Quartet

Quartet in F

COMPOSITIONS FOR THE STAGE

Operas

Life for the Tsar (1836)

Russlan and Ludmilla (1842)

SUGGESTED READING

1.	*CobCM*	I, 472f
2.	*GroutHWM*	584
3.	*GroutSHO*	456-59
4.	*Ul-PiHM*	507-14
5.	*UlSM*	240-42

REFERENCES

BOOKS

1. Abraham, G., *On Russian Music* (1939).
2. Abraham, G., *Studies in Russian Music,* New York: G. Schirmer, 1936.
3. Calvocoressi, M. and Abraham, G., *Masters of Russian Music,* New York: Alfred A. Knopf, Inc., 1936.
4. ———, *Mikhail Ivanovich Glinka: Memoirs,* translated by Richard B. Mudge, Norman: University of Oklahoma, 1963.
5. Montagu-Nathan, M., *Glinka,* London: Constable, 1916.

XXXI. Alexander Dargomyzhsky (1813-1869)

After achieving success as pianist (age twenty), he held a government position (1831-35) and then turned to music exclusively. Visited Germany, Brussels, Paris (his opera *Esmeralda,* after Victor Hugo's *Notre-Dame de Paris,* was successfully given in Moscow on December 17, 1847—eight years after its composition). *Russalka,* given May 16, 1856, in St. Petersburg, firmly secured his position as an outstanding composer. The opera-ballet *The Triumph of Bacchus* was written in 1845 and produced January 23, 1867, in Moscow. Popular also were the orchestral works, *Cossack Dance, Finnish Fantasia,* and *Baba-Yaga.* In his songs (several to satirical texts) as well as in his culminating masterpiece, *The Stone Guest* (posthumous opera after Pushkin's poem of same title; completed by Cui, orchestrated by Rimsky-Korsakov; performed February 28, 1872, at St. Petersburg), he turned from early influences of Rossini and Auber to a musical creed of dramatic realism with nationalistic implications. In *The Stone Guest* (based on the Don Juan legend) he employed a type of continuous recitative. His doctrine of "representation with idealization" was a vital factor as Russian music moved toward its destiny.

COMPOSITIONS FOR THE STAGE

Operas

Russalka (1856)
Kamennyi Gost (The Stone Guest, 1872)

XXXII. Mily Balakirev (1837-1910) and "The Five"

The Mighty Five (actually called by the music critic, Vladimir Stassov, the "Mighty Heap," or the *Kutchka*) was a group of enthusiastic Russian musical amateurs who combined their efforts in the direction of a genuinely national school of Russian music. Coming under the influence of Mily Balakirev and with a central purpose in the direction of a unique nationality, they undertook the development and use of purely Russian elements in their compositions. Although results of their devotion to a conscious nationalism were strongly felt, they exhibited such diverse abilities and technical experiments that their musical endeavors often lacked consistency and strength.

Balakirev, acknowledged leader of the group, was the only one who was a professional musician. Introduced to books and music by his boyhood friend, Alexander Oulibishev, he studied mathematics at the University of Kazan and later (age eighteen), encouraged by Glinka and others, began a career as concert pianist and composer in St. Petersburg. After a period as director of the Free School of Music (St. Petersburg), he became a railway clerk, later a school inspector, and finally, after retiring on a pension, became Director of the Court Chapel. His musical style combined elements of the classical school, Russian folk music, Romanticism (Liszt being an especially strong influence) and an exotic orientalism (the later stemming from several trips to the Caucasus).

ORCHESTRAL MUSIC

Overture on Russian Themes (performed 1859); *Second Overture on Russian Themes* (performed April 18, 1865, first published as *One Thousand Years* to commemorate the millennium of Russia's founding in 862, and renamed *Russia* when revised in 1882); Symphony in C Major (1866-98); Second Symphony in D minor (1907-8; performed St. Petersburg, April 23, 1909); Overture to *King Lear;* symphonic poem, *Tamara* (performed St. Petersburg, March 19, 1883).

Symphonic Poems

Russia
Tamara

CONCERTOS AND PIECES WITH ORCHESTRA

Two for piano (No. 1, 1855; No. 2, begun 1861, continued 1909, completed posthumously by Sergey Liapunov).

SOLO COMPOSITIONS

Piano sonata; piano transcriptions (numbers by Berlioz, Chopin, Glinka—e.g., *The Lark*); oriental fantasy for piano, *Islamey.* Forty Russian folk songs harmonized and published 1866; thirty additional in 1898.

Piano

Islamey

SUGGESTED READING

1. *CobCM* I, 57

REFERENCES

BOOKS

1. Seroff, V. I., *Mighty Five.* New York: Allen, Towne and Heath, 1948.

PERIODICALS

1. Calvocoressi, M. D., "Mily Balakirev," *MQ,* January, 1937 (Centennial article).

XXXIII. Alexander Borodin (1833-1887)

Professionally a scientist (student, professor, writer and lecturer in chemistry), but at the same time an important member of the "Mighty Five." Began composition at fourteen in style of Mendelssohn, but turned toward an aggressive nationalism after meeting Balakirev (1862). Influenced by folk song (although rarely quoting actual tunes) and a Russian type of orientalism, he produced works marked by distinctive themes, a luminous orchestral fabric, sensitive and modally-tinted harmonies, and an effective manner of extending a musical idea into a complete tonal structure. While never achieving full mastery of the mechanics of composition, and while working—of necessity—very slowly, he left significant examples of conscious and idiomatic musical monuments to his country, with exoticism, characteristic rhythmic patterns, lyrical and descriptive melodies, and orchestral coloring of a high order as salient features.

ORCHESTRAL MUSIC

Symphony No. 1 in E-flat major (1862-67, performed 1869; 3rd movement in D major with central portion in D-flat major); Symphony No. 2 in B minor (1876; 4 movements in B minor, F major, D-flat major and B major); Symphony No. 3 (incomplete); Symphonic sketch, *In the Steppes of Central Asia* (1880).

Symphony
No. 2 in B minor (1869-76)

Symphonic Poem
In the Steppes of Central Asia (1880)

CHAMBER MUSIC

Two String Quartets (No. 1 in A, 1875-79; No. 2 in D, 1881-85); *Serenata alla spagnola* (3rd movement of quartet on name *B-la-f*, by Borodin, Rimsky-Korsakov, Liadov and Glazunov; 1886); String Trio (dated 1860, discovered in 1915); Septet for strings (1860); Piano Quintet (discovered in 1915).

A. String Instruments

Quartet
No. 1 in A major
No. 2 in D major

COMPOSITIONS FOR THE STAGE

Prince Igor (opera in 4 acts, begun 1869, on the subject of the famous Russian medieval chronicle, *Tale of Igor's Campaign*; completed posthumously by Rimsky-Korsakov and Glazunov; 1st performed St. Petersburg, November 4, 1890; London, June 8, 1914, in Russian; New York, December 30, 1915, in Italian); *Bogatyry* (*The Valiant Knights*, opera-farce, anonymously produced in Moscow on October 29, 1867, rediscovered 1932, and produced in Moscow November 12, 1936, with a new libretto by Demian Biedny, to serve propaganda purposes in an anti-religious campaign, but two days later banned by the Soviet government for its mockery of Russian nationalism); *Mlada* (sketches for 4th act only; each act was to be composed by a different writer, but never produced).

Opera
Prince Igor

SOLO COMPOSITIONS

For the piano: *Polka, Requiem, March funèbre,* and *Mazurka* (posthumous; in series of paraphrases on the theme of *Chopsticks* Waltz; includes variations by Borodin, other members of the Russian group, and Liszt, 1880); *Petite Suite* (7 numbers: *Au Couvent, Intermezzo, Deux mazurkas, Rèverie, Sérénade, Nocturne*; 1885).

For the voice: *Sérénade de 4 galants â une dame* (comical; no date; for a cappella male quartet); songs (*Sleeping Princess,* 1867; *The Princess of the Sea*; *The Song of the Dark Forest*; *The False Note*; *My Songs are Full of Venom,* 1867-68; *The Sea Shores of Your Distant Country,* 1881; *Conceit,* 1884; *Arabian Melody,* 1885; and *The Wondrous Garden,* 1885).

SUGGESTED READING

1. *CobCM*	I, 147-53
2. *GroutHWM*	584-5
3. *GroutSHO*	464-66
4. *HiSym*	247-60
5. *UlSM*	247-52

REFERENCES

BOOKS

1. Abraham, G., *Borodin: the Composer and the Man,* 1922.

XXXIV. César Cui (1835-1918)

An army engineer by profession (advanced to Lieutenant General), he was also stimulated by Balakirev, who coached him in compositional technique, to the writing of a large number of musical works. Typically Romantic in his musical tastes and an admirer of Schumann, he was best in piano pieces and songs. Wrote caustic articles against Wagner,

Strauss, and Reger, with whose artistic creeds he was not in sympathy. Gave ardent support, however, to the work of Glinka and the Russian Nationalists. His music generally is lacking in elements of greatness, but in the category of miniatures (both vocal and instrumental) he made significant contributions. Wrote many papers and was author of the first comprehensive book on Russian music (*Musique en Russie,* Paris, 1880).

ORCHESTRAL MUSIC

Tarantella, Op. 12 (1859); 4 Suites (No. 2, Op. 38, 1887; No. 4, *À Argenteau,* Op. 40, 1887; No. 3, *In Modo populari,* Op. 43).

CONCERTOS AND PIECES WITH ORCHESTRA

Suite Concertante for violin and orchestra, Op. 25, (1883); *Two Morceaux* for cello and orchestra, Op. 36.

CHAMBER MUSIC

Three String Quartets (Op. 45, 1893; Op. 68; Op. 91, 1913); Violin Sonata (Op. 84).

CHORAL WORKS

Miscellaneous (sacred and secular texts): Op. 4, 28, 46, 53, 58, 59.

COMPOSITIONS FOR THE STAGE

Six operas, including *William Ratcliff* (February 26, 1869; subject taken from an early drama by Heine based on Scottish legends); 4 children's operas; also completed Mussorgsky's *The Fair at Sorotchinsk* (1914).

Opera
William Ratcliff (1869)

SOLO COMPOSITIONS

Wrote violin pieces (*Kaleidoscope,* 24 numbers, Op. 50; Six *Bagatelles,* Op. 51); piano works (including one number in a set of variations on *Chopsticks*—Borodin, Liadov, and Rimsky-Korsakov being also represented); and songs.

SUGGESTED READING

1. *CobCM* I, 305
2. *GroutHWM* 584-5
3. *GroutSHO* 461

XXXV. Modest Mussorgsky (1839-1881)

The least schooled among the Five in theory and details of compositional procedure, he towered above them all in imagination, originality, power and directness. While having early musical instruction from his mother, he entered the cadet school of the Imperial Guard (age thirteen), joining the regiment of the Guard upon his graduation. Still later, when family fortunes made self-support necessary, he took a clerk's position in the Ministry of Communications (for four years) and then entered the Forestry Department. When eighteen, he met Dargomyzhsky, who presented him to Cui and Balakirev. After some formal lessons from the latter, he attempted composition in traditional style (employing Classic and Romantic elements), but was unsuccessful. As expressed by himself, his urge led him to explore "new shores," and thus he moved steadily toward a bold realism in his musical expression, adopting at the same time the banners of aggressive nationalism. Because of lack of technique he was forced to leave many works unfinished (he freely admitted this lack of formal training and his inferiority to his contemporaries). His single completed large opus, however, *Boris Godunov* (written 1868-69), firmly established Mussorgsky as one of the most individual, evocative and impressive of nineteenth-century composers. While the full significance of *Boris Godunov* was not realized at first, its every aspect came ultimately to exercise profound influence on new music everywhere. Unequaled in its portrayal of stirring personal destiny against a background of violent social commotion, its musical language embraced elements of Russian folk music, essential characteristics of Dargomizhsky's methods of voice treatment, great psychological insight, and a harmonic vocabulary compounded of unfamiliarity with standard formulas plus willingness to experiment.

In his vocal writing (*Boris Godunov,* as well as songs and choral works), Mussorgsky translated inflections of speech into natural melody. He avoided both symmetry in phrase structure and lyricism in melodic patterns. Folklike reiteration of rhythmic and melodic units, irregularity of design, use of whole-tone and quartal formulas—these were some of the features of his personal idiom. Called a "musical Folk Drama," *Boris Godunov* is not a continuous development of a situation, but a succession of dramatic episodes held together by the tremendous energy of the music. The tumult of the crowd, the gesture of the individual, and the hidden conflict of designing minds—all are tellingly conveyed by effects often achieved by laborious experiments at the piano.

ORCHESTRAL MUSIC

Scherzo (St. Petersburg, January 23, 1860); *Intermezzo in modo classico* (1867); *A Night on the*

Bald Mountain (1860-66; reorchestrated by Rimsky-Korsakov and performed posthumously, St. Petersburg, October 27, 1886).

Symphonic Poem
A Night on the Bald Mountain

CHORAL WORKS

The Destruction of Sennacherib (with orchestra, on text after Byron; St. Petersburg, March 18, 1867); *Joshua* (contralto, bass, chorus and piano; 1874-77).

COMPOSITIONS FOR THE STAGE

The Marriage (1864; 1st act only; produced, Petrograd, October 26, 1917; finished and orchestrated by Alexandre Tcherepnin and given complete performance in Essen on September 14, 1937); *Boris Godunov* (St. Petersburg, February 8, 1874; revised and reorchestrated by Rimsky-Korsakov in 1896; produced in the new form, St. Petersburg, December 10, 1896; the original score edited by Paul Lamm, published in 1928); *Khovanshtchina* (historical subject from period of Peter the Great; completed and orchestrated by Rimsky-Korsakov and first performed in St. Petersburg, February 21, 1886); *The Fair at Sorotchinsk* (also unfinished, but completed by Cui and given in St. Petersburg, October 26, 1917; also arranged and orchestrated by Nicolas Tcherepnin, and produced at Monte Carlo, March 17, 1923).

Operas
Boris Godunov
The Fair at Sorotchinsk (Sorochintsy)
Khovanshtchina (Khovanshchina)

SOLO COMPOSITIONS

Over 40 songs so sincere, simple and direct that for the listener they create vivid emotional experiences, among them being *Hopak* (1866); *The Nursery* (child's song cycle, 1868-72); *Rayck* (a musical satire directed at contemporaries, 1870); *Sunless* (cycle, 1874); *Songs and Dances of Death* (cycle of 4, 1875-77); and *Mephistopheles' Song of the Flea* (1879).

Several piano works, including *Sonata* for 4 hands (1860); *Intermezzo in modo classico* (piano version of the orchestral number, 1867); and *Pictures at an Exhibition* (his most important contribution to piano literature; musical illustrations of 10 drawings and water colors; introduced and in some cases linked by the "promenade" theme; vividly imaginative; 1874).

SUGGESTED READING

1. *Ca-Jo-WaAM*	409f
2. *GroutHWM*	584-88
3. *GroutSHO*	461-65
4. *UlSM*	249-50

REFERENCES

MUSIC

In 1931, the 50th anniversary of Mussorgsky's death, the *Soviet State Edition* began publication of the complete works, including fragments, variants, notations of folk songs, etc. The editor-in-chief was Pavel Lamm, Russian musicologist (1882-1951).

BOOKS

1. Belaiev, Victor, *Mussorgsky's Boris Godunov* (1928).
2. Calvocoressi, M. D., *Modest Mussorgsky*, Fair Lawn, N.J.: Essential Books, 1956.
3. Layda, J. and Bertensson, S., editors and translators, *Mussorgsky Reader*, New York: W. W. Norton & Company, Inc., 1947.

XXXVI. Nikolai Rimsky-Korsakov (1844-1908)

The most prolific of the Five, Rimsky-Korsakov remains one of Russia's greatest composers. Entered Naval School in St. Petersburg at age twelve, graduating six years later. Having begun piano lessons at age six, he studied music on Sundays and holidays and attempted composition when only nine years old. His moment of decision came in 1861, when he met Balakirev and began formal lessons in composition. Sent abroad with the Russian Navy (1862-65), he continued work on his first symphony by sending it back in fragments for Balakirev's corrections (successfully performed 1865). He accepted a position as teacher of composition and orchestration at the St. Petersburg Conservatory (1871), admitting at the same time his technical deficiencies. With the exception of a few months (in 1905) he remained on the faculty until his death. Leaving the Navy in 1873, he became Inspector of Marine Bands (post was abolished in 1884), with opportunities for careful study of brass, woodwind, and percussion instruments. From 1883 to 1894 he was also assistant director of the Court Chapel, leading the orchestra and chorus.

As a member of the Five his interest in national music was constant (shown in melodic and harmonic characteristics, use of folk tunes, interest in arranging and editing folk songs), but he tended gradually in the direction of musical eclecticism with more varied materials and methods. With Glinka's operatic idiom his first model, and with detailed study of Cui, Seroff, Balakirev and Liszt, he achieved not only a purely Russian style (opera *Snow Maiden* and overture *Russian Easter*), but also one in which oriental color played an important part (*Schehera-*

zade and *Le Coq d'or*), with occasional Wagner traits (e.g., superimposed dissonances as in *The Legend of the Invisible City of Kitezh*). His interest in scales led him to derive patterns of exotic nature (e.g., alternating semitones and whole tones in operas *Sadko* and *Mlada*). Wrote symphonies, chamber music, choruses and songs, but his most important works are his symphonic poems and operas. In these the tendencies of some of his contemporaries toward melancholy on the one hand and stark realism on the other were replaced by poetic refinement, imagination, whimsy and caprice. His tone pictures were painted very objectively, and he was most effective in descriptive orchestration with programmes clearly depicted. His genius for orchestration was outstanding, his treatment of instruments (whether in ensemble or solo) was always idiomatic. In his treatise—which systematized his theories and teaching—he quoted from his own compositions to illustrate registers and tone colors, and demonstrated new and brilliant effects. His tremendous influence is shown in the list of important students: Glazunov, Liadov, Arensky, Ippolitov-Ivanov, Gretchaninov, Nicolas Tcherepnin, Maximilian Steinberg, and Igor Stravinsky (from 1902). Following Dargomyzhsky's death, he orchestrated the posthumous opera, *Kamennyi Gost* (*The Stone Guest*), and also *Prince Igor* of Borodin. From the works of the unfortunate Mussorgsky he reconstructed the following: cycle, *Songs and Dances of Death* (reharmonization); symphonic poem, *Night on the Bald Mountain* (reharmonization); opera, *Khovanshtchina* (orchestration); and *Boris Godunov* (Melodic and harmonic revision, new orchestration).

ORCHESTRAL MUSIC

Symphony No. 1 (Op. 1; Originally E-flat minor; later rewritten and transposed to E minor); symphonic poem, *Sadko* (1867; revised 1869 and 1891); Symphony No. 2, *Antar* (Op. 9; 1868, revised 1876 and 1897; also as a symphonic suite); *Overture on Russian Themes* (Op. 28; 1866, revised 1880); *Capriccio espagnol* (Op. 34; 1887); symphonic suite, *Scheherazade* (St. Petersburg, November 3, 1888); *Grande pâque russe* (*Russian Easter Overture*, Op. 36; 1888).

Symphonies
No. 2, *Antar*, Op. 9

Overtures
Russian Easter, Op. 36
May Night

Suites
Scheherazade, Op. 35
Le Coq d'or

Other Works
Capriccio espagnol, Op. 34

CONCERTOS AND PIECES WITH ORCHESTRA

Piano Concerto in C♯ minor (Op. 30; 1882-83); *Fantasie de concert sur les themes russes* for violin and orchestra (Op. 33); Concerto for trombone and band.

Piano
Concerto in C-sharp minor, Op. 30

CHAMBER MUSIC

String Quartet in F major (Op. 12; 1875); *Serenade* for cello and piano Op. 37; 1903); String Sextet in A major (1876); Quintet in B-flat for flute, clarinet, horn, bassoon and piano (1876); String Quartet in G major (1897); Trio in C minor for violin, cello, and piano (1897); and 1st movement of String Quartet on *B-la-f* (Belaiev; other movements by Borodin, Glazunov, Liadov; 1886).

CHORAL WORKS

Vocal works with orchestra include *Poem about Alexis*, Op. 20 (a folk song for mixed chorus, 1877); *Glory*, Op. 21, for mixed chorus (1876-80); *Svitezyanka*, Op. 44, cantata for soprano and tenor solo and mixed chorus (1897); *From Homer*, Op. 60, for women's voices (1899). Several choruses a cappella, Op. 13, 14, 16, 18, 19, 23.

COMPOSITIONS FOR THE STAGE

Operas: *Snow Maiden* (St. Petersburg, February 10, 1882); *Mlada* (St. Petersburg, November 1, 1892); *Sadko* (Moscow, January 7, 1898; Metropolitan Opera, N.Y., January 29, 1929); *Mozart i Salieri* (after play by Pushkin dealing with supposed poisoning of Mozart; Moscow, December 7, 1898); *The Tsar's Bride* (1899); *Tsar Saltan* (Moscow, November 3, 1900); *Kashchey the Immortal* (Moscow, December 25, 1902); *The Legend of the Invisible City of Kitezh* (St. Petersburg, February 20, 1907); *The Golden Cockerel* (more often given French title, *Le Coq d'or*; posthumous, Moscow, October 7, 1909; only operatic work often given abroad).

Operas
The Snow Maiden (1882)
The Tsar's Bride (1899)
Tsar Saltan (1900)
Kashchey the Immortal (1902)
The Legend of the Invisible City of Kitezh (1907)
The Golden Cockerel (1909)

SOLO COMPOSITIONS

Vocal works with orchestra: Op. 20, 21, 44, 49, 53, 58, 60. Vocal with piano: 77 songs, including *Night, The Hebrew Song, Come to the Kingdom of Roses and Wine.* Piano pieces include Six Fugues (Op. 17) and Six Variations on B-A-C-H (Op. 10).

SUGGESTED READING

1. *CobCM*	II, 297-98
2. *GroutHWM*	588
3. *GroutSHO*	466-71
4. *UlSM*	250-52
5. *VeiCon*	245

REFERENCES

MUSIC

Under auspices of the State Music Publishers in Moscow, a complete edition of the works of Rimsky-Korsakov was inaugurated in 1944, the centennial of his birth. Sixty-four volumes have so far been issued.

BOOKS

1. MONTAGU-NATHAN, M., *Rimsky-Korsakov,* London: Constable and Co. Ltd., 1916.
2. RIMSKY-KORSAKOV, N., *Practical Manual of Harmony,* translated by Joseph Achron, New York: C. Fischer, 1930.
3. RIMSKY-KORSAKOV, N., *Foundations of Orchestration,* 2 vols., St. Petersburg, 1913; English translation by E. Agate, 1912.
4. RIMSKY-KORSAKOV, N., *My Musical Life,* posthumous (1909), 5th edition by his son, Andrey, with annotations and supplement (1935), English translation Joffe, New York: Alfred A. Knopf, Inc., 1942.

BOHEMIAN

XXXVII. Bedřich Smetana (1824-1884)

Bedřich Smetana evidenced musical talent as a child, but was denied systematic study. Managing some piano lessons, however, he became a fine performer, won encouragement from Liszt, and achieved reputation as a Chopin interpreter. Spent several years (from 1856) in Sweden as conductor of the Göteborg Philharmonic Society, composing his first three symphonic poems there. Returned to Prague shortly after 1860 when Austria granted self-government to Bohemia. Caught up in a wave of national enthusiasm he turned to opera, composing his first dramatic work, *The Brandenburgers in Bohemia,* for a new opera house where it was produced on January 5, 1866. A few months later (May 30, 1866) his second opera, *The Bartered Bride,* was received with tremendous acclaim. Smetana was hailed as Bohemia's most important musician, and was appointed first conductor in the new theatre. *Dalibor* (the third opera; May 16, 1868) brought a different reaction. The work was criticized for its use of Wagnerian *leitmotif* technic and its emphasis on the role of the orchestra. A conflict arose between Smetana and his antagonists which lasted many years and contributed greatly to the nervous ailment and deafness which ultimately forced him to resign his post (1874).

Turning to instrumental music, Smetana composed his great cycle of symphonic poems entitled *My Country* and his well-known String Quartet in E Minor. Within a year or two he was again in public favor at the opera, and his *The Kiss, The Secret,* and *Libussa* won enthusiastic response. But his mental health rapidly deteriorated. While trying desperately to complete the opera *Viola* (1884) he had to be committed to an insane asylum, where he died shortly afterwards.

Smetana's musical language was learned from the people and was full of the history and nature of his country. It is an energetic and dramatic language, a mirror of popular feeling, replete with rich orchestral color. Smetana felt little urge to write abstract music, employing programmatic ideas even in his chamber music. With his piano compositions, many of them Lisztian in their virtuosity, he accomplished for his country something akin to what Chopin had done for his.

ORCHESTRAL MUSIC

Festive Overture in D major (1848-49); Festive Symphony in E major (1853-54); symphonic poems *Richard III* (1858; after Shakespeare); *Wallensteins Lager* ("Wallenstein's Camp," 1858-59; after Schiller); and *Haakon Jarl* (1860-61). Cycle of six symphonic poems: *Má Vlast* (My Country; 1874-79) including *Vysehrad* (depicting an ancient castle of kings); *Vltava* (German, *Moldau;* river flowing thru Prague); Sárka (mythological Czech amazon); *Z ceskych luhüv a hayüv* ("From Bohemia's Fields and Groves"); *Tábor* (city associated with Bohemia's struggles for religious and political freedom; music based on Hussite chorale. "All ye who are Warriors of God"); *Blanik* (mountain beneath which Hussite heroes slumber, waiting to take arms for their country).

Symphonic Poems

Má Vlast (My Country)
Richard III
Wallenstein's Camp
Haakon Jarl

CHAMBER MUSIC

String Quartets: No. 1 in E minor (*Z mého Zivota*; German, *Aus meinem Leben*; main events in Smetana's life described in modified classical form, ending with the persistent note which resulted from deafness) and No. 2 in D minor (continues the life story, less successfully); Trio for piano, violin and cello.

String Quartets
No. 1 in E minor
No. 2 in D minor

Trio
G minor, Op. 15 for Piano, Violin and Cello

COMPOSITIONS FOR THE STAGE

The Brandenburgers in Bohemia; The Bartered Bride; Dalibor; Libussa; The Two Widows; The Kiss; The Secret; The Devil's Wall; Viola.

Operas
The Bartered Bride
The Secret

SOLO COMPOSITIONS

Two pieces for violin and piano, various songs, piano music (3 sets of polkas, a set of Bohemian dances, and the concert etude *Am Seegestade*).

SUGGESTED READING

1. *CobCM*	II, 425-32
2. *GleCM*	Outline IX
3. *GroutHWM*	589-90
4. *GroutSHO*	474
5. *RobCM*	201-6
6. *UlCM*	347-48
7. *Ul-PiHM*	518-22
8. *UlSM*	242-43

REFERENCES

BOOKS

1. NEJEDLY, Z., *Frederick Smetana*, London: G. Bles, 1924.

XXXVIII. Antonin Dvořák (1841-1904)

Born near Prague, son of an innkeeper who wished him to enter the butcher's trade. Early studies with local and nearby village musicians. After his father became reconciled to serious music study, young Dvořák went to Prague for three years of training at the Prague Organ School. Played viola in the National Orchestra (1862-73), part of the time with Smetana as conductor. In his thirty-second year he attracted wide notice for a patriotic cantata, *Heirs of the White Mountain.* As his reputation grew he was invited to write an opera for the National Theatre. *The King and the Collier* was the result; after substantial revision it was produced with great success. His music soon came to the attention of Brahms who offered warm encouragement and induced Simrock to publish some of the works. Liszt and von Bülow were similarly helpful.

Dvořák's music became extremely popular in England, and in 1884 the composer began a series of visits to that country, conducting his own works, composing for choral festivals, etc., and finally receiving the honorary degree of Doctor of Music at Cambridge. From 1892 to 1895 he was artistic director of the National Conservatory in New York City. While in America, he composed the symphony *From the New World,* the themes of which suggest Negro spirituals though not derived from authentic materials. Returning to Prague in 1895, he was appointed head of the Conservatorium (1901) and served until he died suddenly on May 1, 1904.

Dvořák is a musical descendant of the "classic" symphonic school, his structural model being Beethoven. As far as his first opera is concerned, reviewers found traces of Wagner. There are also other influences in his music, notably Brahms, Smetana, and Bohemian folk song. His talent, however, was above imitation of any sort, and his works reveal a musical personality of striking individuality. Characteristics of his music include an unlimited wealth of melodic invention, rhythmic variety, a strongly expressive type of harmony, much variety in coloring, and a free use of national folk materials. In both large and small works he reveals a fine sense for form and proportion. When featuring elements of the Bohemian style—especially folk dances such as the "Dumka" and the "Furiant"—he is especially ingratiating.

ORCHESTRAL MUSIC

Seven published symphonies: Op. 60 (D major, 1880), Op. 70 (D minor), Op. 76 (F major; originally Op. 24; 1875, 1887), Op. 88 (G major, 1889), Op. 95 (E minor, *From the New World*; 1893), E♭ major (originally Op. 10, 1873; posthumous), D minor (originally Op. 13, 1874; posthumous, 1912); 2 unnumbered symphonies: C minor (*The Bells of Zlonice*; originally Op. 31, 1865; discovered in Prague, 1936) and B♭ major (originally Op. 41, 1865); symphonic poems *The Watersprite* (Op. 107; 1896); *The Midday Witch* (Op. 108; 1896); *The Golden Spinning-wheel* (Op. 109; 1896); *The Wood Dove* (Op. 110; 1896); overtures *Amid Nature* (Op. 91; 1891), *Carnival* (Op. 92; 1891), *Othello* (Op. 93; 1891-2); *Slavonic Dances* (Op. 46, 72).

Symphonies
D Major, Op. 60
D Minor, Op. 70

F Major, Op. 76
G Major, Op. 88
E Minor, Op. 95, *From the New World*

Overtures
Amid Nature, Op. 91
Carnival, Op. 92
Othello, Op. 93

Symphonic Poems
The Golden Spinning-wheel, Op. 109
The Wood Dove, Op. 110

CONCERTOS AND PIECES WITH ORCHESTRA

Romance for violin (Op. 11; 1873); Piano Concerto in G Minor; Violin concerto in A Minor; Cello Concerto in B Minor.

Violin
A Minor, Op. 53 (1879-80)

Cello
B Minor, Op. 104 (1895)

Piano
G Minor, Op. 33 (1876)

CHAMBER MUSIC

Four Piano Trios (B♭, Op. 21; G minor, Op. 26; F minor, Op. 65; E minor "Dumky," Op. 90); a string trio (2 violins and viola, C major, Op. 74); 3 piano quartets (D major, Op. 23; B♭ major with 2 violins; E♭ major, Op. 87); 13 string quartets (including 5 unpublished); 2 piano quintets (the A major, Op. 81 being best known); 2 string quintets (in G major and E♭ major, pub. as Op. 77 and Op. 97), and a string sextet (A major, Op. 48).

Trio
"Dumky," Op. 90 for Piano, Violin, Cello

Quartet
F Major, Op. 96, "American," for 2 Violins, Viola, Cello

Quintet
A Major, Op. 81 for Piano and String Quartet

CHORAL WORKS

Stabat Mater (Op. 58; 1876-7); cantata, *The Spectre's Bride* (Op. 69; 1884); oratorio, *St. Ludmila* (Op. 71; 1885-86; enlarged as an opera, *Svatá Ludmila,* Prague, November 30, 1901); Mass in D (Op. 86; 1887, 1892); *Requiem* (Op. 89; 1890); cantata, *The American Flag* (Op. 102; 1892); *Te Deum* (Op. 103; 1892).

Hymnus
Die Erben Des weissen Berges ("The Heirs of the White Mountain"), Op. 30 for choir and orchestra on a patriotic theme

Cantata
The Spectre's Bride, Op. 69

Stabat Mater
Op. 58

COMPOSITIONS FOR THE STAGE

Stage works (all of which enjoyed first performances at Prague): *King and Collier* (1874); *The Pigheaded Peasants* (1874); *Vanda* (1875); *The Peasant a Rogue* (1877); *Dimitrij* (1882); *Jakobín* (1888, rev. 1897); *The Devil and Kate* (1899); *Rusalka* (1900; his best opera; revived many times and very popular); *Armida* (1904).

Operas
The Devil and Kate, Op. 112
Rusalka, Op. 114

SUGGESTED READING

1.	*CobCM*	I, 354-70
2.	*GleCM*	Outline X
3.	*GroutSHO*	474-75
4.	*HiCon*	234-45
5.	*HiSym*	276-96
6.	*RobCM*	202-4; 206-14
7.	*UlCM*	348-53
8.	*Ul-PiHM*	546-48
9.	*UlSM*	243-47
10.	*VeiCon*	230-5

REFERENCES

MUSIC

1. Dvořák, A., *Complete Works,* Prague: Artaria, 1955- , to date, thirty-three volumes have been issued.

BOOKS

1. Fischel, V., *Antonin Dvořák,* 1942.
2. Newmarch, R., *The Music of Czechoslovakia,* 1942.
3. Sourek, Otskar, *Antonin Dvořák, His Life and Works,* New York: Philosophical Library, 1954.
4. Robertson, A., *Dvořák,* 1945.

SCANDINAVIAN

XXXIX. Edvard Grieg (1843-1907)

One of Norway's most celebrated composers; often called "the Chopin of the North." After early musical instruction from his mother, and upon the advice of famed violinist Ole Bull, he attended the Leipzig

Conservatory (1858-1862), studying theory under Hauptmann and Richter, composition under Rietz and Reinecke, and piano under Wenzel and Moscheles. In Copenhagen he worked with Gade, and in Denmark he came under the influence of Emil Hartmann. Returning to Norway, Grieg associated himself with those dedicated to a distinctively national form of art, and it was then that his true power was revealed. He formed a close friendship with Richard Nordraak, and until the untimely death of Nordraak (1866) the two worked together toward a Norwegian school of music. Left to carry on alone, Grieg—after travels in Italy—organized a Norwegian Academy of Music (1867) and became conductor of the Harmonic Society in Christiania.

Franz Liszt, whom Grieg met in Rome, was a helpful influence in his life and career. Grieg's performances of his piano concerto in Leipzig (Gewandhaus Concert, 1879) and London (1888) as well as the conducting of his own compositions brought him prominently before the public. In other visits to England (1889, 1894, 1896) he gave joint recitals with his wife, who sang his songs, and he received an honorary degree (Doctor of Music) from Cambridge University.

Grieg is the most original among northern composers who espoused the cause of nationalism. With German Romanticism as a background and the traditions of Mendelssohn and Schumann as his legacy from Leipzig days, he adapted classical patterns to melodies so close to actual traditional themes that they sounded like authentic materials of his own country. At best in the smaller, more lyrical types, he brought to traditional forms a song-like expressiveness and contagious rhythm that depicted in musical terms the melancholy and haunting beauty of his native land. In his music can be found the Lydian fourth, the Aeolian seventh, the use of drone effects, the alternation of 6/8 and 3/4 rhythmic patterns, and the major-minor spelling of the third. Such nationalistic traits, in combination with Grieg's sensitivity for Romantic lyricism, produced a unique, personal style that retains its charm.

ORCHESTRAL MUSIC

Principal compositions for orchestra include the Overture, *I Höst* ("In Autumn," 1866); 2 suites from *Peer Gynt* (1888, 1891); 3 pieces from *Sigurd Jorsalfar* (1892); symphonic dances (1898); suite for strings, *Fra Holbergs Tid* ("From Holberg's Time," 1885).

Suite

Aus Holbergs Zeit, Op. 40 (miniatures for string orchestra)

CONCERTOS AND PIECES WITH ORCHESTRA

Piano

Concerto in A Minor, Op. 16 (1868; revised 1907)

CHAMBER MUSIC

Three sonatas for violin and piano (F major, Op. 8, 1865; G minor, Op. 13, 1867; C minor, Op. 45, 1886-87); a sonata for cello and piano in A minor (Op. 36, 1883). String quartet in G minor (Op. 27, 1877-78); and two movements of a string quartet in F major (1892).

CHORAL WORKS

Included are *Landsighting* (Op. 31, 1872) and *Scenes from "Olav Trygvason"* (Op. 50, 1873). He also wrote *The Bewitched One* for baritone with strings and 2 horns (Op. 32, 1878); and the ballad, *Bergliot,* for declamation and orchestra (Op. 42, 1870-71).

COMPOSITIONS FOR THE STAGE

Incidental Music (from which the suites were taken)

For Ibsen's play, *Peer Gynt,* 8 pieces (Op. 46 and 55, 1874-1875)

For Björnson's *Sigurd Jorsalfar* (Christiania, April 10, 1872)

SUGGESTED READING

1. *CobCM*	I, 497f
2. *GroutHWM*	590-91
3. *HiCon*	246-51
4. *UlCM*	345-46
5. *Ul-PiHM*	522-23
6. *UlSM*	253-54
7. *VeiCon*	235-37

REFERENCES

1. Abraham, G., ed., *Grieg: a Symposium,* Norman, Oklahoma: University of Oklahoma Press, 1950.
2. Monrad-Johansen, D., *Edvard Grieg,* tr. from Norwegian by Madge Robertson. Princeton: Princeton U. Press, 1938.

FRENCH

XL. Édouard Lalo (1823-1892)

Distinguished French composer of Spanish descent. Born at Lille, he studied at the Lille branch of the Paris Conservatory, then in Paris. A performer on both the violin and the viola, he was violist in the Armingaud-Jacquard Quartet. As a composer, he was not well received in his early years. One of his first real successes came when Sarasate performed his violin concerto (January 18, 1874) at a Châtelet concert. Next came his most famous work, *Symphonie espagnole,* which Sarasate also performed (February 7, 1875), and which became one of the great favorites in violin repertory, combining a true virtuoso style with pulsing Spanish rhythms. The *Fantaisie norvégienne,* for violin and orchestra, was rearranged for orchestra alone and performed successfully as *Rapsodie norvégienne* (Colonne Concerts, October 26, 1879). His opera *Le Roi d'Ys* (begun 1875) after several revisions was given at the Opéra-Comique on May 7, 1888, achieving tremendous success, with performances following in other parts of France, elsewhere in Europe, and finally in America (New Orleans, January 23, 1890).

The talent of Lalo was a very individual one and was the result of careful study of such great masters as Beethoven, Schubert, and Schumann—all of whom he admired deeply and attempted to emulate. Essential characteristics of his music are melodic expressiveness, beauty of line, harmonic richness and ingenious orchestration. One of the most notable of French composers, he richly deserved the decoration of the *Légion d'Honneur* which was conferred upon him in July 1880.

In addition to works named above, the following should be noted:

ORCHESTRAL MUSIC

Three symphonies, 2 of which remain unpublished.

CONCERTOS

One for cello (1877), and 1 for piano (1889).

CHAMBER MUSIC

Three piano trios; 1 string quartet; a sonata for violin; a sonata for cello.

COMPOSITIONS FOR THE STAGE

A 3-act opera, *Fiesque* (unperformed), from which successful ballet music was arranged under the title *Divertissement;* 1 act from an unfinished opera, *La Jacquerie* (produced posthumously in 1895 after completion by Artur Coquard); Ballets *Namouna* (1882) and *Néron* (1891).

SOLO COMPOSITIONS

Pieces for violin and piano, songs.

SUGGESTED READING

1. *CobCM* II, 88f
2. *GroutSHO* 434
3. *HiCon* 151-53
4. *VeiCon* 230

XLI. Emmanuel Chabrier (1841-1894)

Largely self-taught as far as music was concerned, Chabrier was a law student in Paris, taking lessons in theory and piano on the side. At twenty-one he entered government service, but his interest in music remained active, and one of the avenues through which he approached it was a private musical society in which Henri Duparc and Vincent d'Indy were also members. A strong admirer of Wagner, he visited Germany with Duparc (1879) to hear Wagner operas performed. Back in Paris, he had some piano pieces published, then left for a tour of Spain. From this experience came his most famous composition, the rhapsody *España* (1883). When the work was programmed by Lamoureux in Paris (1884), it created a real sensation. A second musical result of the travel in Spain was the well-known piano number, *Habanera* (1885). In writing for the stage, Chabrier seemed to alternate between a sensational Wagner style and the more conventional French style of the period. His two operas (*Gwendoline,* Brussels, 1886; *Le Roi malgré lui,* Paris, 1887) have not enjoyed marked success. However, the *Bourrée fantasque* for piano (1891; orchestrated by Felix Mottl) and *Joyeuse Marche* for orchestra (at first titled *Marche française* 1888) have been popular.

Among additional works should be mentioned the following:

CHORAL WORKS

Cantata *La Sulamite* for mezzo-soprano and women's chorus (1884); and *Ode à la musique* for voices and orchestra (1890).

COMPOSITIONS FOR THE STAGE

Two early light operas, *L'Étoile* (1877) and *Une Éducation manquée* (1879), and an unfinished opera *Briséis.*

SOLO COMPOSITIONS

For piano, *Dix Pièces pittoresques* (1880), 4 of which were orchestrated and performed as *Suite pastorale*; for 2 pianos, *Trois Valses romantiques* (1883); many songs.

SUGGESTED READING

1. *GroutHWM* 603-4
2. *GroutSHO* 429-30

SPANISH

XLII. Isaac Albéniz (1860-1909)

Born in Catalonia (NE Spain), Albéniz showed great musical talent at an early age, giving his first piano recital at age four. When he was six, he was taken by his mother to Paris, where he studied privately with Marmontel. Returning to Spain, he and his sister—also very gifted—concertized. Albéniz, however, had an adventurous spirit, and ran away from home. He crossed and recrossed the Peninsula, living from his piano recitals. Fleeing from the police, he stowed away on a boat bound for Puerto Rico. Cuba was the next stopping place, and finally the United States. Life for the young artist was a long series of escapades. In 1883 there was a change. He accepted the help of Count Morphy toward serious music study in Brussels, Leipzig, and Budapest, where he met Franz Liszt. Influenced by Felipe Pedrell's devotion to national Spanish music, and influenced, too, by his affection for Rosita Jordana, he married (1883) and settled down, finally making Paris his home.

In his compositions, Albéniz combined elements of French impressionism with melodic and rhythmic patterns of his homeland. His first work to show national characteristics was the rhapsody *Catalonia* for piano and orchestra (1899). Later (1906-09) came his masterpiece, *Iberia.* This was a suite of twelve piano pieces: *Evocación, El Puerto, Fête-Dieu à Seville, Rondeña, Almería, Triana, El Albaicin, El Polo, Lavapiés, Málaga, Jérez,* and *Eritaña.* Not only is the music fully idiomatic for the instrument, but it is a splendid example of virtuoso writing. Two other piano works were left unfinished: *Azulejos* (completed by Granados) and *Navarra* (finished by D. de Sévérac; orchestrated by Fernandez Arbós). Also transcribed by Arbós, who was a brilliant orchestrator, were the first, sixth, and third numbers from *Iberia* (Leopold Stokowski has also made an orchestration of No. 3). Other piano pieces which have achieved great popularity are the *Seguidillas, Córdova,* and the *Tango* in D major.

While Albéniz is now remembered for his later piano works (*Iberia,* especially), it should be noted that his early compositions were for the theater, as follows:

COMPOSITIONS FOR THE STAGE

Several operas include *The Magic Opal* (written to an English libretto and given in London, 1893); *Enrico Clifford* (1895); *San Antonio de la Florida* (1894; staged in Brussels under the title *Ermitage fleuri* in 1905); *Pepita Jiménez* (1896). He projected an operatic trilogy, *King Arthur,* but completed only the first part, *Merlin.*

SUGGESTED READING

1. *GroutHWM* 596
2. *GroutSHO* 484

XLIII. Enrique Granados (1867-1916)

Granados, of an entirely different temperament than Albéniz, studied piano at the Barcelona Conservatory with Pujol, winning first prize (1883). While attending the Conservatory of Madrid, he worked with Felipe Pedrell, the famous musicologist and composer whose influence has been so strongly felt in modern Spanish music. Granados was known early in his life as a splendid pianist and a composer of characteristic Spanish songs and dances. His spirit was thoroughly Romantic, and his interest went back to the colorful epoch of the painter, Francisco Goya (1746-1828). The work which became his masterpiece began as a set of piano pieces inspired by etchings and paintings and was called *Goyescas.* The six numbers are replete with imagination, color, and idiomatic writing for the piano. Titles are as follows: *Los Requiebros* (Flattery), *Coloquio en la Reja* (Love Duet), *El Fandango de Candíl, Quejas o la Maja y el Ruiseñor* (The Lady and the Nightingale), *El Amor y la Muerte* (Love and Death, with some reference to melodic materials from the preceding number), and *Epilogo* (Serenade of the Spectre). Later, a libretto was written by Fernando Periquet on ideas and scenes shown in the paintings of Goya. In furnishing the musical setting of the text, Granados employed music from the piano suite. The first performance of the opera (also called *Goyescas*) was by the Metropolitan Opera in New York on January 28, 1916. The presentation was an excellent success, and the famous *Intermezzo*—which was composed to provide time necessary for changes of scenery—became one of the most popular compositions of Granados. A week after the performance, the composer and his wife, who were present, sailed for Europe. As an act of war their ship was torpedoed in the English Channel, and they lost their lives.

A partial list of works includes—in addition to numerous piano pieces—seven operas, two symphonic poems (*La Nit del Mort* and *Dante*), three suites and other orchestral works. In chamber music there is a piano trio, a string quartet, a *Serenata* for two violins and piano, and other works. His choral opus, *Cant de las Estrelles,* calls for both organ and piano. The music of Granados is typically Romantic (he has been called "the last Romantic"), with characteristic Spanish melodies (often elaborately ornamented) and rhythmic patterns forming an important element.

SUGGESTED READING

1. *GroutSHO* 484

XLIV. Manuel de Falla (1876-1946)

One of Spain's greatest composers, de Falla studied with J. Tragó (piano) and Felipe Pedrell (composition) in Madrid. His first compositions were *zarzuelas,* later discarded. For his opera, *La Vida breve,* he was awarded (1905) the prize of the Academia de Bellas Artes. In the same year he also won the Ortiz y Cussó piano prize. In 1907 de Falla went to Paris, where he became acquainted with Dukas, Debussy, and Ravel. Under their guidance and with their encouragement, he accepted and put into practice the basic principles of impressionism. At the same time he retained his own personal and national style. The colorful, elegant, and meticulous style of de Falla, then, evolves partly from this seven-year stay in Paris, and partly from his studies with Felipe Pedrell. From Pedrell he learned how to build his art on the Spanish folk idiom, without, however, employing authentic folk material in his music. Returning to Spain from France (1914), he made his home in Granada (1921), from which place he frequently toured Europe as conductor of his own compositions. After the Spanish Civil War de Falla emigrated to Argentina where, in the Alta Gracia district, he lived the remaining years of his life in quietness and detachment.

The works belonging to de Falla's early period are based on the Andalusian style, which is often considered to be the typically "Spanish" way of writing. In this style, the instrumental idiom is frequently colored by effects derived from popular Andalusian guitar music. His later works are based on the idiom of Castile and hence are quite different in character. Typical of this changed idiom is *El Retablo de Maese Pedro,* which is in strictly classical vein. His orchestral style is characterized by a rich and varied texture, *contrast* being the important element of expression. In many ways this style suggests Ravel and the modern French school. In his harpsichord concerto, the keyboard style shows a definite relationship with the musical practices of Domenico Scarlatti, who spent much of his life in Spain. Among the talented students of Manuel de Falla were Ernesto Halffter and Joaquin Nin-Culmell.

ORCHESTRAL MUSIC

Important in this category: *Homenajes* 1. *Pour le Tombeau de Debussy* (1920; originally for guitar); 2. *Fanfare pour Arbós* (1933); 3. *Pour le Tombeau de Paul Dukas* (1935; originally for piano); 4. *Pedrelliana* (1938; 1st perf. entire suite, Buenos Aires, November 18, 1939; composer conducting).

CONCERTOS AND PIECES WITH ORCHESTRA

Noches en los jardines de España (Nights in the Gardens of Spain, 1909-15); Concerto for Harpsichord (or piano), flute, oboe, clarinet, violin, and cello, written at suggestion of Wanda Landowska (Barcelona, November 5, 1926; Landowska soloist, de Falla conducting).

CHAMBER MUSIC

Psyché, for voice, flute, harp, violin, viola, and cello (1924).

CHORAL WORKS

La Atlántida, a large work for soli, chorus, and orchestra, based on M. J. Verdaguer's Catalan poem, was begun in 1928, unfinished at de Falla's death; completed by Ernesto Halffter.

COMPOSITIONS FOR THE STAGE

Operas *La Vida breve* ("The Short Life") for marionettes and singers (Nice, April 1, 1913; Metropolitan Opera, N.Y., March 7, 1936); and *El Retablo de Maese Pedro* (Master Peter's Puppet Show; performed in concert version, Seville, 1919; first complete stage performance in Madrid, March 23, 1923). Ballets *El Amor Brujo* ("Gypsy Love"; Madrid, April 15, 1915; often given as an orchestral suite); *El Sombrero de tres picos* ("The Three-cornered Hat"; London, July 22, 1919).

SOLO COMPOSITIONS

For piano: *Four Pièces espagnoles* including *Aragonesa, Cubana, Montañesa, Andaluza,* and *Fantasia Bética.* For voice: *Trois mélodies* (1909); *Siete canciones populares españolas* (1914); *Soneto a Córdoba* for voice and harp.

SUGGESTED READING

1. *AusMTC*	118-20
2. *CobCM*	I, 384f
3. *GroutSHO*	527-30
4. *Ul-PiHM*	585, 621-22

REFERENCES

1. Chase, G., *The Music of Spain,* 2nd Revised Edition, New York: Dover Publications, Inc., 1959.
2. Trend, J. B., *Manuel de Falla and Spanish Music,* New York: Alfred A. Knopf, Inc., 1929.

CHAPTER

7

The Post-Romanticists

XLV. Sir Edward Elgar (1857-1934)

An English composer with a consistent English slant to his work, his uniqueness and the strength of his personal idiom were so pronounced that the adjective "Elgarian" has a place in the analyst's vocabulary. Beginning life as the fifth son of an obscure organist-violinist, he ended up with most of the honors possible to his profession—numerous honorary degrees and titles, the Order of Merit, Knighthood, Master of the King's Musick, etc. Almost entirely self-taught, he made his way as accompanist, church organist, director of choirs and orchestras, and for a while, bandmaster at an insane asylum. A turning point came with his marriage in 1889. His wife believed in his future as a composer and did everything possible to encourage him, smoothing the way and standing beside him through failure and success. It is significant that all of his important works were composed prior to 1920, the year of his wife's death.

Elgar's compositional style has been described as "functional Romanticism." He is also referred to as "post-Wagnerian," and at least in his superb command of the orchestra he does have something in common with the Master of Bayreuth. In temperament and outlook, however, he seems more akin to Brahms and Dvořák. He is also thoroughly individual, his originality being perhaps most evident in melody and rhythm. Harmonically and texturally he was content to be conservative. Devoutly Roman Catholic he wrote into his oratorios many of the tenets and feelings of his faith. The style of Elgar, with its curious mixture of restraint and sentiment, its frequent touches of humor, its masterly sense of architecture, served well the expressive purposes of a man who was quickly recognized as England's first native musical genius since the time of Purcell. While it is possible to find in his music occasional lapses in unity and coherence, and while it is true that his handling of the English language is often something less than ideal, the magnitude of his creative achievement still justifies the esteem in which he is held.

ORCHESTRAL MUSIC

Two symphonies (1908, 1911); *Enigma Variations* (1899); symphonic poem *Falstaff* (1913). Suites: *The Wand of Youth* (1907-08) and *Nursery Suite* (1933). Overtures: *Froissart* (1890), *Cockaigne* (1901), *In the South* (1904). *Serenade* (1893) and *Introduction and Allegro* (1905) for strings.

Symphonies

No. 1 in A-flat Major, Op. 55 (1908)
No. 2 in E-flat Major, Op. 63 (1911)

Symphonic Poem

Falstaff, "Symphonic Study" in C Minor, Op. 68 (1913)

Symphonic Variations

Variations on an Original Theme, Op. 36 "Enigma" (Publ. 1899)

Overtures

Cockaigne, Op. 40 (1901)
In the South, Op. 50 (1904)

Other Works

Introduction and Allegro for String Quartet and String Orchestra, Op. 47 (publ. 1905)

CONCERTOS AND PIECES WITH ORCHESTRA

Violin

B Minor, Op. 61 (1910)

Cello

E Minor, Op. 85 (1919)

CHAMBER MUSIC

Duo

Sonata for Violin and Piano in E Minor, Op. 9 (1919)

Quartet

E Minor, Op. 83 for 2 Violins, Viola, Cello (1918)

Quintet

A Minor, Op. 84 for Piano and String Quartet (1918)

CHORAL WORKS

Oratorios: *The Light of Life* (1896); *The Dream of Gerontius* (1900); *The Apostles* (1903); *The Kingdom* (1906). Other Choral Works: *The Black Knight* (1893); *Scenes from the Bavarian Highlands* (1896); *King Olaf* (1896); *The Banner of St. George* (1897); *The Music Makers* (1912); *The Spirit of England* (1916).

SOLO COMPOSITIONS

Organ: 2 sonatas (1896, 1933), the second arranged from the *Severn Suite* for brass band. Songs: *Sea Pictures,* with orchestra (1899); songs with piano; part songs.

SUGGESTED READING

1.	*AusMTC*	85-88
2.	*CobCM*	I, 372-77
3.	*GroutHWM*	595
4.	*HiCon*	252-60
5.	*HiSym*	313-25
6.	*RobCM*	338
7.	*SachsCA*	190-92
8.	*Ul-PiHM*	568-70
9.	*UlSM*	273-74
10.	*VeiCon*	255-56

REFERENCES

BOOKS

1. Anderson, W. R., *Introduction to the Music of Elgar,* 1949.
2. McVeagh, D., *Edward Elgar: His Life and Music,* 1955.
3. Maine, B., *Elgar: His Life and Works,* 2 vols., 1933.
4. Newman, E., *Elgar,* 1922.
5. Young, P. M., *Elgar, O. M.: a Study of a Musician,* London: Collins, 1955.

XLVI. Gustav Mahler (1860-1911)

An outstanding conduotor, especially of opera. Not content with the universal tribute given him as an interpreter, he looked for equal distinction as a creative artist. His symphonic concepts were often on a grand scale, with elaborate means being used for the realization of his ideas. Paradoxically, he was a great master of *lieder* composition, sensitive to the miniature and concentrated world of the art song.

Attempted a synthesis of the lyric and the monumental. Taking from the music dramas of Wagner many of his ideas, he shared also with Wagner the ideal of giving expression to the Infinite by means of music.

Sought to reconcile the elements of musical Romanticism, the symphony and the *lied.* Each symphony (of the nine) contains programmatic elements, sometimes explicit through the use of words, sometimes inherent in the expressive nature of the movements. In a letter (1896) he wrote: "Beginning with Beethoven there exists no modern music which hasn't its inner program."

ORCHESTRAL MUSIC

Embraces 9 symphonies, the 10th being left unfinished—the picture thus established showing the composer to be the last great composer of the Viennese Romantic School.

Symphonies

No. 1 in D Major (1888), *Titan*
Nos. 1-4 constitute a group in which a lyric, folkish quality is often present. No. 1 contains themes from the song cycle (1884), *Lieder eines fahrenden Gesellen* ("Songs of a Wayfarer"). Scored for large orchestra (no voices).

No. 2 in C Minor (1894), *Resurrection*
Scored for large orchestra, soprano, alto and chorus. Five movements, conceived as a huge bipartite design, Part I consisting of the lengthy first movement, Part II of the remaining four movements. Third mvt. (Scherzo), 4th (folk song for soprano voice), and 5th (containing the chorale *Auferstehn*) are connected.

No. 3 in D Minor (1896), *Die fröhliche Wissenschaft*
For large orchestra, contralto, and two choruses (women's chorus, boys' chorus). Six movements, again in huge bipartite design, Part I made up of the first mvt. (lasting 45 minutes), Part II of the remaining mvts. "Song of Nature" with symbolic triumph of summer.

No. 4 in G Major (1900)
For small orchestra and (last mvt. only) soprano solo. Returns to normal four-movement plan of moderate dimensions. Introduces new kind of melodic counterpoint somewhat reminiscent of Haydn. Last movement features simple folklike melody for soprano soloist.

No. 5 in C♯ Minor (1902), *The Giant*
For orchestra alone. Typical of 2nd period; reveals change in mental outlook; somewhat disjointed in

form and unsettled in matter. Orchestra normal in size, but great demands made upon it.

No. 6 in A Minor
For orchestra. Tragic in mood; victory of destiny—with all its harshness—over the will.

No. 7 in E Minor (1905)
For orchestra. Full of hope and with energetic finale; romantic qualities with more leanings toward classical form.

No. 8 in E-flat (1907), *Symphony of a Thousand*
Scored for very large orchestra with auxiliary brass choir, 2 double choruses, boys' choir, and 7 vocal soloists. Four movements, but in bipartite scheme. Part I—the first movement—draws its text from the hymn, *Veni creator spiritus*; Part II—the remaining movements (all connected)—uses texts from the second part of Goethe's *Faust*. In effect a large cantata, with striking synthesis of choral and orchestral music.

No. 9 in D Major (1909)
Uses instruments alone. Mood one of resignation—a kind of personal farewell to world in which the composer had not found true sympathy. Bitterness and frustration overcome; music is reflective and reminiscent.

No. 10 (incomplete), *Adagio* and *Purgatorio*
Preliminary sketches only, preserved despite Mahler's instructions that they be destroyed. First and 2nd mvts. (Adagio and Scherzo) completed by Ernst Křenek, performed Vienna 1924. Third mvt. bears inscription "purgatorio." In 4th mvt. (Scherzo) and 5th (Finale) cryptic comments suggesting an autobiographical basis for the symphony.

VOCAL WORKS

Apart from his symphonies, Mahler published only vocal works—songs and song cycles. Included in the catalogue: *Lieder und Gesänge aus der Jugendzeit* (14 songs for voice and piano; 1880-92); *Das klagende Lied* (soprano, contralto, tenor, chorus, and orch.; 1880-99); *Lieder eines fahrenden Gesellen* (4 songs with orch.; 1883-85); *Des Knaben Wunderhorn* (10 songs, with piano or orch.; 1888); 5 songs to poems by Rückert (1902); *Kindertotenlieder* (5 songs with piano or orch.; 1901-04); *Das Lied von der Erde*, for contralto, tenor, and orchestra (1907-10; performed posthumously in Munich, November 20, 1911, Bruno Walter conducting).

Das Lied von der Erde ("The Song of the Earth")
A song cycle and a symphony. Text from German version of a set of melancholy Chinese poems by Li Tai Po. Six mvts., with tenor and alto (or baritone) soloists alternating. Vocal phrases combined with orchestral themes; unification achieved by the cyclical form and the despairing mood.

OTHER COMPOSITIONS

Nothing of importance. Mahler limited himself almost exclusively to symphonic and vocal works.

SUGGESTED READING

1. *AusMTC*	122-130
2. *Ca-Jo-WaAM*	399-403
3. *GroutHWM*	571-576
4. *HiSym*	297-312
5. *Ul-PiHM*	552-557
6. *UlSM*	256-261

REFERENCES

BOOKS

1. ENGEL, GABRIEL, *Gustav Mahler, Song-Symphonist*, New York: Bruckner Society, 1933.
2. MAHLER, A., *Gustav Mahler*, translated 1946.
3. REDLICH, H. F., *Mahler and Bruckner*, 1955.
4. WALTER, BRUNO, *Gustav Mahler*, Vienna, 1936, translated by James Galston with biographical note by E. Křenek, New York: Greystone Corporation, 1941.
5. MITCHELL, DONALD, *Gustav Mahler: the Early Years*, 1958.
6. NEWLIN, DIKA, *Bruckner, Mahler, Schoenberg*, New York: King's Crown Press, 1947.
7. STEFAN, PAUL, *Gustav Mahler: A Study of His Personality and Work*, translated by T. E. Clark, New York: G. Schirmer, 1913.

XLVII. Richard Strauss (1864-1949)

One of the most celebrated of the post-Romantic German composers, Strauss left an indelible mark on the symphonic poem and the opera. While he did not attempt a complete written exposition of his views dealing with the functions of music, as Wagner and others had done, his philosophy can be understood from various comments and statements as well as from a study of his scores. Refusing to concede a distinction between abstract and programme music, he admitted only "good" and "bad" music, the former being defined as that which could express the most. In line with this conviction, Strauss taught that music could do more than merely picture outward happiness and events. To him it could also stimulate in the listener emotions similar to those characteristic of the object or circumstance being described.

Possessed of a prolific imagination, splendid musical and dramatic abilities, and a supreme mastery of orchestral technique, he used orchestral forces similar in size to those employed by Wagner, retaining also the principle of the *leitmotif* as well as the complex, chromatic harmony of the earlier master. Going beyond this, Strauss exploited the possibilities of enharmonic modulations, achieved more and more tension and excitement by such devices as opposing sonorities and tonalities, thus pointing in the direction of a complete negation of the accepted harmonic system.

As he moved toward the close of his compositional career, however, Strauss left the extreme style for which he was then famous and returned to a more lyrical type of writing. His final works, both operatic and instrumental, were examples of musical serenity and repose.

In his songs, which number over 150, he established himself as a true master of the German *lied,* and a worthy successor of earlier composers in the genre.

ORCHESTRAL MUSIC

Symphonic Fantasia *Aus Italien,* 8 tone-poems, the *Alpensinfonie,* Symphony in F minor, Suite from *Le Bourgeois gentilhomme.*

Symphonies and Symphonic Poems

Aus Italien, Op. 16 ("Symphonic Fantasia," 1887)
Written after visit to Italy. A bridge from the absolute to the programmatic. In 4 movements, with the program influencing the form of each.

Macbeth, Op. 23 (1887)
First symphonic poem in 1 movement. Based on Shakespeare, with musical leanings toward Liszt, it constitutes a musical psychological study. Published after *Don Juan.*

Don Juan, Op. 20 (1888)
Inspired by poem of Nikolaus Lenau, the music shows psychological character changes. In sonata form, employing theme transformation and development.

Tod und Verklärung, Op. 24 (1889)
Sonata form with slow introduction and epilogue. More unified than many of his compositions. Ritter's poem added after music had been composed, being an interpretation of the music rather than the other way around.

Till Eulenspiegels lustige Streiche, Op. 28 (1894-1895)
Most popular of Strauss's works, and one of the shortest. Form similar to Rondo with Prologue and Epilogue. Some elements of variation also present, the chief thematic elements recurring in varied form with episodes between.

Also sprach Zarathustra, Op. 30 (1895-1896)
Inspired by Nietzsche's book dealing with the development of the human race. Eight parts, with titles taken from the book. Employs Gregorian *Credo* and the *Magnificat.* Section "Of Science" employs fugal subject containing all 12 tones—this being a distortion of previous "nature" theme. Keys of C major and B major used simultaneously to show contrast between nature and spirit.

Don Quixote, Op. 35 (1897)
"Fantastic variations on a theme of noble character." Consists of Prologue, the Theme and 10 Variations, Epilogue. Realism carried to furthest degree with sounds of sheep and use of wind machine. The variation form employed to show changes in Knight's mind and temperament. Virtuoso solo cello part depicts the Don.

Ein Heldenleben, Op. 40 (1898)
Autobiographical. Composer strikes back at his critics. Themes from earlier works appear in the score. Written in six sections, but with two main subjects.

Symphonia domestica, Op. 53 (1903)
Portrays a day in the life of Strauss's family. Very large orchestra. In one movement and 3 subdivisions (Introduction and Scherzo, Adagio, Double Fugue and Finale).

Eine Alpensinfonie, Op. 64 (1911-1915)
Somewhat autobiographical, being the story of a day in the Alps. Also very large orchestra, including heckelphone, organ, wind machine, thunder machine, celesta, and an additional 12 horns, 2 trumpets, and 2 trombones behind the scenes.

CONCERTOS AND PIECES WITH ORCHESTRA

Violin

D Minor, Op. 8 (1881-1882)

Oboe

D Major (1945-1946)

Horn

No. 1, in E-flat Major, Op. 11 (1882-1883)
No. 2, in E-flat Major (1942)

Clarinet, bassoon, strings, and harp

Duet Concertino (Radio Svizzera Italiana, 1948)

Piano

Burleske (1886)
Parergon zur Symphonia domestica for piano left hand, Op. 73 (1925)

CHAMBER MUSIC

A. String Instruments

Quartet

A Major, Op. 2 (1879-80)

23 Solo String Instruments

Metamorphosen (1944-1945)

B. Piano with Other Instruments

Duos

Sonatas:
E-flat Major, Op. 18 for violin and piano (1887)
F Major, Op. 6 for cello and piano (1882-1883)

Quartet

C Minor, Op. 13 for piano, violin, viola, and cello (1884)

C. Miscellaneous

Large Chamber Ensembles

Suite, Op. 4 for 13 wind instruments (1884)
Serenade, Op. 7 for 13 wind instruments (1881)
Sonatine No. 2 in E-flat Major for 16 wind instruments (1944-45)

COMPOSITIONS FOR THE STAGE

Included are the ballets *Josephslegende* (Paris, 1914) and *Schlagobers* (Vienna, 1924), and 15 operas.

Guntram (1893)
Strauss wrote both text and music; unsuccessful.

Feuersnot (The Fire Famine; 1901)
A confusion of musical styles, combining medieval legend, farce, parody, satire, and eroticism.

Salome, Op. 54 (1905)
Based on German translation of Oscar Wilde's 1-act play. Erotic and psychological subject set to music of tremendously expressive power. The macabre mood of the drama lifted to artistic height by descriptive harmonies, new and strange melodic and rhythmic patterns, and an orchestral fabric both splendid and nerve-shattering. Exceeds the limit of the Wagnerian music drama.

Elektra (1909), Op. 58
First of long line of works in which Strauss and Hugo von Hofmannsthal (1874-1929), the Viennese dramatist, collaborated. Sophocles' play depicting in one act the emotions of hatred and revenge with the horrors of matricide. A score of tremendous strength in which dissonance and harmonic daring reach extremes hitherto unknown.

Der Rosenkavalier, Op. 59 (1911)
Story of the Rose Cavalier in 3 acts with libretto by von Hofmannsthal. The aristocratic and elegant Vienna of the 18th century presented in Romantic, sensuous music replete with chromatic harmonies, turbulent rhythms, orchestral coloring of a high order, and a magical sense of comedy—all held together by a pervading humaneness and sympathy. A perfect combination of comedy and sentiment.

Ariadne auf Naxos (Ariadne at Naxos, 1912)
At first connected with von Hofmannsthal's version of Molière's *Le Bourgeois gentilhomme*. Perfect example of neo-Classical chamber opera, in style of Mozart with recitatives; small orchestra; combination of the legendary and the comic.

Die Frau Ohne Schatten (1919)

Intermezzo (1924)
A small but busy chamber orchestra supports typical comic-opera parts and also furnishes melodically charming interludes; naturalistic recitatives.

Die ägyptische Helena (1928)
Arabella (1933)
Die schweigsame Frau (1935)
Friedenstag (1938)
Daphne (1938)
Die Liebe der Danae (1938-40)
Capriccio (1942)

SOLO COMPOSITIONS

Songs: 4 sets with orchestra (1897-1921); also, *Four Last Songs* (with orchestra; 1949); 26 sets with piano. Piano: Sonata in B minor (1881); 2 sets of short pieces (1881, 1882).

OTHER WORKS

Editions of Gluck's *Iphigénie en Tauride* (1894) and Mozart's *Idomeneo* (1930), also Berlioz's *Instrumentation* (1905).

SUGGESTED READING

1.	*AusMTC*	134-44
2.	*Ca-Jo-WaAM*	393-99
3.	*CobCM*	II, 460f
4.	*GroutHWM*	576-83
5.	*GroutSHO*	515-20
6.	*Ul-PiHM*	561-65
7.	*UlSM*	261-66

REFERENCES

THEMATIC INDEX

1. Mueller von Asow, and Hermann, Erich, *Richard Strauss Thematisches Verzeichnis*, Op. 1-59. Wien-Wiesbaden: Verlag Doblinger, 1959.

BOOKS

1. Armstrong, T., *Strauss's Tone Poems*, London: Oxford University Press, 1931.
2. Berlioz, H., *Treatise on Instrumentation*, enlarged and revised by R. Strauss, New York: Kalmus, 1948.
3. Blom, E., *Strauss—The Rose Cavalier*, 1930, an analysis of the opera.
4. Del Mar, N., *Richard Strauss: A Critical Commentary on his Life and Works*, New York: The Macmillan Company, 1962.
5. Mann, W., *Richard Strauss: A Critical Study of the Operas*, London, 1964.
6. Marek, G. R., *Richard Strauss: The Life of a Non-Hero*, New York: Simon and Schuster, Inc., 1967.
7. Newman, E., *Richard Strauss*, 1921.
8. Strauss, R., *Correspondence between Richard Strauss and Hugo von Hofmannsthal*, 1907-1918, translated by Paul England, New York: Alfred A. Knopf, Inc., 1927.

XLVIII. Jean Sibelius (1865-1957)

Finland's most celebrated composer, he evidenced an individual approach to the use of the orchestra and the treatment of thematic material. Showed no recognized modern tendency and belonged to no "school"—atonal, polytonal, modal, or any other. Not greatly influenced by any of his immediate forerunners. Has never in any of his large works made use of Finnish folk song material or material patterned after Finnish folk songs.

Compositions before Op. 63 show development of the "idee fixe," this trend reaching its consummation in the fourth and sixth symphonies. Beginning with his Opus 22 (*The Return of Lemminkaïnen*) he developed an individual style of motive development. Along with this style there is a building of unity through conciseness, so that (as in Symphony No. 4) the result is a complex form reduced to its bare essentials.

Unity through interrelation of movements was secured by creating an idea that matured as the work progressed. Cyclic form as used by Franck was not an element of his style.

His compositional output shows three distinct phases, which can be considered as matching three periods of his life:

a. The National and Romantic idiom—including the symphonic poems, choral compositions, and works based upon the *Kalevala* or Finnish mythology in general.
b. The Eclectic and Cosmopolitan—including works composed largely while he traveled abroad and attained a European reputation.
c. The Classic and Universal—including the symphonies which were composed in the later part of his life as he lived, secluded, at his home in "Järvenpää."

ORCHESTRAL MUSIC

Seven symphonies, 14 symphonic poems (4 grouped under the title, *Legends from the Kalevala*), and 7 symphonic suites.

Symphonies

No. 1 in E Minor, Op. 39 (1899)
Classical four-movement form. First movement has an introduction which bears no relation to the rest of the movement, but which is heard again as the introduction to the final movement. Second movement in rondo form; third movement a scherzo in sonata form with development containing a new theme; fourth movement in sonata form.

No. 2 in D Major, Op. 43 (1902)
Melodious, in Romantic style. In first movement the themes are developed into a complete melodic unit which is stated at the end of the development section. Second movement a combination of rondo and sonata form. Third movement a scherzo, regular in form. Fourth movement in simple sonata form.

No. 3 in C Major, Op. 52 (1908)
Shows a return to classical patterns. Three movements, with a bright, gay style. First movement in sonata form. Second a large 3-part song form. Third in binary form with allusions to theme of second movement.

No. 4 in A Minor, Op. 63 (1911)
Thought by many to be one of his best works. Four movements in classic sonata form with the exception of the slow movement following the scherzo—this change because first movement is slow. Key relationships similar to those in the Brahms First—a major third apart. Shows elimination of unessentials.

No. 5 in E-flat Major, Op. 82 (1915)
Represents a new trend toward complete unification of all material. Three movements, the first being actually a combination of the usual 1st and 2nd.
In first movement the themes are given in fragments with a new kind of harmonic background, constantly changing with indefinite tonic, many passing tones, changing-tone figures and pedal points. This movement makes some use of polytonal, polychordal effect—otherwise rare in Sibelius.

No. 6 in D Minor, Op. 104 (1924)
A testing ground avoiding all extremes. In formal design, a free sonata form. In first movement, a strong modal character (Dorian). Second movement in two sections, the first being a sonatina-like form with one theme only, the second consisting of a series of 16th-note patterns based on 7th chords; then a return of 1st section, followed by a coda. Third movement in Scherzo-rondo form; very modal. Fourth movement a splendid example of theme and variation form.

No. 7 in C Major, Op. 105 (1925)
Like the Fifth in mood. One movement, but embracing the four-movement idea. Tonality a mixture of modes—major and minor, etc. Shows skillful use of sixteenth-century style of voice leading.

Symphonic Poems

En Saga, Op. 9 (1893)
The Swan of Tuonela, Op. 22, No. 3 (1893)
Finlandia, Op. 26 (1900)
Pohjola's Daughter, Op. 49 (1906)
Aallottaret (*The Oceanides*), Op. 73 (Norfolk, Conn. Festival, June 4, 1914, composer conducting)
Tapiola, Op. 112 (commissioned by Walter Damrosch; 1st performed by him, New York, December 26, 1926)

Symphonic Suites

Karelia, Op. 11 (1893)
Scènes historiques, 2 suites, Op. 25 and Op. 66 (1899, 1912)
Suite champêtre, for strings, Op. 98b (1921)

CONCERTOS AND PIECES WITH ORCHESTRA

Violin

Concerto in D Minor, Op. 47 (1st version, Helsinki, February 8, 1904; 2nd version, Berlin, October 19, 1905)

Six Humoresques, Op. 87b and 89 (1917)

CHAMBER MUSIC

String Quartet in B-flat major, Op. 4 (1889); and *Voces intimae,* Op. 56, also for String Quartet (1909).

CHORAL WORKS

The Origin of Fire, Op. 32, for baritone, male chorus, and orchestra (1902); cantata *Oma maa* for chorus and orchestra, Op. 92 (1918); cantata *Maan virsi* for chorus and orchestra, Op. 95 (1920); *The Song of Väinö* for chorus and orchestra, Op. 110 (1926).

COMPOSITIONS FOR THE STAGE

Opera: *Jungfruburen* (The Maid in the Tower; 1896); *Scaramouche,* a "tragic pantomime" (1913); incidental music to *King Christian II* (1898); *Kuolema* (1903); *Pelléas et Mélisande* (1905); *Belshazzar's Feast* (1906); *Svanevhit* (1908); *Odlan* (1909); *The Language of the Birds* (1911); *Jedermann* (1916); *The Tempest* (1926).

SOLO COMPOSITIONS

For violin and piano: 4 pieces (or cello), Op. 78 (1915); 6 pieces, Op. 79 (1915); Sonatina, Op. 80 (1915); 5 pieces, Op. 81 (1915); *Novellette,* Op. 102 (1923); 5 *Danses champêtres,* Op. 106 (1925); 4 compositions, Op. 115 (1929); 3 compositions, Op. 116 (1929). For cello and piano: *Malinconia,* Op. 20 (1901). For piano solo: sonata, Op. 12 (1893); 111 pieces, arranged in cycles (composed 1894-1929). For voice: 85 songs, mostly early works and without opus numbers.

SUGGESTED READING

1.	*AusMTC*	96-103
2.	*CobCM*	II, 416-19
3.	*GroutHWM*	593-95
4.	*HiCon*	276-81
5.	*HiSym*	326-58
6.	*Ul-PiHM*	576-78, 614-16
7.	*UlSM*	268-73
8.	*VeiCon*	257-58

REFERENCES

BOOKS

1. Abraham, G., *Sibelius: A symposium,* New York: W. W. Norton & Company, Inc., 1947.
2. Ekman, K., *Jean Sibelius,* London: Wilmer, 1936.
3. Gray, C., *Sibelius,* London: Oxford University Press, 1931.
4. ———, *Sibelius: The Symphonies,* London: Oxford University Press, 1935.
5. Johnson, H. E., *Jean Sibelius,* New York: Alfred A. Knopf, Inc., 1959.
6. Ringbom, N. E., *Jean Sibelius,* Norman: University of Oklahoma Press, 1954.

XLIX. Max Reger (1873-1916)

Attracted to the music of Bach and Brahms, he was a master of counterpoint as well as elements of nineteenth-century Romanticism. Erected large musical edifices in Classical and pre-Classical designs using a complex harmonic idiom. Reger Societies were founded in Germany, Austria and elsewhere. A complete edition was begun in 1954 by Breitkopf & Härtel.

Works (147 opus numbers) include orchestral and organ compositions, chamber music, choral works, concertos, piano pieces (including two large pieces for two pianos), and songs. His textbook on modulation is important.

ORCHESTRAL MUSIC

Serenade

G Major, Op. 95 for Small Orchestra

Symphonic Variations

Variations and Fugue on a Merry Theme by John A. Hiller, Op. 100

Variations and Fugue on a Theme by Mozart, Op. 132

CONCERTOS AND PIECES WITH ORCHESTRA

Violin

A Major, Op. 101

Piano

F Minor, Op. 114

SUGGESTED READING

1.	*AusMTC*	144-147
2.	*CobCM*	II, 277-83
3.	*GroutHWM*	583
4.	*UlCM*	361
5.	*UlSM*	266-68

REFERENCES

BOOKS

1. Reger, M., *On the Theory of Modulation,* translated by John Bernhoff from *Beiträge zur Modulationslehre,* Leipzig, 1903. New York: Kalmus, 1948.

CHAPTER 8

The Impressionists

L. Claude Debussy (1862-1918)

Impressionism came into existence during the latter years of the nineteenth century as a protest against the dramatic energy of late Classicism, the exhibitionism of the Wagner style, and the extravagances and emotionalism of the Romantics. The term was first applied to a school of French painting (chief representative was Claude Monet). The so-called "symbolist" poets (led by Verlaine and Mallarmé) joined in the fight against the abuses of Romanticism also. Debussy, with his inquiring mind, his sensitive musical ear, and his unlimited imagination, was the ideal leader for the new musical movement. His early works reveal influences of Massenet, Gounod, Chopin, and others. In Moscow at age seventeen he became acquainted with the music of Borodin, Rimsky-Korsakov, and Mussorgsky. Other influences, such as the Oriental music of the Paris Exposition, contributed to the forming of his mature style, in which formal outlines give way to atmosphere, mood, and shifting colors. In this style the melodic line is usually fragmentary or motif-like. Chromaticism, parallelism, modal, whole-tone and other exotic scales are among the devices used. Orchestration is masterful, all instruments being used throughout their ranges and in all conceivable combinations. Coloristic effects are explored. There is nothing vague, however, in the writing or in the performance instructions—each score showing signs of careful and precise workmanship. The chief impressionistic piano works are found in collections which appeared between 1903 and 1915: *Estampes* (1903), *Images* (two books: 1905, 1907), *Préludes* (two books: 1910, 1913). In orchestral compositions, the first evidence of the new technic appears in the famous *Prélude à l'après-midi d'un faune* (1894). Exemplary for all composers is Debussy's setting of Maeterlinck's symbolist play *Pelléas et Mélisande* (1902), in which the elusiveness and vague imagery of the text are perfectly set to instrumental and vocal sounds that are strange, subdued, and mysteriously expressive.

ORCHESTRAL MUSIC

1. *Printemps* (1887)
2. *Prélude à l'après-midi d'un faune* (1892-94)
3. *Nocturnes* (*Nuages, Fêtes, Sirènes;* 1893-99)
4. *La Mer* ("From Dawn till Noon on the Sea," "Play of the Waves," "Dialogue between the Wind and the Sea"; 1903-5)
5. *Images* (*Ibéria, Rondes de printemps, Gigues*; 1906-12)

CHAMBER MUSIC

String quartet in G minor, Op. 10 (1893); cello sonata (1915); sonata for flute, viola, harp (1915); violin sonata (1916-17). The *Première Rhapsodie* for clarinet and piano and the *Petite Pièce* for clarinet and piano were later orchestrated.

CHORAL WORKS

Cantatas

L'Enfant prodigue, for soprano, tenor, and baritone (1884)

La Demoiselle élue, for solo voices, chorus, and orchestra (1887-88)

COMPOSITIONS FOR THE STAGE

Opera

Pelléas et Mélisande (1892-1902)

Incidental Music

Le Martyre de Saint-Sébastien, for soli, chorus, and orchestra to the mystery play by Gabriele d'Annunzio (1911)

Ballets
Jeux (1912)
Khamma (1912)

SOLO COMPOSITIONS

Piano
Suite bergamasque (1905)
Pour le piano (1901)
Estampes (1903)
Images (1905 & 1907)
Children's Corner (1908)
Préludes (book I, 1910; book II, 1913)
Études (1915)

Two Pianos
En blanc et noir (1915)

Voice
About 60 songs set to texts by Paul Verlaine, Bourget, Villon, Baudelaire, Louÿs, Girod, Mallarmé, and others.

SUGGESTED READING

1. *AusMTC*	1-36, 42-47, 48-50
2. *Ca-Jo-WaAM*	412-18
3. *CobCM*	I, 316-19
4. *GroutHWM*	601-4
5. *GroutSHO*	497-502
6. *RobCM*	279-80; 378-82
7. *Ul-PiHM*	578-82; 619-21
8. *UlSM*	275-80

REFERENCES

1. Debussy, C., *Monsieur Croche, the dilettante hater,* New York: Lear, 1948.
2. Harvey, H. G., *Claude of France,* New York: Allen, Towne, and Heath, 1948.
3. Lockspeiser, E., *Debussy, Man and Artist,* London: J. M. Dent & Sons, Ltd., 1937.
4. Lockspeiser, E., *Debussy: His Life and Mind* 2 vols., London: Cassell & Company, Ltd., 1962-65.
5. Schmitz, E. R., *The Piano Works of Claude Debussy,* New York: Duell, Sloan & Pearce, 1950.
6. Thompson, O., *Debussy, Man and Artist,* New York: Dodd, Mead, 1937.
7. Vallas, L., *Claude Debussy: his Life and Works,* 1933.

LI. Paul Dukas (1865-1935)

Dukas was born in Paris and lived there all his life. He studied composition at the Paris Conservatoire. When he failed to win the *Prix de Rome* (1888), he recommenced his entire musical education steeping himself in the masterworks of earlier periods. Only about a dozen compositions exant. Published nothing in the final quarter of his life, and before his death he destroyed all the manuscripts of that period. His best-known works are the orchestral scherzo *L'Apprenti Sorcier* (1897), the opera *Ariane et Barbe-Bleue* (Paris, 1907; on libretto by Maeterlinck), and the ballet *La Péri* (1912). His Piano Sonata in E-flat minor is noteworthy. Dukas was a significant figure in the musical life of France during the early part of the century, belonging to the Franck-d'Indy line. In *La Péri,* his richest orchestral score, he employed the complete color palette available and introduced exotic instruments in unusual groupings.

SUGGESTED READING

1. *AusMTC*	156
2. *GroutHWM*	606
3. *Ul-PiHM*	62
4. *UlSM*	297

LII. Albert Roussel (1869-1937)

Roussel, whose works in general are not very well known outside of France, planned a career in the French navy, but resigned in 1894 to begin the study of music. At the Schola Cantorum he was a student of d'Indy. Progressing chronologically through his works, one is conscious of a steady growth in Impressionistic method, beginning with the late Romanticism of his teacher and César Franck, and then of a final resolve toward a neo-Classical style.

Most significant works in the line of development: Symphony No. 1 (*Le Poème de la forêt,* 1908); three symphonic *Évocations* (1911); the opera-ballet *Pâdmâvâti* (1914; perf. 1923; reaching new heights in musical treatment of exotic themes, employing Hindu scales in the depiction of Indian scenes and moods); *Suite in F* (1926; marking the transition to neo-Classicism); *Eightieth Psalm* for chorus and orch. (1928); Symphony No. 3 in G minor (1930); and the Sinfonietta for string orchestra (1934).

SUGGESTED READING

1. *CobCM*	II, 306f; III, 27-29

REFERENCES

BOOKS

1. Demuth, N., *Albert Roussel,* 1947.

LIII. Maurice Ravel (1875-1937)

Born in the French Basque country (of a Swiss father and Basque mother), Ravel was taken to Paris as an infant and grew up in the atmosphere of the

French Impressionists. Among his teachers were Fauré (composition) and Gedalge (counterpoint and fugue). In his writing he makes use of many of the same technical devices as are found in the composition of Debussy. His general style, however, developed in a different direction. Based on his fondness for early French harpsichord music, his respect for the orchestration of Rimsky-Korsakov, and his attraction to the piano style of Liszt, he gave more attention to formal outlines and to traditional harmonic practices. To the sharper definitions given his music were added cleverness and wit, the total result being a musical language filled with charm, freshness, vigor and logic—and thoroughly his own. Because the very nature of his writing fitted the idiom of the piano, his piano works are of unusual interest and quite often require a high type of virtuosity.

ORCHESTRAL MUSIC

1. *Rapsodie espagnole* (1907)
2. *Daphnis et Chloé,* 2 suites from the ballet (1909-11)
3. *La Valse* (1920)
4. *Boléro* (1928)

(Mention should be made of Ravel's remarkable orchestration of Mussorgsky's *Pictures at an Exhibition,* 1922.)

CONCERTOS AND PIECES WITH ORCHESTRA

Piano

D Major, for left hand alone (1931; written for the one-armed pianist Paul Wittgenstein)

G Major (given Paris, January 14, 1932, Ravel conducting, Marguerite Long, soloist)

CHAMBER MUSIC

Duos

Sonata for Violin and Piano (1923-27)
Sonata for Violin and Cello (1920-22)

Trio

A Minor, for Violin, Cello, and Piano (1915)

Quartet

F Major, for 2 Violins, Viola, Cello (1903)

Septet

Introduction and Allegro for harp, flute, clarinet, and string quartet (1906)

COMPOSITIONS FOR THE STAGE

Operas

L'Heure espagnole (1-act, text by Franc-Nohain; 1911)

L'Enfant et les sortilèges (a "fantasie lyrique," with libretto by Colette; 1925)

Ballets

Daphnis et Chloé (1912)

Ma Mère l'Oye (from suite for piano duet; 1915)

Le Tombeau de Couperin (choreographic poem from orchestral suite; 1920)

SOLO COMPOSITIONS

Piano: *Jeux d'eau* (1901); *Miroirs* (1905); *Sonatine* (1905); *Gaspard de la Nuit* (1908); *Ma Mère l'Oye* (4 hands; 1905); *Valses nobles et sentimentales* (1911); *Le Tombeau de Couperin* (1917). Songs: *Shéhérazade* (cycle for voice and orch; 1904); *Trois Poèmes de Mallarmé* (voice, piano, 2 flutes, 2 clarinets, and string quartet; 1913); *Histoires naturelles* (1906); *Chansons madécasses* (voice, flute, cello, piano; 1926); *Don Quichotte à Dulcinée* (3 songs with orchestral accompaniment; 1934); 5 *Mélodies populaires grecques* (1905; an additional Greek melody publ. in *La Revue musicale,* December, 1938); *Vocalise en forme d'habanera* (1907); 2 *Mélodies hébraïques* (1914).

SUGGESTED READING

1.	*AusMTC*	169-177
2.	*CobCM*	II, 270-76
3.	*GroutHWM*	604-6
4.	*GroutSHO*	503-05
5.	*HiCon*	307-14
6.	*RobCM*	382-6
7.	*UlCM*	361-2
8.	*Ul-PiHM*	582-4, 621
9.	*UlSM*	297-99

REFERENCES

BOOKS

1. DEMUTH, N., *Ravel,* London: J. M. Dent & Sons, Ltd., Collier paperback, 1962.
2. JANKELEVITCH, V., *Maurice Ravel,* New York: Grove Press, 1959.
3. MEYER, ROLLO H., *Ravel, Life and Works,* London: Gerald Duckworth & Co., Ltd., 1960.
4. SEROFF, VICTOR I., *Maurice Ravel,* New York: Henry Holt Company, 1953.

CHAPTER

9

Composers of Modern and New Music; Conflicting Trends and Styles

Following the Impressionistic period, with its anti-Romantic tendencies and its reaction against the German tradition of the mid-nineteenth-century, a still more radical break occurred. A period in music history was introduced for which the term "New Music" has been generally adopted. About the time of World War I, innovations seemed to find a fertile soil, and a disconcerting list of "isms" was offered by young composers of "serious" music as a means of filling the vacuum left by the rejection of traditional practices. Into the vocabulary of the composer and the musical analyst came such terms as Atonality, Barbarism, Bruitism (Fr., *bruitisme*), Expressionism, Futurism, Jazz (a whole family of terms here, such as Ragtime, Blues, Swing, etc.), Machine music, Microtones, Pandiatonicism, Satire, Twelve-tone technic, and so on.

Beginning with the second quarter of the present century, however, there came another turning in the stream of music. With some of the experiments proven ineffectual and inconclusive, many composers began to show a desire to return to earlier and more traditional principles. Thus was introduced the movement usually termed "neo-Classicism," the extension of which has become a potent influence in the musical output of almost all countries.

The following composers, all active in the first half of the twentieth century, include some of conservative temper who prefer to continue time-tested methods of the past, others of decidedly radical outlook blazing entirely new paths, and still others—moderate progressives—who represent a middle ground. Despite their differences in outlook, all are men of talent who have made an impressive contribution to the art of music.

RUSSIAN

LIV. Alexander Glazunov (1865-1936)

After studies with Rimsky-Korsakov, he became a teacher at the St. Petersburg Conservatoire, and finally its director. He then settled in Paris (1928). He was a prolific composer, and his works became widely popular. While usually thought of as a member of the Nationalist group, he was rather academic in his musical style, never achieving a true individuality. Evidence of technical skill and a certain brilliance and charm are features of his music.

ORCHESTRAL MUSIC

Eight symphonies (1st, 1881; 8th, 1906); *Stenka Razin,* symphonic poem (1884); *The Sea,* symphonic fantasy (1890); *The Kremlin,* symphonic picture (1890); *Chopiniana,* suite on Chopin's themes (1894); 6 overtures, including *Ouverture solennelle* (1901).

CONCERTOS AND PIECES WITH ORCHESTRA

Violin concerto (1904; performed London, October 17, 1905, Mischa Elman, soloist); Piano concerto No. 1 (1911); Piano concerto No. 2 (1922); *Concerto-*

Ballata for cello and orchestra (1933); Saxophone concerto (in collaboration with A. Petiot, 1934) with flute and strings.

CHAMBER MUSIC

Seven string quartets (in D, F, G—*Quatuor Slave*—A, D, B-flat, C); string quintet (1895); suite for string quartet (1929); quartet for brass (*In modo religioso*).

CHORAL WORKS

Coronation Cantata (1894); *Hymn to Pushkin* for female chorus (1899); *Memorial Cantata* (1901); cantata for women's chorus with 2 pianos, 8 hands.

COMPOSITIONS FOR THE STAGE

Incidental music to Grand Duke Konstantin Romanov's mystery play *The King of the Jews* (1914); ballets *Raymonda* (1896, his most popular score), *Ruses d'amour* (1898), and *The Seasons* (1899). Also (with Rimsky-Korsakov) completed Borodin's *Prince Igor,* orchestrating the overture from memory, having heard the composer play it on the piano).

SOLO COMPOSITIONS

Twenty-one songs; *Pensée à Liszt* for cello and piano; *Rêverie* for French horn and piano; *Elegy* for viola and piano; *Oberek* for violin and piano. His piano music includes 2 sonatas (1898; 1899); *Prelude and Fugue*; *Theme and Variations*; and other pieces, including a suite for 2 pianos.

SUGGESTED READING

1.	*CobCM*	I, 462-70
2.	*SachsCA*	192-95
3.	*ToveyEMA*	III, 209-10
4.	*Ul-PiHM*	576
5.	*UlSM*	274
6.	*VeiCon*	245-46

REFERENCES

BOOKS

1. ABRAHAM, G. and CALVOCORESSI, M. D., *Masters of Russian Music,* New York: Alfred A. Knopf, Inc., 1936.
2. ABRAHAM, G., *On Russian Music,* New York: Scribner's Sons, 1939.

LV. Alexander Scriabin (1872-1915)

A brilliant pianist as well as composer, his first compositions show strong influences of Chopin. After absorbing the chromaticism of Wagner and Liszt and some of the elements of musical impressionism, he began the development of his own harmonic vocabulary, and the experiments he carried on were connected with his interest in Theosophy. Unusual sonorities were achieved with chords of fourths and other nontraditional intervals. In his latest works (including the unfinished *Mystery*) he began the development of a synthesis of all the arts as a means of inducing spiritual and emotional ecstasy.

ORCHESTRAL MUSIC

Rêverie, Op. 24 (1899); three symphonies (Op. 26, 1900; Op. 29, 1901; Op. 32, *The Divine Poem,* 1905); *The Poem of Ecstasy,* Op. 54 (1908); *Prometheus, The Poem of Fire,* Op. 60 (1911; requires a "color organ," this being perfected for him by Rimington). The only complete performance of *Prometheus,* with colors on a screen, was in New York in 1914.

CONCERTOS AND PIECES WITH ORCHESTRA

Concerto for piano, Op. 20 (1897); his first major work, performed by the composer with the Odessa Philharmonic the year of its composition.

SOLO COMPOSITIONS

For piano: 10 sonatas (in which is shown the growth of Scriabin's musical language and style); 79 preludes in 15 sets; 24 etudes in 4 sets; 6 impromptus; 21 mazurkas; 2 nocturnes; *Prelude and Nocturne* for left hand (Op. 9); *Poème tragique* (Op. 34) and *Poème satanique* (Op. 36); *Fantaisie* (Op. 28); 18 *Morceaux*; *Polonaise* (Op. 21); *Feuillet d'album* (Op. 58); *Poème-Nocturne* (Op. 61); 2 *Poèmes* (Op. 63); *Vers la flamme* (Op. 72); and 2 *Danses* (Op. 73). Scriabin wrote no chamber music, songs, or choral works.

SUGGESTED READING

1.	*AusMTC*	69-75
2.	*CobCM*	II, 410
3.	*GroutHWM*	588-89
4.	*Ul-PiHM*	565-67
5.	*UlSM*	280-81

REFERENCES

BOOKS

1. ABRAHAM, G. and CALVOCORESSI, M. D., *Masters of Russian Music.*
2. HULL, A. E., *A Russian Tone Poet,* London: K. Paul, Trench, Trubner & Co., 1922.
3. MITCHELL, E., *Scriabin, Catalogue of Piano Works,* London: Hawkes & Son, 1929.

4. Montagu-Nathan, M., *Handbook to the Piano Works of Scriabin,* London: J. & W. Chester, 1922.
5. Swan, A. J., *Scriabin,* London: John Lane, 1923.

LVI. Sergey Rachmaninoff (1873-1943)

A distinguished pianist (known as "the pianist's pianist"), his early works show unmistakable touches of Tchaikovsky. Among the Romantic features of his music are the melancholy moods, the use of minor keys, and certain lush sonorities. The epic sweep of his melodic line, the resonant opulence of his mature harmonic style, and the idiomatic piano writing are his own.

ORCHESTRAL MUSIC

Three symphonies (1897, 1908, 1936); *Andante and Scherzo* for string orchestra (1891); *The Rock,* symphonic fantasy (1893); *The Isle of the Dead,* symphonic poem after painting by Böcklin (1909); *Symphonic Dances* (Philadelphia, January 3, 1941).

CONCERTOS AND PIECES WITH ORCHESTRA

Four piano concertos (F-sharp minor, 1890-91, revised 1917; C minor, 1901; D minor, 1909; G minor, 1927); *Rhapsody on a Theme by Paganini* (1934).

CHAMBER MUSIC

Trio élégiaque (in memory of Tchaikovsky; 1893); *Romance and Danse hongroise,* for violin and piano (1893); Cello sonata (1901).

CHORAL WORKS

The Spring, for baritone, chorus, and orchestra (1902); *Liturgy of St. John Chrysostom,* for chorus a cappella (1910); *The Bells* for solos, chorus, and orchestra (1913; after Edgar Allan Poe); Vesper Mass for chorus a cappella (1915); *3 Russian Songs,* for chorus and orchestra (1927).

COMPOSITIONS FOR THE STAGE

Three operas: *Aleko* (1893; after *The Gypsies* by Pushkin); *The Miserly Knight* (1906); and *Francesca da Rimini* (1906).

SOLO COMPOSITIONS

For Piano: 2 sonatas (D minor, 1907; B-flat minor, 1913); 5 *Morceaux de fantaisie,* Op. 3; *Élégie, Prélude* (the C-sharp minor), *Mélodie, Polichinelle, Sérénade* (1892); 7 *Morceaux de salon,* Op. 10 (1894); 6 *Moments musicaux;* 23 Preludes; 15 *Études-Tableaux* (9 orchestrated by Respighi); Variations on a theme by Chopin; *Polka V.R.,* on a theme by the composer's father; various arrangements and transcriptions. For piano, 4 hands: 6 Duets. For 2 pianos: 2 Suites.

For voice: several sets with a total of 71 songs, all composed before 1916. Best known: *Floods of Spring, Fate* (on Beethoven's 5th symphony), *Lilacs, Christ is Risen,* and *Vocalise.*

SUGGESTED READING

1. *CobCM*	II, 264f
2. *GroutHWM*	588
3. *HiCon*	289
4. *HiSym*	391-401
5. *ToveyEMA*	IV, 100
6. *Ul-PiHM*	575
7. *UlSM*	274
8. *VeiCon*	149, 248-49

REFERENCES

BOOKS

1. Anderson, W. R., *Rachmaninoff and his Pianoforte Concertos,* London: Hinrichsen, 1947.
2. Berntensson, S. and Leyda, J., *Serge Rachmaninoff,* New York: New York University Press, 1956.
3. Culshaw, J., *Rachmaninoff, the Man and his Music,* New York: Oxford University Press, 1949.
4. Rachmaninoff, S., *Rachmaninoff's Recollections,* London: Gallen & Unwin, 1934.
5. Seroff, V. I., *Rachmaninoff,* New York: Simon and Schuster, 1950.

LVII. Reinhold Glière (1875-1956)

A prolific composer, he was especially distinguished in symphonic works, the characteristic features of which show him to be a successor of the Russian National School. Always traditional in his harmonic idiom, he nevertheless achieved effective results. The Symphony No. 3 (*Ilya Murometz,* dealing with exploits of a legendary Russian hero) is his most significant work.

ORCHESTRAL MUSIC

Three symphonies; symphonic poems *The Sirens* (1908), *Cossacks of Zaporozh* (1921), *Trizna* (1915); symphonic poem for narrator and orchestra *Imitation of Jezekiel* (1919); 4 overtures, including *Friendship of Nations* (1941) and *25 Years of the Red Army* (1943).

CONCERTOS AND PIECES WITH ORCHESTRA

Harp concerto (1938); concerto for coloratura soprano and orchestra (1942); cello concerto (1946); horn concerto (1952). A violin concerto was left unfinished.

CHAMBER MUSIC

Five string quartets (No. 4 won the Stalin Prize, 1948), the 5th being left unfinished at his death; 3 string sextets; 1 string octet.

COMPOSITIONS FOR THE STAGE

An opera, *Shakh-Senem* (Baku, 1934); ballets *Chrysis* (1912), *Cleopatra* (1925), *Comedians* (1922-30), *Red Poppy* (Moscow, 1927; on the Russian Revolution), *The Bronze Knight* (1949; after Pushkin); incidental music to *King Oedipus* of Sophocles (1921), *Lysistrata* of Aristophanes (1923), *Marriage of Figaro* of Beaumarchais (1927).

SOLO COMPOSITIONS

In addition to about 200 piano pieces and 200 songs, the following: 20 pieces for violin and piano; 12 duos for 2 violins; ballad for cello and piano; 4 pieces for double bass and piano; 8 pieces for violin and cello; 12 pieces for cello and piano; 10 duos for 2 cellos, etc.

SUGGESTED READING

1.	*CobCM*	I, 470-72
2.	*Ul-PiHM*	575-76

REFERENCES

BOOKS

1. ABRAHAM, G., *On Russian Music.*
2. ABRAHAM, G. and CALVOCORESSI, M. D., *Masters of Russian Music.*

LVIII. Nikolai Medtner (1880-1951)

Born of German parents, this notable Russian composer won distinction (many medals and prizes) as a concert pianist in the European capitals. After leaving Russia, he lived in Berlin and Paris and eventually settled in London. Important works are for his own instrument, the piano, and include 3 concertos; *Sonata-Triad*; 34 *Fairy Tales*; 3 *Dithyrambs*; 4 sonatas (1904-14); *Fairy-tale Sonata* (1912); *Sonata-Ballade* (1913); *Sonata romantica* (1930); *Sonata minacciosa* (1931); and *Sonata idillica* (1935). Included in his 104 songs is a *Sonata-Vocalise,* for voice and piano, without words.

SUGGESTED READING

1.	*CobCM*	II, 126f
2.	*HiCon*	289
3.	*UlSM*	304-6
4.	*VeiCon*	253-4

REFERENCES

MUSIC

1. Collected Works available through Leeds Music Corporation, 322 West 48th Street, New York, N.Y., as follows:
   - Vol. I. Piano Works, Op. 1, 2, 4, 5, 7, 8, 9, 10, 11, 14
   - Vol. II. Piano Works, Op. 17, 20, 22, 23, 25, 26, 27, 30, 31
   - Vol. III. Piano Works, Op. 34, 35, 38, 39, 40, 42, 47
   - Vol. IV. Piano Works, Op. 48, 49, 51, 53, 54, 55, 56, 59

BOOKS

1. HOLT, R., *Medtner and his Music,* London: Dobson, 1955.

LIX. Nikolai Miaskovsky (1881-1950)

Planned a military career, but left it for music study with Glière in Moscow and Rimsky-Korsakov and Liadov at the Conservatoire in St. Petersburg. Was one of the composers denounced by the Soviets in 1948. A true master of his craft, he stayed within the limits of the traditional in tonal relationships, modulation, etc., but demonstrated structural strength and emotional vitality in his compositions. The major portion of his works can be tabulated as follows:

ORCHESTRAL MUSIC

Twenty-seven symphonies (No. 1, C minor, written in 1908 and 1st performed in 1914; No. 27, also C minor, performed posthumously in Moscow, December 9, 1950); 2 symphonic poems: *Silence,* after Edgar Allan Poe (1911), and *Alastor,* after Shelley (1914); 2 works for small orchestra: *Serenade* (1929), and *Lyric Concertino* (1929); *Sinfonietta,* for string orchestra (1930). The *Salutatory Overture* (1939) was written for Stalin's 60th birthday.

CONCERTOS

For violin (1938) and cello (1945)

CHAMBER MUSIC

One sonata for violin; 2 for cello; 13 string quartets

CHORAL WORKS

Cantata, *Kirov Is With Us* (1942)

SOLO COMPOSITIONS

Nine piano sonatas, several sets of piano pieces, and several song cycles

SUGGESTED READING

1. *AusMTC*	431-32
2. *CobCM*	II, 136; III, 133-37
3. *VeiCon*	277

REFERENCES

MUSIC

1. Selected Works (9 vols.) available through Leeds Music Corporation.

BOOKS

1. Ikonnikov, A. A., *Myaskovsky,* New York: Philosophical Library, 1946.

LX. Igor Stravinsky (b. 1882)

Beginning as a student of Rimsky-Korsakov (1907), and writing early works showing the style and orchestral technic of his master, Stravinsky has seemingly accepted as valid every major trend and has written inside the limits of the style to which it points—always definitively. He has employed Russian folk songs and rhythms. He has pushed exotic orientalism and sensuous orchestration to their limits. Startling demonstrations of primitivism and *verismo* have come from his pen. He has reduced orchestral color and contrapuntal texture to their leanest, most economical minimum. Ragtime and other versions of jazz have been given eloquent uses. Baroque forms and technics have been effectively used. The full meaning of "neo-Classicism" has been demonstrated. He has set liturgical texts in the severe style of the "neo-Gothic," and also in the rich "echo" style of the Renaissance Venetians. He has reproduced the eighteenth-century opera style (division into recitatives, arias, and ensembles) and has made vividly expressive use of the twelve-tone technic—using rows of twelve or fewer tones. Each new work of Stravinsky is the cause for marked reaction and surprise. Each new work is conclusive in its genre.

ORCHESTRAL MUSIC

Symphony in E-flat, Op. 1 (1905-07; derivative, showing influences of Tchaikovsky and Glinka); *Fireworks,* Op. 4 (1908); *Ragtime,* for 11 instruments (1918); *Symphonies of Wind Instruments,* in memory of Debussy (1920; perf. 1921); Concerto in E-flat major, *Dumbarton Oaks,* for 16 instruments (1938; Neo-Baroque); Symphony in C (1940); *Dances Concertantes* (1942); Symphony in 3 movements (1946); Concerto in D for string orchestra (1947); *Monumentum Pro Gesualdo* (1960; "re-composed" by Stravinsky; choreographed by George Balanchine for stage presentation); Eight Miniatures for Chamber Orchestra (1962). Of major importance are the orchestral suites derived from the ballets *The Firebird, Petrouchka, Le Sacre du Printemps, Pulcinella.*

CONCERTOS AND PIECES WITH ORCHESTRA

Concerto for piano and wind instruments (1924; neo-Classical in trend); *Capriccio* for piano and orchestra (1929; neo-Classical, but giving strong emphasis to the rhythmic element); Concerto for violin (1931; commissioned by Samuel Dushkin); Concerto for 2 pianos (1935); *Ebony Concerto,* for clarinet and swing band (1946; for Woody Herman); *Movements* for piano and orchestra (1960).

CHAMBER MUSIC

Three Poems from the Japanese, for soprano, 2 flutes, 2 clarinets, piano, and string quartet (1912-13; Schönberg influence); 3 pieces for string quartet (1914); *Pribautki,* songs for voice with 8 instruments (1914); *Berceuses du chat,* 4 songs for female voice and 3 clarinets (1915-16); 3 pieces for clarinet solo (1919); Concertino for string quartet (1920); Octet for wind instruments (1923); *Duo concertant,* for violin and piano (1932); Septet for piano, violin, viola, cello, clarinet, bassoon, and horn (1952); *In Memoriam Dylan Thomas,* for tenor, string quartet, and 4 trombones (1954); Double Canon for string quartet (1959).

CHORAL MUSIC

Symphony of Psalms, for chorus and orchestra (1930); Mass for men's and boys' voices and 10 instruments (1948); Cantata on 4 poems (semisacred) by anonymous English poets of the 15th and 16th centuries (1952); *Canticum sacrum ad honorem Sancti Marci nominis,* for tenor, baritone, chorus, and orchestra (Venice, 1956; using a method of serial composition in manner of Anton von Webern); *Threni,* on Lamentations of Jeremiah from the Vulgate, for solo voices, chorus, and orchestra (International Festival of Contemporary Music, Venice, 1958; use of 12-tone idiom); *The Dove Descending Breaks the Air,* for a cappella chorus on text by T. S. Eliot (1962); *A Sermon, A Narrative, and A Prayer,* cantata for speaker, alto, tenor, chorus, and orchestra (1962; the "sermon" by St. Paul on hope, the "narrative" describing the stoning of Stephen, the "prayer" on words by Elizabethan playwright Thomas Dekker).

COMPOSITIONS FOR THE STAGE

Operas: *Rossignol,* "lyric tale" in 3 acts, after Andersen (1914; impressionistic); *Renard,* burlesque chamber opera (1922; uses quotations from earlier composers); *Mavra,* comic opera after Pushkin, 1-act (1922; together with *Renard* on stories from Russian folk literature); *Oedipus Rex,* opera-oratorio, after Sophocles (concert perf., 1927; stage perf., 1928); *The Rake's Progress,* opera after Hogarth's engravings, libretto by W. H. Auden and C. Kallman (Venice, 1951; Stravinsky's "Mozart opera").

Ballets: *The Firebird* (1910); *Petrouchka* (1911); *Le Sacre du printemps,* "scenes of pagan Russia" (1913; transl. of Russian title "Spring the Sacred"); *Les Noces* (1923; literally, "Little Wedding"); *Histoire du soldat,* stage play for narrator and 7 instruments (1918); *Pulcinella,* "after Pergolesi" (1920; not all themes are authentic, however); *Apollon Musagète,* pantomime with string orchestra (1928; classic restraint and emotional serenity); *Le Baiser de la Fée* on themes by Tchaikovsky (1928); *Perséphone,* "melodrama" with recitation and chorus, to text by André Gide (1934); *Jeux de cartes* in 3 "deals" (1937; "Card Party," written for an American tour); *Orpheus* (1948); *Agon,* for 12 dancers (1957; also based on the serial technic). Many operas and ballets rearranged as orchestral suites.

For television: *Noah and the Flood* (1962; the Bible story in "music, dance, and song").

SOLO COMPOSITIONS

For piano: 2 sonatas (1904, 1922); 4 Etudes (1908); *Piano Rag-Music* (1920); *Les cinq doigts,* 8 melodies on 5 notes (1921); Serenade in A (1925).

For piano 4 hands: *3 Pièces faciles* (1915), and *5 Pièces faciles* (1917).

For 2 pianos: Sonata (1944).

For pianola: Étude (1917).

SUGGESTED READING

1.	*AusMTC*	243-73; 330-44; 523-37
2.	*Ca-Jo-WaAM*	441-54
3.	*CobCM*	II, 461-67; III, 123-30
4.	*GroutHWM*	630-41
5.	*GroutSHO*	568-69
6.	*RobCM*	281-83
7.	*UlCM*	364-65
8.	*Ul-PiHM*	606-11, 630f
9.	*UlSM*	283-87
10.	*VeiCon*	211-280; 285-89

REFERENCES

BOOKS

1. Armitage, M., *Igor Stravinsky,* New York: G. Schirmer, 1936.
2. Belaiev, V., *Igor Stravinsky's "Les Noces,"* London: H. Milford, Oxford University Press, 1928.
3. *Igor Stravinsky, Complete Catalogue of Published Works,* New York: Boosey and Hawkes, 1957.
4. Evans, E., *Stravinsky: The Fire Bird and Petroushka,* London: H. Milford, Oxford University Press, 1933.
5. Leonard, R. A., *A History of Russian Music,* Mussorgsky, Borodin, Rimsky-Korsakov, Tchaikovsky, Scriabin, Stravinsky, Prokofiev, Shostakovich, etc., New York: Marboro Books.
6. Meyers, Rollo H., *Introduction to the Music of Stravinsky,* London: D. Dobson, 1950.
7. Stravinsky, Igor, *Bibliography of Stravinsky's Works,* New York: Ithaca.
8. Stravinsky, Igor, *Stravinsky: An Autobiography,* New York: Steiner, 1958.
9. Tansman, A., *Igor Stravinsky,* New York: Putnam, 1949.
10. White, E. W., *Stravinsky's Sacrifice to Apollo,* New York: Hogarth Press, 1930.
11. ———, *Stravinsky: The Composer and his Works,* Berkeley: University of California Press, 1966.

LXI. Sergey Prokofiev (1891-1953)

Early music already shows remarkable rhythmic impulse, a unique harmonic idiom, and (often) an attractive irony. To these characteristics was later added strong lyrical feeling. He never abandoned the tonal system, although he made brief excursions into such contemporary idioms as polytonality and atonality. He is a master of orchestration and indeed of all phases of instrumental writing.

ORCHESTRAL MUSIC

Seven symphonies, sinfonietta, overtures, symphonic suites, and film music.

Symphonies

D Major, Op. 25, "Classical" (1916-17)
No. 4, Op. 47 (1929-30)
No. 5, Op. 100 (1944)
No. 6 in E-flat Major, Op. 111 (1949)
No. 7, Op. 131 (1953)

Other Works

Scythian Suite, Op. 20 (1914)
Suites from the Ballet, *Romeo and Juliet,* Op. 64 (1935)
Symphonic Fairy Tale, *Peter and the Wolf,* Op. 67 (1936)

CONCERTOS AND PIECES WITH ORCHESTRA

Five piano concertos, 2 violin concertos, 2 cello concertos.

Violin

No. 1 in D Major, Op. 19 (1917)
No. 2 in G Minor, Op. 63 (1935)

Cello

No. 2, Op. 125 (1950-52)

Piano

No. 1 in D-flat Major, Op. 10 (1912)
No. 2 in G Minor, Op. 16 (1913)
No. 3 in C Major, Op. 26 (1921)
No. 4, Op. 53, for Left Hand (1931)
No. 5 in G Major, Op. 55 (1932)

CHAMBER MUSIC

Sonata for 2 violins, Op. 56 (1932). Sonata for flute and piano, Op. 94 (1943). Two sonatas for violin and piano, Op. 80 (1938-46) and Op. 94 *bis* (1944; a transcription of the flute sonata). For cello and piano: *Ballade,* Op. 15 (1912); sonata, Op. 119 (1950). Two string quartets. One string quintet; 1 quintet for winds and strings. *Overture on Hebrew Themes,* Op. 34, for clarinet, piano, and string quartet (1920).

Quartets

No. 1, Op. 50 (1930)
No. 2 in F Major, Op. 92 (1941)

Quintet

Op. 39 for oboe, clarinet, violin, viola, and double bass (1924; perf., 1927)

CHORAL WORKS

Cantata

Alexander Nevsky, Op. 78 (1939)

COMPOSITIONS FOR THE STAGE

Operas: *Magdalen* (1913); *The Gambler* (1916, rev. 1927); *The Love for Three Oranges* (1919); *The Flaming Angel* (1927); *Simeon Kotko* (1939); *Betrothal in the Monastery* (1940); *War and Peace* (1943, rev. 1952). Six ballets, among them: *Chout* (1915, rev. 1920); *Le Pas d'acier* (1925); *L'Enfant prodigue,* Op. 46 (1928; perf. 1929); *Romeo and Juliet,* Op. 64 (1935-36; perf. 1940); *Cinderella,* Op. 87 (1940-44; perf. 1945). Incidental music to *Boris Godunov,* Op. 70 *bis* (1936); *Eugene Onegin,* Op. 71 (1936); *Hamlet,* Op. 77 (1937-38). Music for films: *Lieutenant Kijé* (1934); *The Queen of Spades,* Op. 70 (1938); *Alexander Nevsky* (1939).

SOLO COMPOSITIONS

For piano: 10 sonatas (No. 10 left incomplete); 2 sonatinas; 4 études; 75 "pieces," some from ballets; *Sarcasms,* Op. 17, a suite of 5 pieces (1912-14); *Visions fugitives,* Op. 22, a suite of 20 pieces; *Tales of an old Grandmother,* Op. 31; 4 pieces (1918); Toccata, Op. 11 (1912). For unaccompanied violin: Sonata, Op. 115 (1947).

About 60 songs, including *The Ugly Duckling,* Op. 18, after Andersen; 5 *Songs Without Words,* Op. 35 (1920; also for violin and piano, Op. 35-*bis*); and *Soldiers' March Song,* Op. 121 (1950).

SUGGESTED READING

1. *AusMTC*	451-71
2. *CobCM*	II, 243f; III, 137-40
3. *GroutHWM*	618
4. *HiCon*	380
5. *RobCM*	420
6. *Ul-PiHM*	604-05, 629
7. *UlSM*	305-7
8. *VeiCon*	272, 287

REFERENCES

BOOKS

1. Abraham, G., *Eight Soviet Composers,* New York: Oxford University Press, 1943.
2. Nestyev, I. W., *Serge Prokoviev,* translated by Florence Jonas, Stanford: Stanford University Press, 1960.

LXII. Dmitri Shostakovich (b. 1906)

Early works alternate between the political and the satirical. Official disfavour came as the result of the opera *Lady Macbeth* with its extremity of social caricature. Symphony No. 4 was withdrawn in rehearsal, and the composer offered the Symphony No. 5 as his "reply to just criticism." The seventh symphony is the musical result of the siege of Leningrad in 1941, showing peace, conflict, and victory.

ORCHESTRAL MUSIC

Symphonies

No. 1, Op. 10 (1924-25)
Form: academic, with the orthodox four movements: *Allegretto* (opens with bassoon solo), *Al-*

legro (scherzo), Lento, *Allegro molto-Lento.* Two prominent elements: (a) the gay, and (b) the meditative. Piano employed extensively.

No. 2, Op. 14 ("October") (1927)
Form: one movement with choral ending. Characteristics: polytonality and polyrhythm. Among formal devices is a canon for 9 woodwind instruments. The first attempt of Shostakovich to inject social meaning into his music. The "high tide" of industrial music.

No. 3, Op. 20 ("May First") (1930)
Form: one movement with choral ending—an appeal to revolutionary uprising. Characteristics: like the 1st Symphony in many ways. Principal theme given to clarinet; contains a waltz caricature; has a slow section before the conclusion.

No. 4, Op. 43 (1935-36)
Put into rehearsal by the Leningrad Philharmonic in December, 1936, but withdrawn by the composer when the reactions of the players were observed.

No. 5, Op. 47 ("A Soviet Artist's Reply to Just Criticism") (1937)
Form: Four movements: *Moderato* (sonata form), *Allegretto* (in nature a rapid scherzo), *Largo, Allegro non troppo* (very boisterous; suggests Tchaikovsky). Characteristics: shows a change from the satirical style; begins "second period."

No. 6, Op. 54 (1939)
Form: Three movements, without an opening allegro: *Largo, Allegro* (scherzo-like), *Presto* (rondo). Characteristics: in romantic vein with no political program.

No. 7, Op. 60 ("Leningrad") (1941)
Form: Four movements: *Allegretto* (The Struggle), *Moderato* (recalls glorious episodes of the past), *Adagio* (a hymn to life, merging into 4th mvt. without pause), *Allegro non troppo* (The Will to Victory). Characteristics: unusual length (1 hour, 26 minutes); solemn undertones.

No. 8, Op. 65 (1943)
Form: 5 movements, the first very long, the 2nd, 3rd, and 4th being contrasted marches. *Adagio-Allegro, Allegretto* (Heroic March), *Allegro non troppo* (Scherzo-march), *L'istesso tempo* (Funeral march), *Rondo* (pastoral in character). Characteristics: no program, but an ideology dealing with the beauty of life.

No. 9, Op. 70 (1945)
Form: Five mvts., final three not separated in performance. *Allegro, Moderato, Presto, Largo, Allegretto.* Characteristics: shorter than the 7th or 8th; more unified in its material. The orchestra (except for a large percussion section) is reduced to classic proportions.

No. 10, Op. 93 (1955)
Form: Four mvts.: *Moderato, Allegro, Allegretto, Andante-Allegro.* Characteristics: Moderate orchestra, with pronounced inclination to the woodwind choir at high and low registers.

No. 11, Op. 103 (1957)
Commissioned for the celebration of the 40th Anniversary of the Bolshevik Revolution. Makes liberal use of themes suggested by folk songs and revolutionary songs as well as 2 themes borrowed from an earlier work, *Ten Poems for Chorus without Orchestra* (1951), about the same revolution. Form: Four movements (entitled Palace Square, Ninth of January, Eternal Memory, Alarm).

No. 12, Op. 112 (1961; world première, 1962)
Form: Four mvts., describing (1) the arrival of Lenin in Petrograd and the meeting with the workers in April 1917, (2) the events of November 7, (3) the Civil War, and (4) the victory of the October Socialist Revolution.

No. 13, Op. (?) (1962)
Programmatic choral symphony based on poems by Yevtushenko. Withdrawn when Yevtushenko came under official displeasure.

Other Works

Suite for Jazz Orchestra (1938)

CONCERTOS AND PIECES WITH ORCHESTRA

Violin

Op. 99 (1955)

Piano

No. 1, Op. 35 (1933), with Trumpet and String Orchestra
No. 2, Op. 102 (1957)

Cello

Concerto (1959)

CHAMBER MUSIC

Two pieces for string octet (1925); cello sonata (1934); 6 string quartets (1938, 1944, 1946, 1949, 1952, 1956); piano quintet (1940); 3 pieces for unaccompanied violin (1940); 2 piano trios (1923, 1944).

CHORAL WORKS

Leningrad, suite for chorus and orchestra (1942); *Song of the Forests,* cantata (1949); *Democratic Vistas,* a cycle of 10 poems by Walt Whitman, for chorus and orchestra (1951).

COMPOSITIONS FOR THE STAGE

Operas: *The Nose* (1930), *Lady Macbeth of the District of Mtzensk* (1934).

Ballets: *The Golden Age* (1930; contains the celebrated *Polka*); *Bolt* (1931); and *The Limpid Brook* (1935).

Operetta: *Moskva Cheromushlsi* (1958).

Incidental Music: *The Bedbug* (1929; to a comedy by Mayakovsky); *The Human Comedy* (1934; after Balzac).

Music for films: numerous scores, including *Golden Mountains* (1931); *The Days of Volotchayev* (1937); *A Great Citizen* (1939); and *Fall of Berlin* (1949).

SOLO COMPOSITIONS

For Voice: 4 songs to texts by Pushkin (1936); 6 songs to words by Burns, Shakespeare, and Walter Raleigh (1942); cycle, *From Jewish Folk Poetry* (1948).

For Piano: *3 Fantastic Dances* (1922); 2 sonatas (1926, 1943); *Aphorisms,* suite of 10 pieces (1927); 24 Preludes (1933); 24 Preludes and Fugues (1951).

OTHER WORKS

Reorchestration of Mussorgsky's opera *Boris Godunov* (1939-40), and Schumann's Cello Concerto in A Minor (1963).

SUGGESTED READING

1. *AusMTC* 432-36
2. *CobCM* II, 416; III, 142-49
3. *GroutHWM* 618
4. *GroutSHO* 552-53
5. *RobCM* 420-21
6. *Ul-PiHM* 605-6
7. *UlSM* 281-83, 303-4

REFERENCE

1. Seroff, V. I., *Dmitri Shostakovich,* New York: Alfred A. Knopf, Inc., 1943.

SCHOENBERG AND HIS FOLLOWERS

LXIII. Arnold Schoenberg (1874-1951)

Schoenberg, who was largely self-taught, changed his conception of music radically during his lifetime, much of his thinking being influenced by Freud's analysis of the unconscious. Wagnerian influence is shown in *Verklärte Nacht,* Op. 4 (1899; originally a string sextet, then scored for chamber orchestra and rescored in 1943) and *Gurre-Lieder* (1900-1913; showing, in its composition, a complete change in style). There came next a period of experimentation seen in *3 Klavierstücke,* Op. 11 (1909; real atonality used for first time); *Das Buch der hängenden Gärten,* Op. 15 (1908; cycle of fifteen poems by Stefan George); the monodrama *Erwartung,* Op. 17 (1909; "Expectation"); *Die glückliche Hand,* Op. 18 ("The Lucky Hand"; 1913); and *Pierrot lunaire,* Op. 21 (1912; *sprechstimme* with piano, flute, piccolo, clarinet, bass-clarinet, violin, viola, cello; on twenty-one poems by Albert Giraud). The new style, plus intricate contrapuntal passages, and a wealth of new instrumental colors, brought forth opposition and controversy, and about 1920 the composer for "higher and better order" proposed his principle of "composition with twelve tones." The working-out of this principle is seen in such works as the *5 Klavierstücke,* Op. 23 (1923); the Piano Suite, Op. 25 (1925); the *Serenade,* Op. 24 (1923; septet of instruments with bass-baritone voice); the quintet for wind instruments, Op. 26; the third string quartet, Op. 30 (1926); and the Variations for Orchestra, Op. 31 (1928).

In many of his American works, Schoenberg turned again to traditional principles of tonality and form. The string suite in G major (1935), for example, employed a key signature (first since second string quartet of 1907). Most significant among the works of his final period were the fourth string quartet, Op. 37 (1936); the violin concerto, Op. 36 (1936); the *Ode to Napoleon,* Op. 41 (1943; setting for piano, strings, narrator, of Byron's poem); the piano concerto, Op. 42 (1943); the string trio, Op. 45 (1946); and *A Survivor from Warsaw,* Op. 46 (1947; for narrator, male chorus, and orchestra). His opera *Moses und Aron* was incomplete at his death.

In addition to works listed above, the following should be noted:

ORCHESTRAL MUSIC

Pelleas und Melisande, symphonic poem after Maeterlinck, Op. 5 (1902); *Kammersymphonie,* for 15 instruments, Op. 9 (1906); *5 Orchester-Stücke,* Op. 16 (1909; revised, 1949); Variations, Op. 31 (1928); *Begleitungsmusik zu einer Lichtspielscene* (Accompaniment to a Cinema Scene, Op. 34; 1930); Suite in G for strings (1934); Second Chamber Symphony, Op. 38 (1940); *Theme and Variations,* Op. 43 (1943; originally for band).

CHAMBER MUSIC

String quartet in D (1897; assumed lost, but brought to the U.S. by the composer and performed at Library of Congress, 1952); sextet for strings, Op. 4 (1899; arr. for string orchestra, 1917; revised, 1943); string quartet No. 1, in D minor, Op. 7 (1904); string quartet No. 2, in F-sharp minor, Op. 10, with voice (1907); suite for 2 clarinets, bass clarinet, violin, viola, cello, and piano, Op. 29 (1927); string quartet No. 3, Op. 30 (1927); string quartet No. 4, Op. 37 (1936); *Fantasia,* for violin and piano (1949).

CHORAL WORKS

Friede auf Erden, Op. 13 (1907); 4 pieces for mixed chorus, Op. 27 (1926); *3 Satires,* Op. 28 (1925); 6 pieces for men's chorus, Op. 35 (1930); *Kol Nidre,* for speaker, chorus, and orchestra, Op. 39 (1938); *3 German Folksongs,* for chorus a cappella, Op. 49 (1948); *Dreimal Tausend Jahre,* for chorus a cappella, Op. 50a (1949); *De Profundis,* for chorus a cappella, to Hebrew text, Op. 50b (1951). An oratorio, *Die Jacobsleiter* was begun (1913), but remained unfinished.

COMPOSITIONS FOR THE STAGE

Von Heute auf Morgen, opera in 1 act, Op. 32 (1928; presented in Frankfurt, 1930).

SOLO COMPOSITIONS

Twenty-seven songs with piano; 10 with orchestra —mostly in early opus numbers. In addition: *Herzgewächse,* Op. 20, after Maeterlinck, for soprano with celesta, harmonium, and harp (1915).

For piano: *Drei Klavierstücke,* Op. 11 (1909; No. 2 arr. for concert performance by Busoni); *6 kleine Klavierstücke,* Op. 19 (1911); *Klavierstück,* Op. 33a (1929); *Klavierstück,* Op. 33b (1932).

For organ: *Variations on a Recitative,* Op. 40 (1940).

Various arrangements and transcriptions.

Schoenberg's *Harmonielehre* (1911; incomplete Eng. transl. D. Adams, 1946) is an important treatise on harmony. His book of essays, *Style and Idea* (1949) and *Models for Beginners in Composition* (1942) are also significant.

SUGGESTED READINGS

1. *AusMTC*	194-222; 294-318
2. *Ca-Jo-WaAM*	422-35
3. *CobCM*	11, 343-53; 111, 1-6
4. *GroutHWM*	646-53
5. *GroutSHO*	571-72
6. *RobCM*	390-400
7. *UlCM*	356-372
8. *Ul-PiHM*	590-95, 622-23
9. *UlSM*	303

REFERENCES

BOOKS

1. Leibowitz, R., *Schoenberg and his School,* translated by Dika Newlin, New York: Philosophical Library, 1949.
2. Newlin, D., *Bruckner, Mahler, Schoenberg,* New York: King's Crown Press, 1947.
3. Perle, George, *Serial Composition and Atonality, An Introduction to the Music of Schoenberg, Berg, and Webern,* Berkeley: University of California Press.
4. Stuckenschmidt, H. H., *Arnold Schoenberg,* New York: Grove Press, 1960.
5. Wellesz, E., *Arnold Schoenberg,* New York: E. P. Dutton & Co., Inc., 1925.

LXIV. Anton von Webern (1883-1945)

Schoenberg's first and most fanatically faithful disciple. At the same time he had a strong individuality of his own. In his application of the principles of his teacher, he wrote with economy and extreme concentration, employing the abstract, mathematical relationships of the twelve tones with utmost strictness. His music, at first rarely heard, is now receiving more and more attention.

Webern's compositions (complete) are available on eight LP record surfaces.

ORCHESTRAL MUSIC

Passacaglia, Op. 1 (1908); *6 Orchestral Pieces,* Op. 6 (1913); *5 Orchestral Pieces,* Op. 10 (1913); Symphony for chamber orchestra, Op. 21 (1928); Variations, Op. 30 (1940).

CHAMBER MUSIC

Five movements for string quartet, Op. 5 (1909); *6 Bagatelles* for string quartet, Op. 9 (1913); trio for violin, viola, and cello, Op. 20 (1927); quartet for violin, clarinet, tenor saxophone, and piano, Op. 22 (1930); Concerto for 9 instruments, Op. 24 (1935); string quartet, Op. 28 (1938); *4 Pieces* for violin and piano, Op. 7 (1910); 3 Little Pieces for cello and piano, Op. 11 (1914).

CHORAL WORKS

Entflieht auf leichten Kähnen, Op. 2, for unaccompanied chorus (1908); 2 songs, to words by Goethe, Op. 19, for chorus, celesta, guitar, violin, clarinet, and bass clarinet (1926); *Das Augenlicht* for chorus and orchestra, Op. 26 (1935); 2 cantatas, Op. 29 and Op. 31 (1940 and 1943).

SOLO COMPOSITIONS

For Piano: Variations, Op. 27 (1926).

For Voice: Song cycles with piano accompaniment: Op. 3, 4, 12, 23, 25; Song cycles with instrumental accompaniment: Op. 8, 13, 14, 15, 16, 17, 18.

Orchestral arrangements: Schubert's *Deutsche Tänze*; Bach's *Ricercare a 6* from *Das musikalische Opfer.*

SUGGESTED READING

1. *AusMTC*	345-70
2. *Ca-Jo-WaAM*	440f
3. *CobCM*	11, 371-74; 111, 7-11
4. *GroutHWM*	655-659
5. *RobCM*	406
6. *Ul-PiHM*	596-98
7. *UlSM*	303-04

REFERENCES

BOOKS

1. Eimert, H. and Stockhausen, K., editors, "Anton Webern," *Die Reihe* II, Bryn Mawr, Pa.: Theodore Presser Co., 1958.
2. Leibowitz, R., *Schoenberg and his School.*
3. Webern, A., *The Path to the New Music,* English translation by L. Black, Bryn Mawr, Pa., 1963.

LXV. Alban Berg (1885-1935)

Also employed twelve-tone music as a basis for composition, but with more flexibility and imagination than either Schoenberg or Webern. In the violin concerto, for example (his last completed work, and the expression of a deeply-felt tragedy), the row is constructed to include major and minor triads, and its final four notes are identified with the opening notes of the Lutheran chorale *Es ist genug.*

ORCHESTRAL MUSIC

Three Pieces (1914); *Chamber Concerto* for piano, violin, and 13 wind instruments (1925).

CONCERTOS AND PIECES WITH ORCHESTRA

Violin Concerto, *"Dem Andenken eines Engels"* (commissioned and 1st performance given by Louis Krasner, 1936).

CHAMBER MUSIC

String Quartet (1910); 4 pieces for clarinet and piano (1913); *Lyrische Suite* for string quartet (1926), 3 mvts. arr. by Berg for string orchestra.

COMPOSITIONS FOR THE STAGE

Operas: *Wozzeck* (1925) and *Lulu* (on 2 plays by Wedekind; left unfinished; 2 acts and 2 fragments of 3rd act perf. Zürich, 1937).

SOLO COMPOSITIONS

Seven *Frühe Lieder* (1905-08); 4 songs (1909); 5 songs with orch. (1912); *Der Wein* for soprano and orch. (1930; after Baudelaire).

For piano: Sonata (1908).

Berg also made piano arrangements of Schoenberg's *Gurre-Lieder* and F-sharp minor quartet, and wrote analyses of Schoenberg's *Kammersymphonie, Pelleas und Melisande,* and the *Gurre-Lieder.*

SUGGESTED READING

1. *AusMTC*	493-96
2. *Ca-Jo-WaAM*	435-40
3. *CobCM*	1, 119-21; 111, 6
4. *GroutHWM*	654-5
5. *GroutSHO*	572-74
6. *HiCon*	362
7. *RobCM*	400-406
8. *Ul-PiHM*	595-6, 623-25
9. *VeiCon*	276-7

REFERENCES

BOOKS

1. Leibowitz, R., *Schoenberg and His School,* New York, 1949.
2. Redlich, H. F., *Alban Berg,* New York: Abelard, Schumann, 1957.
3. Reich, W., *Alban Berg's Wozzeck, The Text and Music of the Opera,* New York: G. Schirmer & Co., 1952.
4. ———, *The Life and Works of Alban Berg,* London, 1965.

ITALIAN

LXVI. Ferruccio Busoni (1866-1924)

A remarkable piano virtuoso (with an intellectual approach to interpretative problems), composer, and teacher, Busoni is often called "the first neo-Classicist." Included in his compositions are the operas *Die Brautwahl* (1912); *Turandot* (1917); and *Doktor Faust* (completed in Dresden, 1925, by Philipp Jarnach); orchestral suites; piano concerto with male chorus; 6 piano sonatinas; *Fantasia contrappuntistica* for piano; chamber music; songs and a large number of arrangements and transcriptions.

Busoni wrote librettos for his operas and was author of *Entwurf einer neuen Aesthetik der Tonkunst* (1907; essay on aesthetics). In addition to the above:

ORCHESTRAL MUSIC

2 Symphonic Suites (1888; 1895); *Lustspielouvertüre* (1897); *Turandot Suite* (1904); *Nocturne symphonique* (1912); *Romanza e scherzoso* (1921).

CONCERTOS AND PIECES WITH ORCHESTRA

Indianische Fantasie for piano and orch. (1913); violin concerto (1897); clarinet concerto (1919).

CHAMBER MUSIC

Two string quartets (1880; 1889); 2 violin sonatas (1890; 1898).

COMPOSITIONS FOR THE STAGE

Opera: *Arlecchino* (perf. Zürich, May 11, 1917).

SOLO COMPOSITIONS

For piano: *Una festa di villaggio* (6 characteristic pieces, 1882); *Tre pezzi nello stilo antico* (1882); *Macchiette medioevali* (1883); *Zwei Tanzstücke* (1914); 10 variations on Chopin's prelude in C minor (1922).

SUGGESTED READING

1. *AusMTC*	110-115
2. *CobCM*	1, 218-21
3. *HiCon*	282, 288
4. *ToveyEMA*	VI, 97, 107
5. *UlSM*	289, 90

REFERENCES

BOOKS

1. BUSONI, F. B., *The Essence of Music, and Other Papers,* London: Rockliff, 1957.
2. ———, *Letters to His Wife,* London: E. Arnold, 1938.
3. DENT, E. J., *Ferruccio Busoni,* London: Oxford University Press, 1933.
4. DIEREN, B. VAN, *Down Among the Dead Men,* London: Oxford University Press, 1935.

LXVII. Ottorino Respighi (1879-1936)

Studied under Rimsky-Korsakov in St. Petersburg, where he played viola in the opera orchestra. Well-known in America as a composer of stature and talent.

ORCHESTRAL MUSIC

Symphonic Poems (Each consisting of 4 tone paintings of the Roman vista):

Le Fontane di Roma (1917)
I Pini di Roma (1924)
Le Feste romane (1929)

Suites

Rossiniana, from Rossini's piano pieces (1925)
Gli Uccelli, for small orch. on themes by Rameau, Bernardo Pasquini, and others (1927)

Other Works

Notturno (1905)
Antiche arie e danze per liuto; 3 sets, No. 3 for string orch. (1916, 1923, 1931)
Vetrate di chiesa, symphonic impressions in 4 mvts. (1927)
Metamorphoseon modi XII, theme and variations (1930, commissioned by Boston Symphony)

CONCERTOS AND PIECES WITH ORCHESTRA

Violin

Concerto gregoriano (1922)

Piano

Concerto in modo misolidio (1925)

Two or More Solo Instruments

Concerto a cinque, for violin, oboe, trumpet, double bass piano, and strings (1932)

CHAMBER MUSIC

Eleven pieces for violin and piano (1904-07); string quartet in D major (1907); *Quartetto dorico,* for string quartet (1924); *Il Tramonto* for mezzo-soprano and string quartet (1917; after Shelley); violin sonata (1917).

CHORAL WORKS

La Primavera, cantata for soloists, chorus, and orch. (1923); *Lauda per la Natività* for soloists, chorus, and orch. (1930).

COMPOSITIONS FOR THE STAGE

Operas: *Belfagor* (1923, comic opera); *La Campana sommersa* (1927, "The Sunken Bell"); *Maria Egiziaca* (N.Y., 1932, Mystery Play); *La Fiamma* (1934, "The Flame"); and a free transcription of Monteverdi's *Orfeo* (1935).

Ballets: *La Boutique fantasque,* on themes by Rossini (1919); *Belkis, Regina di Saba* (1930, Biblical Ballet).

SOLO COMPOSITIONS

Forty-five songs; 3 vocalises without words; various arrangements.

SUGGESTED READING

1. *CobCM*	11, 288-90
2. *ToveyEMA*	111, 217-20
3. *Ul-PiHM*	584
4. *UlSM*	302-3

REFERENCES

BOOKS

1. RENSIS, R. DE, *Ottorino Respighi,* Torino, Milano: G. P. Parovia, 1935.

LXVIII. Ildebrando Pizzetti (b. 1880)

A product of the Romantic trend in modern Italy; employs chromatic harmony with diatonic melodies. In his operas, which he calls "dramas" and which are on tragic or religious themes, the mystical element is very strong. Has written books on Italian composers and on dramatic music.

ORCHESTRAL MUSIC

Concerto dell 'Estate (1928); 3 Symphonic Preludes for *Oedipus Rex* (1961).

CHAMBER MUSIC

Sonata for Violin and Piano in A Major.

COMPOSITIONS FOR THE STAGE

Operas: *Fedra* (1915); *Fra Gherardo* (1925-27, his most famous work); *Assassinio nella cattedrale,* after T. S. Eliot's *Murder in the Cathedral* (1958; received with high acclaim); *La sacra rappresentazione di Abram e d'Isaac,* a mystery play (1917; expanded version perf. 1926).

SUGGESTED READING

1. *CobCM*	11, 225-27; 111, 52f
2. *GroutSHO*	540
3. *Ul-PiHM*	621
4. *VeiCon*	278

REFERENCES

BOOKS

1. GATTI, G. M., *I. Pizzetti,* Turin, 1934, translated in London, 1951, important as biography, with list of works, new Italian edition, 1955.

LXIX. Gian Francesco Malipiero (b. 1882)

Is known to American students as editor of the complete works of Monteverdi, as well as editor of music by Stradella and Frescobaldi. Stands for the neo-Baroque in modern Italian music. His first successful work was *Pause del silenzio* (1918), seven orchestral "Impressions" of states of mind. The first string quartet (*Rispetti e Strambotti*) won the Coolidge Prize in 1920. Among his works are nine symphonies, operas and stage works, oratorios, chamber music, piano music, and songs. He has written essays on Monteverdi (1930) and Stravinsky (1945), and has published a book on *The Orchestra* (Italian and English).

ORCHESTRAL MUSIC

Symphony No. 7, "Delle canzoni" (1949); *Pause del silenzio* (his best-known orchestral work; 1st pt., 1918; 2nd pt., 1927).

Twelve Concerti, Op. 3.

PIECES WITH ORCHESTRA

Concerto for Violin (1933).

CHAMBER MUSIC

Fourth String Quartet (1934); 7th String Quartet (1950); *Musica da Camera* for wind quintet (1960).

CHORAL WORKS

La Cena for soli, chorus, orch. (Rochester, N.Y., April, 1929).

Passer mortuus est, for a cappella chorus (1952).

COMPOSITIONS FOR THE STAGE

Operas: *L'Orfeide,* 3 parts (*La Morte delle maschere; Sette Canzoni; Orfeo*), with 7 short detached scenes plus prologue and semi-satirical epilogue, in which a puppet show is presented; *Giulio Cesare* (1936).

SUGGESTED READING

1. *CobCM*	11, 110f; 111, 51, 53f
2. *GroutSHO*	548
3. *UlSM*	303

REFERENCES

BOOKS

1. MALIPIERO, G. F., *The Orchestra,* translated by Eric Blom, London: J. and W. Chester, 1921.
2. ———, *G. Francesco Malipiero,* London: J. and W. Chester, 1922.

LXX. Alfredo Casella (1883-1947)

His early works are adventuresome and experimental; later ones are more neo-Classical. May be said to combine contemporary technics with traditional forms. Among his works are three symphonies; two concertos (one for string, one for full orchestra); violin concerto; organ concerto; cello concerto; concerto for trio and orchestra. Three operas; four ballets; chamber music; piano works; and songs complete the list. His literary works include *L'Evoluzione della musica . . .* (It., Fr., and Eng. in parallel columns; 1919); *Igor Stravinsky* (new ed., 1951); and *21 + 26* (about Rossini, Tolstoy, Busoni, etc.; 1931).

ORCHESTRAL MUSIC

Symphony No. 3, Op. 63 (1941).
Orchestral Rhapsody, *Italia,* based on folk themes (1909).
Paganiniana, on themes by Paganini (1942).

WITH ORCHESTRA

Scarlattiana, on themes by Scarlatti, for piano (1927).

CHAMBER MUSIC

Five *Pezzi* (pieces) for String Quartet (1920); *Pupazzetti,* for 9 instruments (1916).

FOR THE STAGE

La Giara (1924; a "choreographic comedy" after Pirandello; his most successful opus); *Il deserto tentato* (1937, Conquest of the Desert, a mystery in one act).

SOLO COMPOSITIONS

For the Harp: Sonata, Op. 68. For the piano: 2 sets of stylistic imitations, titled *A la manière de . . .* (presenting Wagner, Fauré, Brahms, Debussy, Strauss, Franck, 1911; also—in collaboration with Ravel—Borodin, d'Indy, Chabrier, Ravel, 1913); Sonatina (1916); 11 *Pezzi infantili* (1920); 3 pieces for pianola.

OTHER WORKS

Orchestrated Balakirev's *Islamey*; edited Beethoven's Piano Sonatas and piano works of Albéniz; arranged Mahler's 7th symphony for piano 4 hands.

SUGGESTED READING

1. *CobCM*	1, 228-31; II, 602; III, 52, 54-56

REFERENCES

BOOKS

1. Casella, A., *Evolution of Music throughout the History of the Perfect Cadence,* Italian, French, and English in parallel columns, London: J. and W. Chester, 1924.
2. ———, *I Segreti della Giara,* translated into English as *Music in My Time: The Memoirs of Alfredo Casella,* Norman: University of Oklahoma Press, 1955.
3. ———, *Alfredo Casella,* London: J. and W. Chester, 1923.

ITALIAN OPERA WRITERS OF LATE NINETEENTH CENTURY–VERISM

LXXI. Giacomo Puccini (1858-1924)

The most important opera composer in late nineteenth-century and early twentieth-century Italy, an eclectic successfully expressing in musical terms such diverse attitudes as emotional tenderness (*Manon Lescaut,* 1893), artistic power of reality (*La Bohème,* 1896), acceptance of the ugly on grounds of truth and aesthetic value (*Tosca,* 1900), and charm of the exotic (*Madama Butterfly,* 1904; *Turandot,* 1926—final duet completed by Alfano after composer's death).

Other Operas

Le Villi (1884)
Edgar (1889)
La Fanciulla del West (MOH, 1910; on Belasco's *The Girl of the Golden West*)
La Rondine (1917)
Il Trittico, three one-act operas (1918):
1. *Il Tabarro*
2. *Suor Angelica*
3. *Gianni Schicchi*

SUGGESTED READING

1. *AusMTC*	107-10
2. *GroutHWM*	607-8
3. *GroutSHO*	441-445
4. *Ul-PiHM*	616-18

REFERENCES

BOOKS

1. Carner, M., *Puccini: A Critical Biography,* New York: Alfred A. Knopf, Inc., 1959.
2. Merek, G. R., *Puccini,* New York: Simon and Schuster, 1951.
3. Puccini, G., *Letters of Giacomo Puccini,* Philadelphia: J. B. Lippincott Co., 1931.

LXXII. Ruggiero Leoncavallo (1858-1919)

Known for one of the most successful of the Italian veristic operas, *Pagliacci* ("The Clowns," 1892). Toured America (1906) with an opera company. Among the operas for which he wrote both libretto and music was *La Bohème,* which appeared 15 months after the work by Puccini. He also composed a ballet and a symphonic poem.

COMPOSITIONS FOR THE STAGE

Operas

I Pagliacci (1892; based on actual story of passion and murder in a Calabrian village)

La Bohème (1897; although successful, lost by comparison with Puccini's masterpiece, which came a year earlier)

Zazà (1900)

Der Roland von Berlin (1904; on a German historic theme; commissioned by Emperor Wilhelm II; a failure)

SUGGESTED READING

1. *GroutSHO* 440
2. *Ul-PiHM* 531

LXXIII. Pietro Mascagni (1863-1945)

Composer of another Italian veristic opera *par excellence*: *Cavalleria rusticana* ("Rustic Chivalry," 1889). This work, dealing with scenes of peasant life, is in one act and brought Mascagni world-wide fame. No later composition of Mascagni equalled the success of this one.

SUGGESTED READING

1. *GroutSHO* 440

FRENCH

LXXIV. Erik Satie (1866-1925)

Student at the Paris Conservatoire (from 1879) and at the Schola Cantorum (1905-08) under d'Indy and Roussel. A musical eccentric, his aesthetic creed was one of irony and whimsicality. Features of his style include use of chords of fourths, omission of bar lines, surrealistic titles, and directions in the music which are plainly satirical. Most of his works are for piano. His style and individuality were of tremendous influence in the careers of many composers.

ORCHESTRAL MUSIC

Socrate, a "symphonic drama" after Plato, for 4 sopranos and small orchestra (1918, perf. 1920).

CHORAL WORKS

Mass for the Poor, for voices and organ.

COMPOSITIONS FOR THE STAGE

Le Piège de Méduse (1913, a lyric comedy); the ballets *Parade* (1917), *Mercure* (1924), *Relâche* (1924); incidental music to Péladan's *Le Fils des Étoiles* (1891, prelude orch. by Ravel), *Le Prince de Byzance* (1891), J. Mazel's *Le Nazaréen* (1892), J. Bois' *La Porte heroïque au ciel* (1893), and M. de Féraudy's *Pousse l'Amour* (1905).

SOLO COMPOSITIONS

For voice: four sets of songs.

For the piano: many pieces, most of which are given satirical titles. *Gymnopédies,* an early suite (1888), was orchestrated by Debussy. Other titles include *Pièces froides; Trois Morceaux en forme de poire; Choses vues à droite et à gauche (sans lunettes); Aperçus désagréables; Croquis et agaceries d'un gros bonhomme en bois.*

SUGGESTED READING

1. *AusMTC* 157-69
2. *GroutHWM* 606-7
3. *Ul-PiHM* 585-6

REFERENCES

BOOKS

1. Myers, R. H., *Erik Satie,* London, 1948.
2. Van Vechten, C., *Erik Satie* (in *Interpreters and Interpretations*), New York: Alfred A. Knopf, Inc., 1917.

LXXV. Florent Schmitt (1870-1958)

An outstanding composer with a long catalogue of works (wrote until his death at age eighty-seven). Along with elements of French Impressionism (such as programmatically conceived orchestral music) he perfected his own individual style by careful attention to the contrapuntal fabric and to asymmetrical rhythmic patterns. Use of humor and primitivistic effects (percussion) are also elements of his writing.

ORCHESTRAL MUSIC

Ballets: *La Tragédie de Salomé* (1907; rewritten as a symphonic poem, 1910); *Le Petit Elfe Ferme-l'oeil,* Op. 58 (after Hans Christian Andersen). Other Works: *Trois Rapsodies,* Op. 53 (1903-4); Symphonies No. 1 (perf. 1958) and No. 2 (perf. 1960).

CHAMBER MUSIC

Sonatine en trio for flute, clarinet, and harpsichord (1935).

Piano Quintet (1901-08).

CHORAL WORKS

Psaume XLVII (in the Vulgate XLVI) for soprano solo, chorus, organ, and orchestra (1904).

SUGGESTED READING

1. *CobCM*	II, 336-41
2. *RobCM*	285

LXXVI. Arthur Honegger (1892-1955) and "The Six"

Les Six was the name given to a group of young French composers who followed the leadings of Erik Satie about 1917. The poet Jean Cocteau and other artists were part of the movement, the general aim of which was to free music from the modern "isms" and to find a new musical language by turning to the dance hall and other places where popular taste was shown.

While Honegger helped to secure a hearing for the experimentalists and innovators, he soon left the ideals of the *Six*. A prolific composer, he wrote in many forms. Perhaps is best known for *Pacific 231* (orchestra, 1923); *Le Roi David* (oratorio, 1921); and his setting of Claudel's *Jeanne d'Arc au bûcher* (1935). He also wrote operas, ballets, 5 symphonies, chamber music, piano music, and songs.

ORCHESTRAL MUSIC

Symphonies

No. 2, for string orchestra (1942); No. 3, "Liturgique" (1946); No. 5, *Di tre re* (1951)

Other Works

Pastorale d'été (Summer Pastorale, 1920); *Horace Victorieux*, a "mimed symphony" (1921); *Pacific 231*, "mouvement symphonique No. 1" (1923); *Rugby*, "mouvement symphonique No. 2" (1928)

CONCERTOS AND PIECES WITH ORCHESTRA

Piano

Concertino (1925)

CHAMBER MUSIC

Strings

Three quartets (1916-17; 1934; 1936); sonatina for 2 violins (1920); *Hymn*, for 10 strings (1920); sonatina for violin and cello (1932)

Piano with other instruments

Rhapsody for 2 flutes, clarinet (or 2 violins, viola), and piano (1917); 2 violin sonatas (1918; 1919); viola sonata (1920); cello sonata (1920); sonatina for clarinet and piano (1922)

Other Works

Trois Contrepoints, for flute, English horn, violin, and cello (1922); *Danse de la Chèvre* (*Program miniature*) for flute unaccompanied.

CHORAL WORKS

Oratorios and other works

Cantique de Pâques, for soli, women's chorus, and orch. (1918)

Pâques à New York, for voice and string quartet (1920)

La Danse des morts, oratorio for soli, chorus, and orch. (1940)

Chant de Libération, for baritone, chorus, and orch. (1944)

Cantate de Noël (1953)

COMPOSITIONS FOR THE STAGE

Operas

Antigone (1927); *Judith*, biblical opera (1926); *Amphion*, melodrama (1931); *Les Aventures du Roi Pausole*, operetta or *opera comique* (1930; "The Adventures of King Pausole")

Other Works

Le Roi David, an oratorio or "dramatic psalm," with text by René Morax (1921); *Jeanne d'Arc au bûcher*, "stage oratorio," or "a vast popular fresco" written as a modern *Chanson de Geste*, text by Paul Claudel, with 5 speaking parts, 5 soloists, mixed choir, children's chorus, large orchestra (1938)

SOLO COMPOSITIONS

Voice

Four Poèmes (1914-16); *6 Poésies de Jean Cocteau* (1920-23); *5 Mélodies-minute* (1941)

Piano

Trois pièces (1910); *Hommage à Ravel* (1915); *Toccata et Variations* (1916); *Prélude et danse* (1919); *Le Cahier romand* (1923); *Hommage à Roussel* (1928); *Prélude, arioso et fughetta sur le nom de Bach* (1932). For 2 pianos: *Partita* (1928; arr. from *Trois Contrepoints*)

SUGGESTED READING

1. *AusMTC*	474-75
2. *CobCM*	I, 569-72; III, 39-42
3. *GroutHWM*	625-26

4. *GroutSHO* 561-63
5. *Ul-PiHM* 588, 628f

REFERENCES

BOOKS

1. Delannoy, M., *Honegger,* Paris: Editions Pierre Horay, 1953.

LXXVII. Darius Milhaud (b. 1892)

A student in Paris under Gédalge and Widor, he became a member of *Les Six.* He has taught composition at Mills College, California, since 1940. A composer with splendid craftsmanship and sparkling humor, he has a long list of successful works to his credit.

ORCHESTRAL MUSIC

Symphony No. 4, "1848 Revolution" (1948); ballets *Le Boeuf sur le toit* (1919, "The Ox on the Roof") and *La Création du monde* (1924, "The Creation of the World"); *Saudades do Brasil,* suite of dances (1920-21, also for piano); *Suite française* (1945, for both band and orchestra); 5 symphonies for small orchestra; 8 symphonies for large orchestra; *Ouverture Philharmonique* (1962).

PIECES WITH ORCHESTRA

Piano: *Cinq études* (1921); *Ballade* (1921); *Le Carnaval d'Aix* (1926); 4 concertos (1934, 1941, 1946, 1950). For 2 pianos: Concerto (1942).

Other concertos: 2 for violin (1927, 1948), plus *Concertino de printemps* (1935); viola (1929); 2 cello (1935, 1946); clarinet (1941); trombone and strings (1953, *Concertino d'hiver*); harp (1954); percussion (1930, small orch.); harmonica (1942, a suite written for Larry Adler; also for violin); marimba and vibraphone (1949). For harpsichord and strings: *L'Apothéose de Molière* (1948).

CHAMBER MUSIC

Violin and Piano

2 sonatas (1911, 1917); *Le Printemps* (1914); *Impromptu* (1926); *3 Caprices de Paganini* (1927); *Danses de Jacarémirim* (1945)

Violin and Harpsichord

Sonata (1945)

Two violins and piano

Sonata (1914); Sonatina (1940)

Piano and other instruments

Flute (Sonatina, 1922); clarinet (Sonatina, 1927); flute, clarinet, oboe (Sonata, 1918); viola (*Quatre Visages,* 1943; 2 sonatas, 1944); cello (*Elegie,* 1945)

String Combinations

Duo for 2 violins (1945); Sonatina for violin and viola (1941); *Sonatine à trois* for violin, viola, and cello (1940); String Trio (1947); *Sonatine* for viola and cello (1959)

Wind Combinations

Pastorale for oboe, clarinet, and bassoon (1935); Suite for oboe, clarinet, and bassoon (1937); *La Cheminée du Roi René,* suite for flute, oboe, clarinet, horn, and bassoon (1939)

String Quartets

Fifteen, with Nos. 14 and 15 playable together as an octet (1949)

Other Works

Aspen Serenade for 9 instruments (1958); *Concert de Chambre* for 11 instruments (1962)

CHORAL WORKS

Cantatas

Le Retour de l'enfant prodigue, 5 voices and orch. (1917); *Psalm 136,* for baritone, chorus, and orch. (1918); *Pan et Syrinx* (1934); *Cantate nuptiale,* after *Song of Songs* (1937); *Naissance de Vénus,* for mixed voices a cappella (1949); etc.

Sacred text

Sabbath Morning Service, for baritone, chorus, and organ (1947)

COMPOSITIONS FOR THE STAGE

Operas

Agamemnon (1913); *Les Malheurs d'Orphée* (1926); *Cristophe Colomb,* grand opera in 26 scenes, the book by Paul Claudel (1930); *Le Jeu de Robin et Marion,* mystery play after Adam de la Halle (1951); *David,* in 5 acts and 12 scenes (1954, for 3,000th anniversary of Israel); *Fiesta* (1960)

SOLO COMPOSITIONS

Voice

Many songs to texts by Francis Jammes, Paul Claudel, Tagore, Christina Rossetti, Mallarmé, and others. Song cycles: *Le Château* (1914), *Rêves* (1942); other collections include *3 Poèmes de Jean Cocteau* (1920), *Catalogue de fleurs* for voice and piano or 7 instruments (1920), *6 Chants populaires hébraïques* (1925)

Piano

Many pieces, including 2 sonatas (1916, 1949); *Saudades do Brasil,* 12 numbers in 2 books (1921); *La Muse ménagère,* suite of 15 pieces (1944; also for orch.); *Scaramouche,* a 2-piano version (1939); *Le Bal martiniquais,* a 2-piano version (1944); *Paris,* suite of 6 pieces for 4 pianos (1948)

Milhaud has written film music, incidental music for plays by Claudel, Romain Rolland, etc.

SUGGESTED READING

1. *AusMTC*	478-82
2. *CobCM*	II, 140-45 III, 29-39
3. *GroutHWM*	625-29
4. *RobCM*	388-89
5. *Ul-PiHM*	586-88, 628
6. *UlSM*	299-301

REFERENCES

BOOKS

1. Milhaud, D., *Notes Without Music, an Autobiography,* London: D. Dobson, 1952.

LXXVIII. Francis Poulenc (1899-1963)

Another member of the Six—a composer who adhered more closely to the stated ideals of the group than did Honegger or Milhaud. French wit, clever satire, irrepressible humor, classical clarity, and seriousness when demanded—these are elements of his style. Illustrative of some of the many sides to his genius are the *Concerto champêtre* (for harpsichord and small orchestra; 1928); Mass in G for chorus *a cappella* (1937); and *Dialogues des Carmélites* ("Dialogues of the Carmelites"; 1956; 3-act serious opera; extremely effective). Among other works to be noted:

ORCHESTRAL MUSIC

Rapsodie nègre, for small orchestra (1917); *Gloria* (1961).

PIECES WITH ORCHESTRA

Concertos: piano (1950); 2 pianos (1932); organ, strings, and timpani (1938, perf. 1941); *Aubade,* for piano and 18 instruments (1929).

CHAMBER MUSIC

Sonata for violin and piano (in memory of Garcia Lorca, 1943); sonata for clarinet and piano; sonata for flute and piano; *Elegy* for horn and piano; sonata for 2 clarinets (1918); *Le Bestiaire* for voice, flute, clarinet, bassoon, and string quartet (1919); sonata for clarinet and bassoon (1922); trio for oboe, bassoon, and piano (1916); string quartet (1946).

CHORAL WORKS

Mass (1937); 2 books of traditional French songs, arr. for chorus a cappella; *Stabat Mater,* for chorus a cappella (1951); *Figure humaine* (1954); *Office for Holy Saturday* (1962).

FOR THE STAGE

Opéra bouffe, Les Mamelles de Tirésias (1947); 1-act opera, *La Voix Humaine* (1959); ballet, *Les Biches* (1924). Incidental music for plays, film scores, etc.

SOLO COMPOSITIONS

Piano: many pieces, including *Mouvements perpétuels* (1918); *12 Improvisations; Suite française*; Sonata for 2 pianos. Voice: Song cycles *Le Bestiaire* (1919); *Poèmes de Ronsard* (1925); *Chansons gaillardes* (1926); *Banalités* (1940); *Chansons villageoises* (1942); *La Courte Paille* (1962); many separate songs; *Histoire de Babar le petit éléphant,* for narration and piano (1940).

SUGGESTED READING

1. *AusMTC*	516-520
2. *CobCM*	II, 236f; III, 42-44
3. *GroutHWM*	629-30
4. *RobCM*	388-89
5. *Ul-PiHM*	588, 629

REFERENCES

BOOKS

1. Hell, Henri, *Francis Poulenc,* New York: Grove Press, 1959.

LXXIX. Olivier Messiaen (b. 1908)

Composer and organist; student at the Paris Conservatoire under Dukas and Dupré. Combines neo-Romantic traits with Catholic mysticism, employs complicated rhythmic and melodic formulae of his own devising, includes exotic instruments, electronic instruments, and bird-song motives in his musical materials. Compositions include:

ORCHESTRAL MUSIC

Le Banquet eucharistique (1928); *Hymne au Saint Sacrement* (1933); *L'Ascension,* transcribed from organ original (1934, 4 Meditations); *Turangalila* (1949; grandiose work in 10 mvts., title a Hindu term meaning "love song").

PIECES WITH ORCHESTRA

For Piano: *Réveil des Oiseaux* (1953); *Oiseaux Exotiques,* for piano and small orch. (1955-56).

CHAMBER MUSIC

Le Merle Noir, flute and piano; *Mort du nombre,* for soprano, tenor, violin, and piano (1931); *Quatuor pour la fin du temps* ("Quartet for the End of Time") for violin, clarinet, cello, and piano; written in a prison camp in Silesia, 1941).

CHORAL WORKS

Mass for 8 sopranos and 4 violins (1933); *O sacrum convivium* (1937); *Choeurs pour une Jeanne d'Arc,* a cappella (1941); *Trois Petites Liturgies de la Présence Divine* ("Three Short Liturgies of the Divine Presence"), cantata for unison chorus of women's voices and orchestra; 1945).

SOLO COMPOSITIONS

Piano: *La Vision de l'Amen* for 2 pianos (1942); *Mode de valeurs et d'intensité* (1949); *Harawi,* "chant d'amour et de mort" for dramatic soprano and piano; *Vingt regards sur L'Enfant-Jésus* (1944). Organ: *Messe de la Pentecôte; Livre d'orgue* (7 pieces); *La Nativité du Seigneur,* 9 meditations ("The Nativity of the Lord"); *Le Banquet céleste* (1928); *Les Corps glorieux* (7 visions).

SUGGESTED READING

1. *AusMTC*	390-95
2. *CobCM*	III, 44-48
3. *GroutHWM*	630
4. *RobCM*	388-89
5. *Ul-PiHM*	611-12
6. *UlSM*	301

REFERENCES

1. MESSIAEN, O., *The Technique of My Musical Language,* Paris: Alphonse Léduc, 1956.

GERMAN

LXXX. Hugo Wolf (1860-1903)

A zealous Wagnerian, he employed many elements of Wagner's style in the accompaniments to the 250 *Lieder* for which he is best known. Achieving a new and highly communicative union between poetry and music, he continued the tradition of Romantic song by careful attention both to vocal declamation and to logical development of musical ideas in the piano part.

ORCHESTRAL MUSIC

Italian Serenade for small orchestra (1892), first written as a string quartet movement in 1887; G Major.

CHAMBER MUSIC

String Quartet in D Minor (1878-84).

CHORAL WORKS

Sechs geistliche a cappella Chöre (1881; ed. by E. Thomas; arr. for men's voices by Max Reger); *Christnacht* for solo voices, chorus, and orch. (1886-89); *Elfenlied* for soprano solo, chorus, and orch. (1889-91); *Dem Vaterland* for male chorus and orch. (1890, many revisions).

FOR THE STAGE

Der Corregidor, 4-act comedy opera, after Alarcón's *El Sombrero de tres picos* (1896, revised version 1898); *Manuel Venegas,* 3-act tragic opera, after Alarcón's *El Niño de la Bola* (1903; parts have been given in concert form).

SOLO COMPOSITIONS (SONGS)

12 *Lieder aus der Jugendzeit* (1888).
31 *Lieder nach verschiedenen Dichtern* (1877-97).
53 *Gedichte von Mörike* (1888).
20 *Gedichte von Eichendorff* (1886-88).
51 *Gedichte von Goethe* (1888-89).
44 songs in *Spanisches Liederbuch,* after Geibel and Heyse (1889-90).
46 songs in *Italienisches Liederbuch* (2 part, after Heyse).
22 songs (1890-91).
24 songs (1896).

Orchestral versions from the above written by Wolf (20 songs) and Max Reger. *Nachgelassene Werke,* ed. by R. Haas and H. Schultz, containing 40 previously unpublished songs (mostly from the composer's early period), published in 4 volumes (Leipzig, 1936). A complete edition of the songs published by Peters (Leipzig, 1935).

SUGGESTED READING

1. *CobCM*	II, 589f
2. *GroutHWM*	569-71
3. *ToveyEMA*	IV, 172-6; VI, 148
4. *Ul-PiHM*	557-559

REFERENCES

BOOKS

1. NEWMAN, E., *Hugo Wolf,* London: Methuen & Co., 1907.
2. SAMS, ERIC, *The Songs of Hugo Wolf,* New York: Oxford University Press, 1962.
3. WALKER, F., *Hugo Wolf, a biography,* London: J. M. Dent & Sons, Ltd., 1951.

LXXXI. Paul Hindemith (1895-1963)

An extremely versatile musician, he is noted as a composer, theorist, performer, teacher, and conductor. He is also known as an exponent of *Gebrauchsmusik* (workaday music, music for practical use). His musical philosophy is set forth in *A Composer's World: Horizons and Limitations* (1952). In *The Craft of Musical Composition* (English translation, 1941; revised 1945) he outlines his theories regarding tones, the forces that reside in them, and their arrangement and use. In his music (which must be studied in detail) his early contrapuntal, dissonant idiom is seen to move in the direction of Baroque and Classical formal designs, neo-Romantic feeling, and a harmonic vocabulary founded on a systematic extension of the principles of tonality.

ORCHESTRAL MUSIC

Symphonic

Lustige Sinfonietta, Op. 4; *Konzertmusik,* for brass and strings (1931; for 50th anniversary of Boston Symph.); *Philharmonisches Konzert* (1932; for Berlin Philharmonic); *Symphonic Dances* (1937); *Symphony in E-flat* (1941); *Symphonic Metamorphosis on Themes by Weber* (1943); *Symphonia Serena* (1947); *Sinfonietta in E* (Louisville, 1950); Symphony for Concert Band (1951); *Marsch über den alten Schweizerton* for orch. (1960); *Pittsburgh Symphony* (1958); *Konzertmusik* for violin and large chamber orch. (1962)

CONCERTOS AND PIECES WITH ORCHESTRA

One Solo Instrument

Violin (1940); 2 for viola (*Der Schwanendreher,* 1935; *Trauermusik,* with strings, 1936); 2 for cello (early work, Op. 3; later work, 1941); clarinet (1940, perf. 1944); horn (1950); 3 for piano (concertos Op. 29, 1924; 1947; *The Four Temperaments,* theme with 4 variations, strings only, 1944); harp (with woodwinds, 1949); organ (1962)

Instrumental Combinations as Soli

Oboe, bassoon, and violin, Op. 38 (1925); trumpet, bassoon, and strings (1948; 2nd version, 1953)

CHAMBER MUSIC

Solo Unaccompanied

Sonatas for viola, Op. 11, No. 5 (1923); violin, Op. 11, No. 6 (1923); viola, Op. 25, No. 1 (1923); cello, Op. 25, No. 3 (1923); 2 violin, Op. 31, Nos. 1 and 2 (1924)

Duo Unaccompanied

Canonic Sonatina for 2 flutes, Op. 31, No. 3 (1924); 14 easy duets for 2 violins (1932); 2 canonic duets for 2 violins (1932)

One Instrument with Piano

Drei Stücke for cello, Op. 8 (1917); 2 sonatas for violin, Op. 11, Nos. 1 and 2 (1920); cello, Op. 11, No. 3 (1922); viola, Op. 11, No. 4 (1922); viola d'amore, Op. 25, No. 2 (1929); viola, Op. 25, No. 4 (1924); *Meditation* for violin (or viola, or cello; 1938); 3 violin sonatas (1935, 1938, 1939); flute (1936); oboe (1938); bassoon (1938); viola (1939); clarinet (1939); horn (1939); trumpet (1939); English horn (1941); trombone (1941); *Echo* for flute (1942); *A Frog He Went A-Courting,* variations for cello (1946); cello sonata (1948)

Trios

Clarinet, horn, and piano, Op. 1 (unpublished); viola, heckelphone, and piano, Op. 47; violin, viola, and cello, Op. 34 (1924); 2nd trio for violin, viola, and cello (1934)

String Quartets

Seven: C Major, Op. 2; F Minor, Op. 10 (1919); C Major, Op. 16 (1922); Op. 22 (1922); Op. 32 (1924); 1944; 1945

Kammermusik

Kammermusik No. 1 (Op. 24, No. 1; 1922); *Kleine Kammermusik* for flute, oboe, clarinet, horn, and bassoon (Op. 24, No. 2; 1922); *Kammermusik* No. 2 for piano and 12 instruments (Op. 36, No. 1; 1925); *Kammermusik* No. 3 for cello and 10 instruments (Op. 36, No. 2; 1925); *Kammermusik* No. 4 for violin and small ensemble (Op. 36, No. 3; 1925); *Kammermusik* No. 5 for solo viola and small ensemble (Op. 36, No. 4; 1927); *Kammermusik* No. 6 for viola d'amore and chamber ensemble (Op. 46, No. 1; 1928); *Kammermusik* No. 7 for organ and chamber ensemble (Op. 46, No. 2; 1928)

Other Combinations

Piano quintet, Op. 7; quintet for clarinet and string quartet, Op. 30; *3 Stücke,* for 5 instruments (1925); *Konzertmusik* for wind instruments, Op. 41 (1927); *Spielmusik,* for strings, flutes, and oboes, Op. 43, No. 1 (1927); octet (1958)

VOCAL AND CHORAL WORKS

Melancholie for contralto and string quartet, Op. 14 (1921); *Des Todes Tod,* Op. 23, No. 1, for soprano, 2 violas, and cello (1922); *Die junge Magd,* 6 poems, Op. 23, No. 2, for contralto, flute, clarinet, and string quartet (1922); *Die Serenaden,* little cantatas on romantic poems, Op. 35, for soprano, oboe, viola, and cello (1925); *In Praise of Music* (a revision of *Frau Musica,* written 1928); *8 Canons* for 2 voices and instruments, Op. 45, No. 2 (1928); *Martinslied,* Op. 45, No. 3, for voice and instruments (1931); *Das Unaufhörliche,* oratorio (1931); Requiem on words of Walt Whitman, "When lilacs last in the dooryard bloom'd" (1946); *Apparebit Repentina Dies,* for chorus and brass (1947); *The Demon of the Gibbet,* for chorus a cappella (1949); *Cantique de l'Espérance,* for mezzo soprano, chorus, and 2 orchestras (1952); *6 Chansons* for mixed voices (1939); 5 songs on old texts for mixed voices (1943); *Ite Angeli Velores,* cantata (U.S. première 1958); 6 Madrigals for chorus a cappella (1958). *Lehrstück* with narrator, 2 small choruses, off-stage band, chamber orchestra, several singers and dancers (1919).

COMPOSITIONS FOR THE STAGE

Operas

Cardillac (1926, revised 1952); *Hin und Zurück,* Op. 45a (1927); *Neues vom Tage* (1929, revised 1954); *Wir bauen eine Stadt,* children's opera (1930); *Mathis der Maler* (1938; symphony arr. in 3 mvts.: Angel Concert, Temptation of Saint Anthony, Entombment); *Die Harmonie der Welt* (1957; partly adapted from 3-mvt. orchestral work of 1951); *The Long Christmas Dinner* (1961; on a play by Thornton Wilder)

Ballets

Der Dämon, a pantomime (1922); *Nobilissima visione* (on episodes in life of Saint Francis of Assisi, a "dance legend," orchestral suite arr., 1938); *Der Ploner Musiktag,* a pantomime (1932)

SOLO COMPOSITIONS

Piano

In einer Nacht, Op. 15, a set of 15 pieces (1922); piano sonata, Op. 17 (1917); *Tanzstücke,* Op. 19 (1922); *1922 Suite,* Op. 26 (1922); *Klaviermusik,* Op. 37 (1927); *Uebung in drei Stücken,* Op. 37, No. 1 (1927); *Reihe kleiner Stücke,* Op. 37, No. 2 (1927); 3 sonatas (1936); sonata for 2 pianos (1942); *Ludus Tonalis* (1943)

Voice and Piano

Drei Hymnen, after Walt Whitman, Op. 13; 8 songs for soprano, Op. 18 (1922); *Das Marienleben,* a cycle of songs after Rilke, Op. 27 (1923; radically revised and perf., 1948); *Bal des pendus* (1946)

Other Works

Three organ sonatas; a sonata for harp

SUGGESTED READING

1.	*AusMTC*	396-416
2.	*Ca-Jo-WaAM*	421-22
3.	*CobCM*	I, 556-62; III, 13-21
4.	*GroutHWM*	641-645
5.	*RobCM*	406-9
6.	*UlCM*	373-36
7.	*Ul-PiHM*	601-13; 626f

REFERENCES

BOOKS

1. HINDEMITH, P., *Catalogue of published works and recordings,* New York: Associated Music Publishers, 1954.
2. HINDEMITH, P., *A Composer's World, Horizons and Limitations,* Cambridge: Harvard University Press, 1952.
3. ———, *The Craft of Musical Composition,* New York: Associated Music Publishers, 1945.

LXXXII. Carl Orff (b. 1895)

Stage works fall into three general types: cantatas with optional action and dance (*Carmina Burana,* 1937; *Trionfo di Afrodite,* 1953); operas (*Der Mond,* 1939; and *Die Kluge,* "The Wise Woman," 1943—both based on fairy tales from Grimm and developed with a primitive type of rhythmic declamation); and plays with music (*Die Bernauerin,* 1947; *Antigonae,* 1949—in which percussive color combinations are further elaborated).

ORCHESTRAL MUSIC

Präludium (1925); *Entrata,* based on melodies of William Byrd (1928, revised 1940).

PIECES WITH ORCHESTRA

Concertino for harpsichord and wind instruments (1927).

COMPOSITIONS FOR THE STAGE

Scenic Cantatas

Trionfi (consisting of three large choral works often performed separately, with or without staging)

1. *Carmina Burana,* "cantiones profanae cantoribus et choris cantandae comitantibus instrumentis atque imaginibus magicis" (1935-36)
2. *Catulli Carmina,* "Ludi Scaenici" after Catullus (1943)
3. *Trionfo di Afrodite* (1953)

Musical Plays

Die Bernauerin, a Bavarian piece (1944-45, perf. 1947); *Antigonae,* a tradedy of Sophocles by Friedrich Hölderlin (1949); and the dance-play, *Der Feuerfarbene* (1925)

Operas

Der Mond (1939); *Die Kluge* (1943); and *Astutuli,* opera-ballet (1953)

Revisions: Monteverdi's *Orfeo* (1925; 2nd version, 1929; 3rd version, 1940); *Ballo delle Ingrate; Lamento d'Arianna;* and *L'Incoronazione di Poppea*

SUGGESTED READING

1. *AusMTC* 387-90
2. *CobCM* III, 21
3. *GroutHWM* 617
4. *Ul-PiHM* 627

REFERENCES

1. WARNER, K., "Egk and Orff," in *The Music Review* vol. XIV.

CZECH

LXXXIII. Leoš Janáček (1854-1928)

Studied in Prague, later in Leipzig and Vienna. A collector and student of folk music, his musical style is built on the melodic and rhythmic inflections found in the speech and songs of his countrymen. Recognition began with the performance of his opera *Jenufa* (1902). Among his later operas is the striking *From a Death-House* (1928). Among his choral music the *Glagolitic Mass* (1926; on text in Old Slavic) is outstanding. He has written chamber music, orchestral works, piano music, and songs. He also published several collections of Moravian folk songs.

ORCHESTRAL MUSIC

Symphonic Rhapsody, *Taras Bulba,* after Gogol (1918, perf. 1924); Suite for string orchestra; Sinfonietta (1926).

SOLO PIECES WITH CHAMBER GROUPS

For piano: Concertino (1926) with 6 instruments; *Capriccio* (left hand only, with 7 wind instruments; 1928).

CHAMBER MUSIC

Piano Trio (1908, subtitled *From Tolstoy's Kreutzer Sonata*); 3 sonatas for violin and piano (1879, 1913, 1921); 3 string quartets (1880, 1923, 1928); Sextet for wind instruments (1924).

CHORAL WORKS

Chorus with orch.: *Amarus* (1898); *Na Soláni Carták* (1911); *Otče Náš* ("The Lord's Prayer"); *Glagolitic Mass* (*Slavonic Mass,* or *Festival Mass*), for soli, chorus, and orch. (1927).

Chorus a cappella: *Potulny šilenec, Maryčka Magdónova.*

FOR THE STAGE

Ten operas, including *Jenufa* (Her Foster Daughter, 1894-1903, perf. 1904); *Kata Kabanová* (based on Ostrovsky's play, *The Storm;* 1921); *The Cunning Little Vixen* (1924); *From the House of the Dead* (after Dostoyevsky; 1928, perf. 1930). Ballet: *Rákocz Rákoczy* (1891).

SOLO COMPOSITIONS

Piano: a sonata and smaller pieces. Voice: song cycles, *Ryhadly* (nursery songs) and *Zápisnik zmizelého* (Diary of a Vanished Man); many arr. of folksongs.

SUGGESTED READING

1. *AusMTC* 77-82
2. *CobCM* II, 27f; III, 71-77
3. *GroutHWM* 590
4. *RobCM* 311
5. *Ul-PiHM* 619
6. *VeiCon* 288

REFERENCES

BOOKS

1. HOLLANDER, H., *Leoš Janáček: his Life and Work,* transl. by P. Hamburger, London: 1963.
2. STEDRON, B., *Leoš Janáček: Letters and Reminiscences,* Prague, 1954, translated by G. Thomsen, 1955.
3. SEDA, J., *Leoš Janáček,* Prague, 1956 in Czech and English.

PERIODICALS

1. HOLLANDER, H., "Leoš Janáček and His Operas," *Musical Quarterly,* January, 1929.
2. ———, "The Music of Leoš Janáček—Its Origin in Folklore," *Musical Quarterly,* April, 1955.

LXXXIV. Bohuslav Martinů (1890-1959)

Student of Suk in Prague and Roussel in Paris. Won the Coolidge Prize in 1933 with his string sextet. Wrote copiously, with operas, ballets, four symphonies, symphonic poems, two piano concertos, concertos for violin and cello, and chamber music to his credit. His style was neo-Classical, but with some Impressionistic additions. Excelled in counterpoint, and showed his greatest fluency in chamber works.

ORCHESTRAL MUSIC

Serenade (1930); Partita (Suite No. 1) for string orchestra (1931); *Sinfonietta giocosa* for orchestra with piano (1942); *Estampes* (Louisville, 1959); *Intermezzo* (Louisville, 1959); 6 symphonies, No. 6, *Fantaisies symphoniques* (Boston, 1955), being most successful; *Sinfonia* for 2 orchestras (1932); *Concerto grosso* (1938, perf. 1941); concerto for orchestra (1949); *The Parables* (1958); Suite on Frescos of Piero della Francesa (1958).

PIECES WITH ORCHESTRA

Concerto for string quartet (1931); cello concerto (1931); piano concerto (1935); concerto for 2 string orchestras, piano, and kettledrums (1940); concerto for 2 pianos (1943); violin concerto (1943); *Rhapsody-Concerto* for viola (1953).

CHAMBER MUSIC

Sonata for flute and piano (1945); Piano quartet (1942); 6 string quartets (1921-47); string quintet (1929); wind quintet (1930); Piano Trio (1930); string sextet (1931, Coolidge Prize); 2 violin sonatas (1931, 1933); sonata for 2 violins (1932); piano quintet (1934); string trio (1935); trio for flute, violin, and piano (1936); *Madrigals* for oboe, clarinet, and bassoon (1937); 2 cello sonatas (1940, 1941); *Madrigal Sonata* for flute, violin, and piano (1942); Sonata for clarinet and piano (1957).

FOR THE STAGE

Ten operas, inc. *The Marriage*, after Gogol (N.B.C. Television Opera Theater, 1953); and *What Men Live By*, after Tolstoy (1953). Ballets, such as *Istar* (1922); *La Revue de Cuisine* (1927, for chamber ensemble); *The Butterfly that Stamped*, after Kipling (1929); *Špalíček* (with voices, 1932); and *The Judgement of Paris* (1935); *The Greek Passion* (1959; a fusion of opera and oratorio).

SOLO COMPOSITIONS

Several piano pieces, including *3 Czech Dances* and *Ritournelles*.

SUGGESTED READING

1.	*AusMTC*	492-93
2.	*CobCM*	II, 117
3.	*UlSM*	309

REFERENCES

BOOKS

1. Šafránek, M., *Bohuslav Martinů: the Man and his Music*, New York: Alfred A. Knopf, Inc., 1944.

PERIODICALS

1. Šafránek, M., *"Bohuslav Martinů," Musical Quarterly*, July, 1943.

HUNGARIAN

LXXXV. Ernst von Dohnányi (1877-1960)

Noted composer, pianist, and teacher. From 1940 until his death, lived in the United States. His principal compositions represent the last flowering of the Hungarian Romantic period, are strongly reminiscent of Brahms, and are sometimes marked by flashes of musical wit.

ORCHESTRAL MUSIC

Ruralia Hungarica, Op. 32a, in 7 mvts. (1924, also for piano); Suite for orchestra, Op. 19, F-sharp minor; *Symphonic Minute*, Op. 36; Symphony No. 1 in D minor, Op. 9; Symphony No. 2 (1944; radically revised, and perf. in new version, Minneapolis, 1957); *Festival Overture*, Op. 31; *American Rhapsody* (1954).

PIECES WITH ORCHESTRA

Piano: *Variations on a Nursery Song*, Op. 25 (1912; perf. 1916); Concerto in E minor (1899); Concerto in D-flat, Op. 22; Concerto (1946). Other instruments: *Konzertstück* for cello, Op. 12; Violin concerto, Op. 27; 2nd Violin concerto (1952, for orchestra without violins); Concertino for harp (1952).

CHAMBER MUSIC

Trio, Op. 10 in C (*Serenade*) for strings; string quartets (Op. 7 in A Major; Op. 15 in D-flat); quintets for piano and strings (Op. 1 in C minor; Op. 26); Sonata for cello and piano in B-flat minor, Op. 8; Sonata for violin and piano in C-sharp minor, Op. 21; Sextet in C major for clarinet, horn, violin, viola, cello, and piano, Op. 37.

CHORAL WORKS

Szegedin Mass (1930).

FOR THE STAGE

Operas: *Tante Simona,* Op. 20 (1913, 1-act); *A Vajda Tornya* ("The Tower of the Voivod," 1922); *Der Tenor* (1929, comic opera). Pantomime: *Der Schleier der Pierrette* ("The Veil of Pierrette," 1910).

SOLO COMPOSITIONS

Piano: Passacaglia, Op. 6; 4 rhapsodies, Op. 11; *Winterreigen,* Op. 13 (10 bagatelles); *Suite in the Olden Style,* Op. 24; Variations on a Hungarian Folk song, Op. 29; 12 Etudes (1950); *Humoresken in Form einer Suite,* Op. 17; *5 Klavierstücke,* Op. 3; Variations for piano in G, Op. 4.

Voice: Six songs, Op. 14; *Im Lebenslenz,* Op. 16 (6 songs).

SUGGESTED READING

1. *CobCM*	I, 327-31
2. *HiCon*	327-440
3. *ToveyEMA*	III, 173-6
4. *UlCM*	355
5. *UlSM*	308
6. *VeiCon*	280, 282, 289

REFERENCES

BOOKS

1. DOHNANYI, E., *Message to Posterity from Ernst von Dohnányi,* Jacksonville, Fla.: H. & W. Drew Co., 1960.

LXXXVI. Béla Bartók (1881-1945)

With Kodály, studied and collected genuine folk music—not only of Hungary but also of Roumania and other sections of Asia Minor and North Africa. Among the many important elements of his style is the use of "barbaric" rhythm. May be said to have achieved a unique synthesis of the best in national folk literature and the highest forms of Western art music. His compositions fall into the categories of orchestral music, concertos, operas and pantomimes, chamber music, choral works, and music for the piano. In the latter division the 153 graded pieces (6 books) titled *Mikrokosmos* furnish both an introduction to his style and a summary of many of its features.

ORCHESTRAL MUSIC

Suites: No. 1 (1905), No. 2 (1907, revised 1943), and Dance Suite (1923). Other works: *Kossuth,* a symp. poem (1904); *Scherzo* (1904); 4 Pieces (1912); *Two Portraits* (1908); *Divertimento* for String Orchestra (1939); Concerto for Orchestra (1944).

PIECES WITH ORCHESTRA

Violin Concerto (1937-8); viola concerto (unfinished; orchestrated by Tibor Serly; perf. 1949); three concertos for piano (1927, 1931, 1945—unfinished).

CHAMBER MUSIC

Sonata for solo violin (1944); 2 sonatas for violin and piano (1922, 1923); 2 Rhapsodies for violin and piano (1928); *Contrasts* for violin, clarinet, and piano (1938, commissioned by Benny Goodman and Joseph Szigeti); Sonata for Two Pianos and Percussion (1937; transc. as Concerto for 2 pianos and orch.); Music for Strings, Percussion, and Celesta (1936); 7 string quartets: No. 1, Op. 7 (1910); No. 2, Op. 17 (1915-17); No. 3 (1927); No. 4 (1928); No. 5 (1934); No. 6 (1939); No. 7 (1944—incomplete); *Rhapsody* for cello and piano.

CHORAL WORKS

Cantata profana (1930; perf. 1934) for tenor and baritone soloists, double chorus, and orchestra.

FOR THE STAGE

Opera: *The Castle of Duke Bluebeard,* Op. 11, in 1 act (1911; perf. 1918). Ballets: *The Wooden Prince,* Op. 13, in 1 act (1915; perf. 1917); and *The Miraculous Mandarin,* a "Pantomime," (1919; perf. 1926).

SOLO COMPOSITIONS

Piano: Sonatina (1915); Sonata (1926); *Rhapsody,* Op. 1 (1904, also for orch.); *Allegro barbaro* (1911); *Mikrokosmos* (1926-37); 14 *Bagatelles,* Op. 6 (1908); 7 *Sketches* (1910, revised 1945); 3 Études, Op. 18 (1918); 2 Rumanian Dances (1909); 3 *Burlesques* (1910); 8 *Improvisations* on Hungarian peasant songs, Op. 20 (1920).

Many arrangements of folk songs for voices and various instrumental combinations, e.g., 40 Hungarian folk songs, 15 Hungarian peasant songs, 9 Slovak folk songs.

SUGGESTED READING

1. *AusMTC*	223-42; 319-29
2. *Ca-Jo-WaAM*	419-21
3. *CobCM*	I, 60-65; III, 61-70
4. *GroutHWM*	612-17
5. *HiCon*	327-56

6. *RobCM* 20-252, 283-84, 317-18
7. *Ul-PiHM* 598-601, 622
8. *UlSM* 287-89

REFERENCES

BOOKS

Béla Bartók's works in the catalog of Boosey & Hawkes, London: Boosey & Hawkes, 1945.

1. STEVENS, HALSEY, *The life and music of Béla Bartók*, New York: Oxford University Press, 1953.
2. HARASZTI, EMIL, *Béla Bartók, his life and works*, Paris: The Lyrebird Press, Louise B. M. Dyer, 1938.
3. BACSKAI-PAYERLE, B., *Béla Bartók, pianist, Hungary's outstanding composer*, New York, 1940, eight-page pamphlet from the Hungarian reference library, pamphlet series 1, no. 3.

LXXXVII. Zoltán Kodály (1882-1967)

Also shows results of his work with Hungarian folk songs in his music although national styles are perhaps less pointedly exemplified than in the music of Bartók. Among the works for which he is best known are the opera, *Háry János* (1926) and the *Psalmus hungaricus* for tenor soloist, chorus, and orchestra (1923–perhaps his most famous composition).

ORCHESTRAL MUSIC

Dances of Galánta (1933; for 80th anniversary of the Budapest Philharmonic, 1934); *Peacock Variations* (1939, "On a Hungarian Folksong"); Concerto for Orchestra (1941); *Summer Evening*, tone poem (1906, revised 1930); *Ballet Music* (1925); *Theater Overture* (1927); *Marosszék Dances* (1930); Symphony No. 1 (1961).

PIECES WITH ORCHESTRA

Viola Concerto (1947); Concerto for string quartet (1947).

CHAMBER MUSIC

Sonatas for cello unaccompanied, Op. 8 (1915); and for cello with piano, Op. 4 (1910); 2 string quartets (1908, 1917); Duo for violin and cello (1914); *Serenade* for 2 violins and viola (1919-20).

CHORAL WORKS

Psalmus Hungaricus (on the 55th Psalm) for tenor solo, mixed chorus and orchestra, with children's chorus ad. lib. (1923); *Te Deum* (*Budavari*) for soli, chorus, and orch. (1936), written for 250th anniversary of delivery of Budapest from the Turks; *Missa brevis* (1945); many choruses (e.g., *Transylvanian Lament, Jesus and the Traders, Ode to Franz Liszt*).

FOR THE STAGE

Operas: *Székely Fonó* (The Spinning Room of the Szekelys, lyric scenes based on Hungarian folk songs and dances; 1932); *Háry János* (1926, an orchestral suite was extracted from the opera); *Czinka Panna* (1948).

SOLO COMPOSITIONS

Piano: *Meditation* (1907); *9 Pieces* (1910); *Marosszék Dances* (1930); *24 Little Canons on the Black Keys* (1945); *Children's Dances* (1946).

Voice and piano: *20 Hungarian Folksongs* (1906, with Bartók); *Magyar nepzene* (Hungarian Folk Music, 57 arr., 1917-32); many songs, choruses, reading exercises for children and students.

SUGGESTED READING

1. *AusMTC* 486-87
2. *CobCM* II, 56-64
3. *GroutHWM* 617

ROUMANIAN

LXXXVIII. Georges Enesco (1881-1955)

Won the *premier prix* for violin playing at the Paris Conservatoire (1899), going on to a distinguished career as composer, violinist, teacher, and conductor. Yehudi Menuhin was his pupil. In 1912 Enesco founded a prize for works by young Rumanian composers.

ORCHESTRAL MUSIC

Poème roumain, Op. 1 (1898); 2 *Rapsodies roumaines* (1901, 1902); 3 suites (1904; 1915; 1939–*Villageoise*); 3 symphonies (1906, 1913, 1921); *Poème symphonique* (1950); *Concert Overture on Motifs in the Rumanian Character* (1948); *Symphonie de chambre* (1954); *Pastorale-Fantaisie* (1899).

PIECES WITH ORCHESTRA

Concertos: Violin (1921); cello, *Symphonie concertante* (1909).

CHAMBER MUSIC

Three violin sonatas (1897; 1899; 1926, *Dans le caractère populaire roumain*); Octet for 4 violins, 2 violas, 2 cellos (1900); Trio, *Aubade,* for violin, viola, and cello (1901); Piano quartet (1911); 2 strings quartets (1921, 1945); *Impressions d'enfance* for violin and piano (1940).

CHORAL WORKS

Chorus and piano: *Trois Mélodies de Fernand Gregh* (1897); *7 Chansons de Clément Marot* (1907-08).

FOR THE STAGE

Opera *Oedipe* (1932, revived 1955).

SOLO COMPOSITIONS

Piano: 2 Suites (No. 1, *Dans le style ancien,* 1897; No. 2, 1903); *Pièces impromptues* (1915-16); 3 sonatas (1924, 1927, 1934). Two pianos: Variations on an original Theme (1899).

SUGGESTED READING

1. *CobCM* I, 380

SWISS

LXXXIX. Ernest Bloch (1880-1959)

Shared in the legacy left by Debussy and in his music shows a fondness for mood, color, and harmonic luxuriance. Intensity and pathos are still other qualities which can be related to his racial heritage.

ORCHESTRAL MUSIC

Symphony in C-sharp minor (1901); *Hiver-Printemps,* symphonic poem (1904-05); *Israel,* symphony with 2 sopranos, 2 contraltos, and bass (1912-16); *Trois poèmes Juifs* (1913); 2 Concerti grossi (1924-25, for strings and piano; 1953 for strings); 2 symphonic poems: *America* (1926) and *Helvetia* (1928); *Voice in the Wilderness,* a symphonic poem with cello obbligato, 6 mvts. (1936); *Suite symphonique* (1945); *Sinfonia breve* (1953); Symphony in E-flat (1954-55); *Evocations,* symphonic suite in 3 mvts. (1937); *Suite Modale* (string orch. version; New York première, 1959).

PIECES WITH ORCHESTRA

For violin, Concerto (1938); for viola, *Suite hebraïque* (1953); for cello, *Schelomo,* Hebrew rhapsody (1916); for trumpet, *Proclamation* (1955); for trombone, *Symphony,* for trombone solo and orch. (1953-54); for piano, *Concerto symphonique* (1949), and *Scherzo fantasque* (1950).

CHAMBER MUSIC

Two violin sonatas (1920; 1924—*Poème mystique*); *Baal Shem,* for violin and piano (1923; also arr. for orch.); Suite for viola and piano (1919); 2 suites for string quartet (1925); 4 string quartets (1916, 1946, 1951, 1953); *Méditation hébraïque* and *From Jewish Life,* for cello and piano (1925); Piano quintet (1923, uses quarter tones); Piano quintet No. 2 (1958); Suite No. 1 for Cello alone (1956).

CHORAL WORKS

Avodath Hakodesh, Sacred Service, a modern Hebrew ritual for baritone, mixed chorus, and orch. (1932-34).

FOR THE STAGE

Operas *Macbeth* (1910) and *Jézabel* (*c.* 1918, unfinished).

SOLO COMPOSITIONS

Piano: Sonata (1935); *Poems of the Sea; In the Night* (both arr. for orch.); *Nirvana; 5 Sketches in Sepia; Visions and Prophecies.*

Voice: *Historiettes au crépuscule,* 4 songs for mezzo soprano and piano (1903), *Poèmes d'Automne* (mezzo soprano and orch. 1906); *Psalm 22,* baritone and orch. (1914).

SUGGESTED READING

1. *AusMTC* 485
2. *CobCM* I, 129-134; III, 182-87
3. *GroutHWM* 604
4. *HiCon* 315-16
5. *RobCM* 215-19
6. *UlSM* 317-18

XC. Frank Martin (b. 1890)

Has received wide recognition as a composer of great strength and originality. Beginning as a French Impressionist, he created a personal style marked by contrapuntal and harmonic mastery, and a feeling for emotional logic and power. Later works have shown a modified twelve-tone method. His stylization of folk material in modern harmonic settings with incisive rhythmic patterns is a noteworthy feature of his writing.

ORCHESTRAL MUSIC

Symphonie pour orchestre burlesque (1915); *Rhythmes* (1929); *Symphonie* (1938); *Petite symphonie concertante,* for harp, harpsichord, piano, and 2 string orchestras (1946); *Études* for string orchestra (1956).

PIECES WITH ORCHESTRA

Concertos for violin (1952); piano (1936); harpsichord (1955); and 7 wind instruments, strings, and percussion (1949). *Ballades* for piano (1939) and cello (1951).

CHAMBER MUSIC

Piano trio (1925, on popular Irish themes); piano quintet (1920); string trio (1936); string quartet (1936); 2 violin sonatas (1913, 1931); *Ballades* with piano for flute (1939) and trombone (1941), both arr. for orch.

CHORAL WORKS

Oratorios: *Le vin herbé* (1942); *In terra pax* (1945); *Golgotha* (1949), on a text by St. Augustine.

FOR THE STAGE

Operas: *The Tempest,* after Shakespeare (1956); and *Monsieur de Pourceaugnac,* on a farcical play, text by Molière, partly spoken, partly sung.

Incidental music: *Oedipus Rex* (1923); *Romeo and Juliet* (1927), *Athalie* (1946).

SUGGESTED READING

1. *AusMTC* 496-97
2. *CobCM* III, 78

AUSTRIAN

XCI. Ernst Křenek (b. 1900)

Came to the United States in 1938 and has since been affiliated with various colleges and universities. Now resident in California. Compositions show preoccupation with jazz, use of the twelve-tone technic, and an underlying Romantic tendency.

ORCHESTRAL MUSIC

Five symphonies (1921, 1922, 1922, 1947, 1950); 2 *Concerti Grossi* (1921); *Symphonische Musik* for 9 solo instruments (1922); *Symphonie* for brass and percussion (1924-25); *Kleine Symphonie* (1928); *Symphonic Piece* for string orch. (1939); *Symphonic Elegy* for strings, on the death of Anton von Webern (1946); *Eleven Transparencies* (1955). *Hexahedron* for chamber orchestra (perf. 1960); *Quaestio Temporis* (perf. 1962).

PIECES WITH ORCHESTRA

Four piano concertos (1923; 1938; 1946, not in the 12-tone system otherwise employed after 1936; 1950); Violin concerto (1924); Concertino for flute, violin, harpsichord, and strings (1924); Double concerto for violin, piano, and chamber orch. (1952); Concerto for harp and chamber orch. (1952); Concerto for 2 pianos and orch. (1953).

CHAMBER MUSIC

Three violin sonatas (1919, with piano: 1924-25 and 1942, solo); viola sonata (1948); string trio (1948), and *Parvula Corona Musicalis ad honorem J. S. Bach* for string trio (1950); 8 string quartets (1921, 1921, 1923, 1923-24, 1930, 1937, 1943, 1952), and *Serenade* for string quartet (1919); Suite for clarinet and piano (1924); Suite for cello solo (1939); Sonatina for flute and viola (1942).

CHORAL WORKS

Cantata, *Von der Vergänglichkeit des Irdischen* (1932); *Reisebuch aus den Oesterreichischen Alpen* (1935); *Proprium Missae in Festo SS. Innocentium,* for women's voices (1940); *Lamentatio Jeremiae Prophetae* (1941); *Cantata for Wartime* (1943); *The Santa Fe Time Table,* for a cappella chorus, on names of stops between Albuquerque and Los Angeles (1945); *Sestina* for voice, piano, flute, clarinet, violin, guitar, vibraphone, marimba, and percussion (1957).

FOR THE STAGE

Operas: *Orpheus und Eurydike* (1926); *Jonny spielt auf* (1927); *Leben des Orest* (1930); *Karl V* (1938); *Dark Waters* (1951); *The Bell Tower* (1957). Revised and orchestrated Monteverdi's *L'Incoronazione di Poppea* (1937).

SOLO COMPOSITIONS

Voice: *Medea,* for contralto and orch. (1953).
Organ: Sonata (1941).

Piano: 6 sonatas (1919, 1928, 1943, 1948, 1950, 1951); 5 sonatinas (1920); Double Fugue (1918); *Dance Studies,* in "Grotesken-Album" (1922); *Toccata and Chaconne* on the chorale, *Ja, ich glaub' an Jesum Christum* (1922, a suite also on the chorale); 2 suites (1924); 5 pieces (1925); 12 short pieces (1938); *Hurricane Variations* (1944); *8 Pieces* (1946); *George Washington Variations* (1950).

SUGGESTED READING

1. *AusMTC*	446-47
2. *CobCM*	II, 76-79; III, 11-13
3. *Ul-PiHM*	625f
4. *UlSM*	317-18

REFERENCES

1. KŘENEK, E., *Music here and now,* New York: W. W. Norton & Company, Inc., 1939.
2. ———, *Self-Analysis,* Albuquerque, N.M., 1953.

ENGLISH

XCII. Frederick Delius (1862-1934)

A solitary and tragic figure in music. Born in England of German blood, found his first success as a composer in Germany, then moved to France after a short period in Florida. In his later years, blind and paralyzed, he dictated a number of compositions to Eric Fenby, who lived and worked with him. His work is difficult to categorize. Features include an opulent use of shifting chromatic sonorities in conjunction with folkish melodic patterns—the music usually requiring a large orchestra. There are flashes of intimacy, and other flashes of robust vigor. Among important works may be mentioned *Over the Hills and Far Away* (1895), *Brigg Fair* (1907) for orchestra; concerto for violin and cello (1916), violin (1916), and cello (1921); *Sea-Drift* (1903), *Requiem* (1916) for chorus; operas *Irmelin* (1892), *Koanga* (1897), *A Village Romeo and Juliet* (1901; one of the best known); 3 violin sonatas, a cello sonata, and 2 string quartets. Significant works in addition to the above:

ORCHESTRAL MUSIC

Paris: The Song of a Great City (1898); *Appalachia,* orchestral variations with final chorus (1902); *In a Summer Garden* (1908); *A Dance Rhapsody* (1909); *Summer Night on the River* and *On Hearing the First Cuckoo in Spring* (1913); *North Country Sketches* (1913-14); *Dance Rhapsody No. 2* (1916); *Eventyr,* symphonic poem (1919).

CHORAL WORKS

A Mass of Life (1909) for soloists, chorus, and large orchestra; *A Song of the High Hills* (1911-12); *A Song Before Sunrise* (1918); *Cynara and Arabesk* (1929).

COMPOSITIONS FOR THE STAGE

Opera: *Fennimore and Gerda* (1919). Incidental music to *Hassan* (1920).

SUGGESTED READING

1. *AusMTC*	88-92
2. *CobCM*	I, 320
3. *UlSM*	309
4. *ToveyEMA*	III, 203-5

REFERENCES

BOOKS

1. BEECHAM, SIR THOMAS, *Frederick Delius,* New York: Alfred A. Knopf, Inc., 1960.
2. HESELTINE, P., *Frederick Delius,* London: John Lane, 1923, new enlarged edition by H. Foss, New York, 1952.
3. HULL, R. H., *Delius,* London: L. & Virginia Woolf, 1928.
4. HUTCHINGS, A., *Delius,* London: Macmillan & Co. Ltd., 1948.

XCIII. Ralph Vaughan Williams (1872-1958)

Son of a clergyman, student at Charterhouse and Cambridge, and at the Royal College of Music. Additional study with Max Bruch in Berlin and with Ravel in Paris. In 1918 appointed professor of composition at the Royal College of Music, and from 1920 to 1926 conducted the London Bach Choir. With his colleague, Gustav Holst, he early became interested in English folk music and in Tudor church music. Served as president of the English Folk Dance and Song Society in 1932. Although strongly influenced by folk song and by sixteenth-century English polyphony, his compositional style is unmistakably individual. Some features are colorful use of modal scales, successive triads in unusual relationships, effective cross relations, simultaneous streams of chords making a counterpoint of harmonies. His expressive gamut is wide, ranging from extremely subdued, mystical effects to outbursts of surprising violence. A sincere idealist and master craftsman, Vaughan Williams is widely respected as England's greatest symphonist.

ORCHESTRAL MUSIC

Nine symphonies (No. 1, *A Sea Symphony* is for soprano, baritone, chorus, and orchestra, on texts of Walt Whitman); *Serenade* for small orchestra (1901); *Bucolic Suite* (1902); 2 *Impressions* (1902); 3 *Norfolk Rhapsodies* (No. 1, 1906. Nos. 2 and 3, 1907); *Fantasia on a Theme by Tallis* for strings (1910); 5 *Variants of "Dives and Lazarus"* for string orchestra and harp (1939).

Symphonies

No. 2, *A London Symphony* (1914, rev. 1920)
No. 3, *Pastoral Symphony* (1922)
No. 4, F Minor (1935)
No. 5, D Major (1943)
No. 6, E Minor (1948)
No. 7, *Sinfonia antartica* (1951-52, material taken from film music titled *Scott of the Antarctic*, 1949)
No. 8, (1956)
No. 9, (1958)

Variations

Variations on a Theme by Tallis, for strings (1910)

CONCERTOS AND PIECES WITH ORCHESTRA

Concerto accademico for violin and orchestra (1925); piano concerto (1933; also arranged for 2 pianos and orchestra); concerto for oboe and strings (1944); concerto for bass tuba and orchestra (1954). *The Lark Ascending,* romance for violin and orchestra (1914); *Flos Campi,* suite for viola, small chorus, and small orchestra (1925); *Fantasy on Sussex Folk Tunes* for cello and orchestra (1930); suite for viola and orchestra (1934); *Romance* for harmonica and orchestra (1952).

CHAMBER MUSIC

Two string quartets (No. 1, 1908, rev. 1921; No. 2, 1945); *Fantasy Quintet,* for 2 violins, 2 violas, and cello (1910); *On Wenlock Edge,* for tenor, string quartet, and piano (1909); *6 Studies in English Folksong,* for cello and piano (1927); *Introduction and Fugue* for 2 pianos (1946).

CHORAL WORKS

Toward the Unknown Region (after Walt Whitman; 1905, rev. 1918); *A Sea Symphony* (1910); *Five Mystical Songs* (1911); *Fantasia on Christmas Carols* (1912); Mass in G Minor (1923); *Sancta Civitas* (1926); *Benedicite* (1930); 3 choral hymns (1930); Magnificat (1932); *Dona nobis pacem* (1936); *Five Tudor Portraits* (1936); *Te Deum* (1937); *Serenade to Music* (1938); *The Sons of Light* (1950).

COMPOSITIONS FOR THE STAGE

Operas: *The Shepherds of the Delectable Mountains* (1922); *Hugh the Drover* (1911-14); *Sir John in Love* (1929); *The Poisoned Kiss* (1936); *Riders to the Sea* (1937); *The Pilgrim's Progress* (1949). Ballets: *Old King Cole* (1923); *On Christmas Night* (1926); *Job,* a masque for dancing (1931). Incidental music to several plays and music for a number of films.

SOLO COMPOSITIONS

Many songs and arrangements of English folk songs. Several short piano pieces. Pieces for organ. Hymn tunes and carols.

SUGGESTED READING

1.	*AusMTC*	487-91
2.	*GroutHWM*	618-22
3.	*GroutSHO*	532
4.	*HiCon*	401-02
5.	*Ul-PiHM*	571-72
6.	*UlSM*	310-11

REFERENCES

BOOKS

1. DAY, JAMES, *Vaughan Williams,* London: J. M. Dent & Sons, Ltd., New York: Farrar, Straus and Cudahy, 1961.
2. DICKINSON, A. E. F., *Vaughan Williams,* London, 1963.
3. FOSS, H., *Ralph Vaughan Williams: a Study,* London, 1950.
4. HOWES, F. S., *The Music of Ralph Vaughan Williams,* London & New York: Oxford University Press, 1954.
5. PAKENHAM, S., *Ralph Vaughan Williams,* New York, 1957.
6. VAUGHAN WILLIAMS, RALPH, *National Music and Other Essays,* London, 1963.

XCIV. Gustav Holst (1874-1934)

British, in spite of his name, and a close friend of Vaughan Williams. Pupil of Stanford at the Royal College of Music. Organist, choral conductor, and professional trombonist for several years in the Carl Rosa Opera orchestra. Taught composition at the Royal College for a time but devoted his last years entirely to composition. His style was influenced not only by English folk song but also by Hindu mysticism. His music is often austere, sometimes astringent. Among important works, the following: *The Hymn of Jesus,* for double chorus and orchestra

(1917); the orchestral suite *The Planets* (1916); and his setting of Walt Whitman's *Ode to Death* (1919). Also:

ORCHESTRAL MUSIC

Somerset Rhapsody, Op. 21b (1910); *St. Paul's Suite* for strings (1913); *Fugal Overture* (1923); *Egdon Heath* (1928); *Hammersmith* (1931). Two suites for military band.

CHAMBER MUSIC

Fantasy Pieces for oboe and strings, Op. 2 (1896); piano quintet, Op. 3 (1896). Woodwind quintet, Op. 14 (1903).

CHORAL WORKS

Hymns from the Rig-Veda, Op. 26 (1910); *The Cloud Messenger,* Op. 30 (1910); *Choral Symphony,* for soprano solo and mixed voices, Op. 41 (1925); *Choral Fantasia,* for soprano, chorus, organ, and orchestra, Op. 51 (1930).

COMPOSITIONS FOR THE STAGE

Operas: *Sāvitri,* Op. 25 (1908); *The Perfect Fool,* Op. 39 (1923); *At the Boar's Head,* Op. 42 (1925); *The Wandering Scholar,* Op. 50 (1929).

SUGGESTED READING

1. *AusMTC*	94-96
2. *ToveyEMA*	II, 42; 208-12 IV, 169-70
3. *UlSM*	311

REFERENCES

BOOKS

1. DYER, LOUISE B., *Gustav Holst,* catalogue of his works published up to March, 1931, London: Oxford University Press, 1931.
2. HOLST, IMOGEN, *Gustav Holst,* London & New York: Oxford University Press, 1938.
3. ———, *The Music of Gustav Holst,* London & New York: Oxford University Press, 1951.
4. RUBBRA, E., *Gustav Holst,* Paris, 1948.

XCV. John Ireland (b. 1879)

Student, then teacher, at the Royal College of Music in London. Among his compositions are *The Forgotten Rite* (1913) and *Mai-Dun* (1921) for orchestra; concerto (1930); a choral work *These Things Shall Be* (1937); and many suites and single numbers for piano; song cycles and songs; with some chamber music of interest.

XCVI. Sir Arnold Bax (1885-1953)

Bax represents the Celtic side of modern British music. Studied at the Royal Academy of Music under Frederick Corder. Knighted in 1937, made Master of the King's Music in 1942. His natural Romanticism was colored by his fondness for Irish folklore. He composed much chamber music and several symphonies. He could be gay (e.g., the "jig" finale of his Oboe Quartet; two of the movements in the G Major Quartet), his harmony was elaborate and chromatically rich, and his counterpoint exemplified complete independence of component melodies.

ORCHESTRAL MUSIC

Seven symphonies; *The Garden of Fand* (1916); *Tintagel* (1917); *November Woods* (1917); *Overture to a Picaresque Comedy* (1930).

CONCERTOS AND PIECES WITH ORCHESTRA

Symphonic Variations for piano and orchestra (1917); cello concerto (1932); violin concerto (1937).

CHAMBER MUSIC

Nonet; octet; string quintet; piano quintet; oboe quintet; 3 string quartets; trio for flute, viola, and harp; 3 violin sonatas; sonatas for viola, cello, clarinet and piano; sonata for viola and harp.

SOLO COMPOSITIONS

Four sonatas for piano. Songs and folk song settings.

SUGGESTED READING

1. *AusMTC*	427
2. *HiSym*	402-16
3. *ToveyEMA*	VI, 141

REFERENCES

BOOKS

1. HULL, R. H., *A Handbook on Arnold Bax's Symphonies,* London: Murdoch, 1932.

PERIODICALS

1. EVANS, EDWIN, *"Arnold Bax," Modern Music,* December 1927, pp. 25-30.

XCVII. Arthur Bliss (b. 1891)

Trained at Cambridge and the Royal College of Music; was in California 1923-25. Knighted in 1950, made Master of the Queen's Music in 1953. Early works (*Rout* for soprano and ten instruments, 1919; and *Conversations* for five instruments, 1919) seem experimental. In his mature style he is characterized by vigorous expression and independence, and leanings in the direction of English Romanticism.

XCVIII. Edmund Rubbra (b. 1901)

Composer and pianist. Main influence in his musical style is sixteenth-century polyphony, resulting in extreme contrapuntal elaboration. It is in his instrumental works that his talent for thematic development best comes into use. In his orchestration he seemed at the first to be severe and strict; later, more interest in color seems evident. Among his works are seven symphonies, concertos for viola and piano, *Festival Overture,* three Masses, motets, madrigals, two string quartets, piano trio, two violin sonatas, cello sonata, and songs. Of special interest:

ORCHESTRAL MUSIC

Symphony No. 5, Op. 63, in B-flat (1949).

CONCERTOS AND SOLO PIECES WITH ORCHESTRA

Improvisation for Violin and Orchestra, Op. 89 (1955).

CHAMBER MUSIC

String Quartet No. 2 (1950; perf. 1952).

SUGGESTED READING

1. *RobCM*	350-52
2. *CobCM*	II, 566

REFERENCES

BOOKS

1. RUBBRA, E., *Counterpoint; a Survey,* London: Hutchinson University Library, 1960.

XCIX. Sir William Walton (b. 1902)

Mostly self-taught as a composer. He became known by *Façade* (series of instrumental pieces designed to be given with recitation of Edith Sitwell poems), added to his reputation with his viola concerto (1929) and the oratorio *Belshazzar's Feast* (1931), and achieved world-wide attention with the opera *Troilus and Cressida* (1954). An early overture *Portsmouth Point* (1925) and a powerful symphony (1935) should also be mentioned.

ORCHESTRAL MUSIC

1. *Façade* ("entertainment" for declamation, flute, clarinet, saxophone, trumpet, cello, and percussion) (1923, revised 1942 with augmented orchestra).
2. Overture, *Portsmouth Point* (1925).
3. *Partita* (1958).

CHORAL WORKS

1. *Belshazzar's Feast,* for baritone solo, chorus and full orchestra plus a large percussion section and two brass bands (1931).

SUGGESTED READING

1. *AusMTC*	506-7
2. *ToveyEMA*	III, 220-26

REFERENCES

BOOKS

1. HOWES, F. S., *The Music of William Walton* 2 vols., London: Oxford University Press, 1942-1943, new edition, 1965.
2. WALTON, W. T., *The Music of William Walton,* London: Oxford University Press.

PERIODICALS

1. AVERY, K., "William Walton," *ML* (January, 1947).
2. EVANS, E., "William Walton," *MT* (1944).
3. FOSS, H. J., "William Walton," *MQ* (October, 1940).

C. Michael Tippett (b. 1905)

An idealist and a pacifist (spent some months in prison during the war for failing to register as a conscientious objector). When he decided to be a composer he also decided against any appointments which might restrict him. In 1940 became music director at Morley College, but has steadfastly refused to let routine school work occupy very much of his time. He has composed the oratorio *A Child of our Time* (1941), the operas *The Midsummer Marriage* (1952) and *King Priam* (1961), two symphonies, a concerto for double string orchestra, a piano concerto (1955), a *Concerto for Orchestra* (1963), choral works, chamber music, and piano pieces.

CI. Benjamin Britten (b. 1913)

England's most prominent composer and musical figure at the middle of the twentieth century. Pupil of Frank Bridge and John Ireland, graduate (1934) of the Royal College of Music, he began composing as a child and chose to make his career as a professional composer. A capable pianist and conductor, he has made a particularly fine impression as a piano accompanist. Public appearances as conductor or performer remain, however, a side line. He is regarded by many as the first really significant composer of English opera since Purcell, and his *Peter Grimes* has entered the repertoire of opera companies the world over. Revealing the composer's remarkable affinity for vocal writing, the choral works and song cycles have earned high praise and, in the case of the recent *War Requiem,* international renown. But Britten is also a master of instrumental writing, and his symphonic and chamber works are important additions to the literature. Although his music makes no radical break with the past, it is progressive and unmistakably of the twentieth century. In his style one looks in vain for a predominating influence from a single other composer; rather, one finds an amalgam of many influences conditioned and made individual by the operation of a powerful musical temperament. A professional in the best sense, Britten is prolific in output and fluent in his musical speech. But he is also a man of feeling, with poetic and dramatic gifts of a high order.

ORCHESTRAL MUSIC

Sinfonietta (1932); *Simple Symphony* for strings (1925, rev. 1934); *Variations on a Theme by Frank Bridge* for strings (1937); *Canadian Carnival* (1939); *Sinfonia da Requiem* (1940); *The Young Person's Guide to the Orchestra* (variations and fugue on a theme by Purcell; 1946); *Divertimento* for chamber orchestra (1952).

Variations

Variations on a Theme by Frank Bridge, Op. 10 (1937)

The Young Person's Guide to the Orchestra, Op. 34 (1946)

Symphony

Sinfonia da Requiem, Op. 20 (1940)

CONCERTOS AND PIECES WITH ORCHESTRA

Piano concerto in D Major, Op. 13 (1928, rev. 1946); violin concerto in D Minor, Op. 15 (1939); *Diversions on a Theme,* for piano (left hand) and orchestra, Op. 21 (dedicated to Paul Wittgenstein; 1940); *Scottish Ballad* for 2 pianos and orchestra, Op. 26 (1941); *Symphony for Violoncello and Orchestra,* Op. 68 (1963). For solo voice and orchestra: *Our Hunting Fathers,* Op. 8 (text by W. H. Auden; 1936); *Les Illuminations,* Op. 18 (cycle of 9 songs for high voice and strings; text by Rimbaud; 1939); 4 British Folksongs (1942); *Serenade* for tenor, horn, and strings, Op. 31 (cycle of 8 songs to texts by several poets; 1943); *Nocturne* for tenor, 7 obbligato instruments and string orchestra, Op. 60 (1958).

Les Illuminations, Op. 18 (1939).

Serenade for tenor, horn, and strings, Op. 31 (1943).

Symphony for Violoncello and Orchestra, Op. 68 (1963).

CHAMBER MUSIC

Two string quartets (No. 1 in D Major, Op. 25, 1941; No. 2 in C Major, Op. 36, 1945); *Fantasy Quartet,* Op. 2, for oboe, violin, viola, and cello (1932); suite, Op. 6, for violin and piano (1935); *Lacrymae,* Op. 48, for viola and piano (1950); sonata in C Major, Op. 65, for cello and piano (1961).

CHORAL WORKS

Hymn to the Virgin (1933); *A Boy Was Born,* Op. 3 (1933); *Friday Afternoons,* Op. 7, for children's voices (1934); *Ballad of Heroes,* Op. 14 (1939); *A Ceremony of Carols,* Op. 28, for boys' chorus and harp (1942); *Hymn to St. Cecelia,* Op. 27 (unaccompanied chorus; 1942); *St. Nicholas,* Op. 42 (cantata; 1948); *Spring Symphony,* Op. 44, for soloists, chorus, and orchestra (1949); *Noye's Fludde,* Op. 59 (boys' choir; 1957); *Missa brevis* in D, Op. 63 (boys' choir and organ; 1959); *War Requiem,* Op. 66 (for soloists, chorus, and orchestra; 1961).

A Ceremony of Carols, Op. 28 (1942).

Spring Symphony, Op. 44 (1949).

War Requiem, Op. 66 (1961).

COMPOSITIONS FOR THE STAGE

Operetta: Paul Bunyan (1941). Operas: *Peter Grimes,* Op. 33 (1945); *The Rape of Lucretia,* Op. 37 (1946); *Albert Herring,* Op. 39 (1947); *The Beggar's Opera* (new version of Gay's text; 1948); *Let's Make an Opera,* Op. 45 (1949); *Billy Budd,* Op. 50 (1951); *Glorianna,* Op. 52 (1953); *The Turn of the Screw,* Op. 54 (1954); *A Midsummer Night's Dream,* Op. 64 (1960). Incidental music to a number of plays. Radio music and music for many films.

Operas

Peter Grimes

The Rape of Lucretia

Billy Budd

SOLO COMPOSITIONS

Many song cycles; a few independent songs. The cycles include: *On this Island,* Op. 11 (1937); *Seven Sonnets of Michelangelo,* Op. 22 (1940); *The Holy Sonnets of John Donne,* Op. 35 (1945); *A Charm of Lullabies,* Op. 41 (1947); *Winter Words,* Op. 53 (1953). Three volumes of folk song arrangements. *Six Metamorphoses after Ovid,* Op. 49, for oboe solo (1951). A few pieces for piano solo. *Prelude and Fugue* on a theme by Victoria, for organ (1947).

SUGGESTED READING

1. *GroutSHO* 543-44
2. *Ul-PiHM* 606; 629

REFERENCES

1. Britten, B., and Holst, Imogen, *The Wonderful World of Music,* Garden City, N.Y.: Garden City Books, 1958.
2. ———, *Britten, Benjamin,* Bonn: Boosey & Hawkes, 1954.
3. Mitchell, D., and Keller, H. eds., *Benjamin Britten: a Commentary on His Works, from a Group of Specialists,* New York: Philosophical Library, 1953, 1952.
4. Stein, E., *Orpheus in New Guises,* London: Rockliff, 1953.
5. White, E. W., *Benjamin Britten: a Sketch of His Life and Works,* London & New York: Boosey & Hawkes, 1954.

BRAZILIAN

CII. Heitor Villa-Lobos (1887-1959)

Mainly self-taught as a composer, he is the principal representative of nationalism in Brazil. His works, which are numerous, reveal the influence of Indian music (which he studied in 1912), and the folk materials of Brazil. Compositions include five operas, six symphonies, symphonic poems, cello concerto, a number of *chôros* (serenades) for various media, chamber music, choral works, piano solos, and songs. Best known, perhaps, are the *chôros,* which utilize Brazilian sonorities and rhythms. From his enormous output the following are singled out for attention:

ORCHESTRAL MUSIC

1. *Dawn in a tropical forest* (*Alvorada na floresta tropical*) (1954)
2. *Erosion* (*Erosào*), the Origin of the Amazon River (*Sorimáo u Ipirungáva*) (1951)
3. Ballet, *Uirapurú* (1935)

CONCERTOS AND SOLO PIECES WITH ORCHESTRA

1. Piano Concerto (1945)

CHAMBER MUSIC

1. Trio for Oboe, Clarinet and Bassoon (1921)
2. Quartet for flute, oboe, clarinet, and bassoon (1928)
3. Wind Quintette *en forme de Chôros* (1928)
4. *Bachianas Brasilieras* No. 1, for 8 cellos (1932)
5. *Bachianas Brasilieras* No. 3 for piano and orch. (1934)
6. *Bachianas Brasilieras* No. 5 for voice and 8 cellos (1939)
7. String Quartet No. 6 in E Major (1938)

CHORAL WORKS

1. *Mass of St. Sebastian,* 3 voices a cappella (1937)
2. *Ave Maria* No. 20 (1938)
3. *Lendas Amerindias* and *O lurupari o menino*

SUGGESTED READING

AusMTC 483-4

REFERENCES

1. Mariz, V., *Heitor Villa-Lobos,* Rio de Janeiro, 1950, abridged English translation, Gainesville, Fla., 1963.
2. Smith, C. S., *Heitor Villa-Lobos,* in *Composers of the Americas* III, 1957.

MEXICAN

CIII. Carlos Chávez (b. 1899)

Composer, conductor, and Director of the National Conservatorio in Mexico City. As the chief representative of nationalism in his country, he presents in his music a modern version of characteristic elements of Indian folk music. Compositions include four symphonies, a piano concerto, a violin concerto, three string quartets and other chamber music, ballets, choral works, piano music, and songs.

ORCHESTRAL MUSIC

1. *Sinfonia India* (1935)
2. *Sinfonia* No. 5 for string orchestra (1953)
3. *Toccata* for percussion instruments (1947)

CHORAL WORKS

1. *Arból que te sequeste* for unaccompanied chorus (1942)

REFERENCES

BOOKS

1. Chávez, Carlos, *Musical Thought,* Cambridge: Harvard University Press, 1961.
2. ———, *Toward a New Music; Music and Electricity,* New York: W. W. Norton & Company, Inc., 1937.
3. ———, *Pan American Union,* catalog of his works, with a preface by Herbert Weinstock, Washington, D.C.: Music Division, Pan American, 1944.

General Bibliography

1. *ApelHD* — Apel, W., *Harvard Dictionary of Music,* 10th printing, Cambridge: Harvard University Press, 1956.
2. *AusMTC* — Austin, W. W., *Music in the 20th Century,* New York: W. W. Norton & Company, Inc., 1966.
3. *BurST* — Burrows, R., and Redmond, B. G., *Symphonic Themes,* New York: Simon and Schuster, Inc., 1942.
4. *Ca-Jo-WaAM* — Cannon, B. C., Johnson, A. H., and Waite, W. G., *The Art of Music,* New York: Thomas Y. Cromwell Company, 1960.
5. *CobCM* — Cobbett, W. W., *Cyclopedic Survey of Chamber Music,* with supplementary material edited by Colin Mason, 3 vols., London: Oxford University Press, 1963.
6. *FergHMT* — Ferguson, D. N., *A History of Musical Thought,* 3rd ed., New York: Appleton-Century-Crofts, 1959.
7. *GleCM* — Gleason, H., *Chamber Music from Haydn to Ravel,* Rochester: Levis Music Stores, 1955.
8. *GroutHWM* — Grout, D. J., *A History of Western Music,* New York: Columbia University Press, 1960.
9. *GroutSHO* — ———, *A Short History of Opera,* New York: Columbia University Press, 1947, 2nd ed., 1965.
10. *Har-MelMHM* — Harman, A., and Mellers, W., *Man and His Music,* the story of musical experience in the West, New York: Oxford University Press, 1962.
11. *HiCon* — Hill, R., *The Concerto,* London: Penguin Books, 1952.
12. *HiSym* — ———, *The Symphony,* London: Penguin Books, 1956.
13. *LangMWC* — Lang, P. H., *Music in Western Civilization,* New York: W. W. Norton & Company, Inc., 1941.
14. *LeichMHI* — Leichtentritt, H., *Music, History, and Ideas,* Cambridge, Mass.: Harvard University Press, 1938.
15. *LeichMWN* — ———, *Music of the Western Nations,* ed. and amplified by Nicolas Slonimsky, Cambridge: Harvard University Press, 1956.
16. *McKin-AndMH* — McKinney, H. D., and Anderson, W. R., *Music in History;* the evolution of an art, New York: American Book Co., 1940.

17. *PahMW* — PAHLEN, K., *Music of the World; A History,* translated by J. A. Galston, New York: Crown Publishers, 1949.

18. *PaulyMCP* — PAULY, R. G., *Music in the Classic Period,* Englewood Cliffs, N.J.: Prentice-Hall, Inc., 1965.

19. *RobCM* — ROBERTSON, A., *Chamber Music,* London: Penguin Books, 1957.

20. *SachsCA* — SACHS, C., *The Commonwealth of Art,* New York: W. W. Norton & Company, Inc., 1946.

21. *SachsOMH* — ———, *Our Musical Heritage,* 2nd ed., Englewood Cliffs, N.J.: Prentice-Hall, Inc., 1955.

22. *ToveyEMA* — TOVEY, D. F., *Essays in Musical Analysis,* London: Oxford University Press, 1937.

23. *UlCM* — ULRICH, H., *Chamber Music,* New York: Columbia University Press, 1948.

24. *Ul-PiHM* — ULRICH, H., and PISK, P. A., *A History of Music and Musical Style,* New York: Harcourt, Brace & World, Inc., 1963.

25. *UlSM* — ULRICH, H., *Symphonic Music,* New York: Columbia University Press, 1952.

26. *VeiCon* — VEINUS, A., *The Concerto,* Garden City, New York: Doubleday, Doran and Co., 1945.

Index of Composers

Date Due

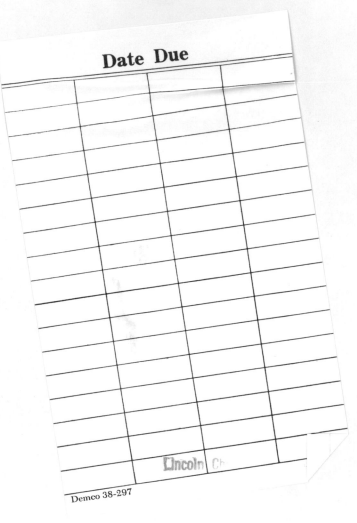

Date Due

MAY 12 '79			
APR 28 '88			